Criminal Law for A2

Criminal Law for A2

Jacqueline Martin

Orders: please contact Bookpoint Ltd, 130 Milton Park, Abingdon, Oxon OX14 4SB. Telephone: (44) 01235 827720. Fax: (44) 01235 400454. Lines are open from 9.00 -6 .00, Monday to Saturday, with a 24 hour message answering service. You can also order through our website www.hoddereducation.co.uk

If you have any comments to make about this, or any of our other titles, please send them to educationenquiries@hodder.co.uk

British Library Cataloguing in Publication Data
A catalogue record for this title is available from the British Library

ISBN-10: 0 340 91452 1
ISBN-13: 978 0 340 914526

This Edition Published 2006
Impression number 10 9 8 7 6 5 4 3 2
Year   2011 2010 2009 2008 2007 2006

Hodder Headline's policy is to use papers that are natural, renewable and recyclable products and made fromwood grown in sustainable forests. The logging and manufacturing processes are expected to conform to the environmental regulations of the country of origin.

Typeset by Dorchester Typesetting Group Ltd, Dorchester, Dorset.
Printed in Great Britain for Hodder Arnold, an imprint of Hodder Education, a member of the Hodder Headline Group, 338 Euston Road, London NW1 3BH by Martins the Printers, Berwick-upon-Tweed.

Contents

Acknowledgements

The publishers wish to thank the following for permission to use copyright material:

Oxford Cambridge and RSA Examinations for OCR examination questions and source material.
Welsh Joint Education Committee for WJEC examination questions.
Daily Telegraph for extract from 'Mercy for mother who was driven to kill her Down's Syndrome son', page 83.
Kent Messenger Group for extract from 'Thug jailed for stamping on policeman's face', page 119.
Courier Newspapers for extracts from '£2,000 stolen in cash scame', page 142; 'Armed raid at off-license', p. 145; 'Clingfilm-wrapped yob wrecks lights', page 164.
Daily Mail for extract from 'Jury in rape trial accepts the defence of sleepwalking', page 176.

Every effort has been made to trace and acknowledge ownership of copyright. The publishers will be glad to make suitable arrangements with any copyright holders whom it has not been possible to contact.

Preface

This book is aimed at the criminal law topics on the specifications for OCR and WJEC examining boards. It covers the general principles of criminal law: *actus reus, mens rea*, strict liability, participation, inchoate offences and general defences. It also covers the law on the offences of murder, manslaughter, assaults, theft, robbery, burglary and criminal damage.

The aim has been to explain the topics as clearly as possible. I have used a similar style to that of my best-selling text, *The English Legal System*. Features include text broken down with the use of many subheadings, diagrams and activities. There are also key facts charts and key cases charts to help students to revise topics.

As the book is aimed at two boards and also as the OCR specification will be changing for teaching from 2007, the following table makes the coverage for each specification clear.

After the chapters on substantive law, there are appendices for each board which set out the examination style used and other relevant information. As OCR's specification is changing after 2007, there are separate sections for the current specification and for the new one.

Finally, Appendix 5 gives students help with how to answer examination questions. These tips are applied to some of the past examination questions which feature at the end of most chapters.

The law is stated as I believe it to be on 1st January 2006.

Chapter	OCR 2006-07	OCR 2007 onwards	WJEC
1 Introduction	√	√	√
2 *Actus reus*	√	√	√
3 *Mens rea*	√	√	√
4 Strict liability	√	√	√
5 Participation	√		
6 Inchoate offences	√	Attempts only	
7 Murder	√	√	√
8 Voluntary manslaughter	√	√	√
9 Involuntary manslaughter	√	√	√
10 Non-fatal offences against the person	√	√	√
11 Theft	√	√	
12 Robbery and burglary	√	√	
13 Criminal damage	√		
14 Defences	√	√	√

Table of Acts of Parliament

Table of Cases

CHAPTER 1

Introduction to criminal law

Murder, Manslaughter, Robbery, Rape and Theft

Virtually everyone can identify these as criminal offences. But how many others can you name? There are thousands of different offences. They vary from the most serious, such as murder and manslaughter, to minor breaches of regulations, such as selling a lottery ticket to someone who is under the age of 16. Fortunately, for A level, you only have to learn about a small number of offences. But you will have to understand the general principles involved in criminal law.

1.1 DEFINING A CRIME

With such a wide range, it is difficult to have a general definition covering all offences. The only way in which it is possible to define a crime is to say that it is:

■ conduct forbidden by the State
■ for which there is a punishment.

Lord Atkin supported this definition when, in the case of *Proprietary Articles Trade Association v Attorney-General for Canada* (1931), he said:

'The criminal quality of an act cannot be discerned by intuition (made out by "gut feeling"); nor can it be discovered by reference to any standard but one: is the act prohibited with penal consequences?'

This is the only definition which covers all crimes. However, there have been other definitions. An American legal writer, Herbert Packer, thought that, to be a crime:

■ the conduct must be wrongful and
■ it must be necessary to condemn or prevent such conduct.

However, what is considered criminal will change over time. This can be caused by changing views in society; or changes in technology which lead to the need for new offences to cover new situations.

Changing views on what is criminal can be demonstrated by the changes in the law on consenting homosexual acts. In 1885 the Criminal Law Amendment Act made consenting homosexual acts criminal even if they were in private. This remained as the law until 1967 when the Sexual Offences Act 1967 decriminalised such behaviour between those aged 21 and over. The age was reduced to 18 in 1994 and finally, in 2000, it was further reduced to 16. This age brings the law into line with consenting sexual acts between heterosexuals.

New technology can lead to new areas of criminal law. For example, the invention of the motor car over a hundred years ago led to new road traffic laws. These have been added to over the years so that we now have such offences as driving without a licence, driving while over the legal limit of alcohol, having tyres which do not have the right level of tread, up to causing death by dangerous driving.

Computers and the internet have led to new offences being created to protect people from internet fraud and to prevent pornographic material from being viewed or downloaded.

1.1.1 The role of the State

As the criminal law is set down by the State, a breach of it can lead to a penalty, such as imprisonment or a fine, being imposed on the defendant in the name of the State. Therefore, bringing a prosecution for a criminal offence is usually seen as part of the role of the State. Indeed, the majority of criminal prosecutions are conducted by the Crown Prosecution Service which is the State agency for criminal prosecutions.

However, it is also possible for a private individual or business to start a prosecution. Big shops often conduct their own prosecutions in shoplifting cases and organisations such as the RSCPA regularly bring prosecutions. But it is unusual for an individual person to bring a prosecution.

Even where an organisation or an individual brings a prosecution, the State still has control over the case as the Attorney-General can stay (halt) the proceedings at any time. This is done by the Attorney-General entering what is called a *nolle prosequi*. This stops the case from going on, even if the original prosecutor wants it to continue.

1.1.2 Conduct criminalised by the judges

Although, in the vast majority of offences, the State decides what conduct is considered to be criminal, some conduct is criminalised not by the State but by judges. This occurs where the judges create new criminal offences through case law. In modern times this only happens on rare occasions because nearly all law is made by Parliament. An example of conduct criminalised by judges is the offence of conspiracy to corrupt public morals. This offence has never been enacted by Parliament. However, the judges recognised that it existed in *Shaw v DPP* (1962).

> ### *SHAW v DPP* (1962)
> The defendant published a *Ladies Directory* which advertised the names and addresses of prostitutes, with their photographs and details of the 'services' they were prepared to offer. He was charged with conspiracy to corrupt public morals. The House of Lords accepted that there was an offence of conspiracy to corrupt public morals, as there did not appear to be any other offence which covered the situation.

Another offence which has been created by the judges in modern times is marital rape. This was declared a crime in *R v R* (1991). Before that case, the law held that a husband could not be guilty of raping his wife, as she was assumed, by the fact of marriage, to consent to sexual intercourse with him. When the Law Lords decided the case of *R v R* they pointed out that society's views on the position of women had changed. The Law Lords said:

'The status of women and the status of a married woman in our law have changed quite dramatically. A husband and wife are now for all practical purposes equal partners in marriage.'

The Law Lords ruled that if a wife did not consent to intercourse, then the husband could be guilty of raping her.

1.2 ELEMENTS OF A CRIME

So, there are many offences aimed at different 'wrong' behaviour. However, there are general principles which apply to all offences. The most important principle is that for all crimes, except crimes of strict liability (see Chapter 4), there are two elements which must be proved by the prosecution. These are:

- *actus reus* and
- *mens rea*.

These terms come from a Latin maxim (*actus non facit reum nisi mens sit rea*) which means 'the act itself does not constitute guilt unless done with a guilty mind'. Both an act (or omission) and a guilty mind must be proved for most criminal offences. (See Figure 1.1.)

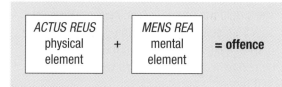

Figure 1.1 The elements of an offence

1.2.1 *Actus reus*

'*Actus reus*' has a wider meaning than 'an act', as it can cover omissions or a state of affairs. The term '*actus reus*' has been criticised as misleading. Lord Diplock in *Miller* (1983) preferred the term 'prohibited conduct', while the Law Commission in the Draft Criminal Code (1989) used the term 'external element'. We will look at the concept of *actus reus* in detail in Chapter 2.

1.2.2 *Mens rea*

'*Mens rea*' translates as 'guilty mind' but this is also misleading. The Law Commission in the Draft Criminal Code (1989) used the term 'fault element'. The levels of 'guilty mind' required for different offences vary from the highest level, which is specific intention for some crimes, to much lower levels, such as negligence or knowledge of a certain fact, for less serious offences. The levels of *mens rea* are explained in detail in Chapter 3.

1.2.3 Examples

The *actus reus* and *mens rea* will be different for different crimes. For example, in murder the *actus reus* is the killing of a human being and the *mens rea* is causing the death 'with malice aforethought' which means that the killer must have intended to kill or to cause grievous bodily harm. For theft, the *actus reus* is the appropriation of property belonging to another while the *mens rea* is doing this dishonestly and with the intention permanently to deprive the other of the property.

The *actus reus* and the *mens rea* must be present together, but if there is an ongoing act, then the existence of the necessary *mens rea* at any point during that act is sufficient. This is explained fully in Chapter 3 at section 3.7. However, even where the *actus reus* and *mens rea* are present, the defendant may be not guilty if he has a defence (see section 1.3).

1.2.4 Strict liability offences

There some crimes which are an exception to the general rule that there must be both *actus reus* and *mens rea*. These are crimes of strict liability, where the prosecution need prove only the *actus reus*; no mental element is needed for guilt. (See Chapter 4 for discussion of strict liability.)

1.3   DEFENCES

Although the defendant may have done the required act, there are a number of general defences that may be available which will lead to a 'not guilty' verdict. These defences are:

- insanity
- automatism
- mistake
- self-defence
- duress
- necessity and
- intoxication.

The first four of these (insanity, automatism, mistake and self-defence) can be a defence to any offence. Duress and necessity are not defences to a charge of murder. Intoxication is only a defence where, because of his intoxication, the defendant did not have the required specific intention for the offence charged. If the defendant, even though he was drunk, had the required specific intention, then he cannot use intoxication as a defence. Also intoxication is never a defence to any offence where recklessness is sufficient for the *mens rea*. Each of these defences is considered in detail in Chapter 14.

1.4 STANDARD AND BURDEN OF PROOF

The prosecution has to prove the case against the defendant. There are rules about the level to which the case has to be proved. This is referred to as the 'standard of proof'.

1.4.1 Standard of proof

The standard of proof in criminal cases is 'beyond reasonable doubt'. This is usually explained by the judge telling the jury that they should only convict if they are satisfied on the evidence, so that they are sure of the defendant's guilt.

This is a higher standard than the one used in civil cases. Civil cases have to be proved only 'on the balance of probabilities'. The reason that criminal cases require a higher standard of proof is because the defendant is at risk of losing his liberty if he is found guilty.

1.4.2 Presumption of innocence

An accused person is presumed innocent until proven guilty. The burden is on the prosecution to prove the case. This means that it must prove both the required *actus reus* and the required *mens rea*. An important case on these principles is *Woolmington* (1935).

WOOLMINGTON v DPP (1935)
D's wife had left him and gone to live with her mother. D went to the mother's house and shot his wife dead. He claimed that he had decided to ask his wife to come back to him and, if she refused, that he would commit suicide. For this reason he was carrying under his coat a loaded sawn-off shotgun. When his wife indicated that she would not return to him, he threatened to shoot himself and brought the gun out to show her he meant it. As he brought it out, it somehow went off, killing his wife. He claimed that this was a pure accident.

The judge at the trial told the jury that the prosecution had to prove beyond reasonable doubt that the defendant killed his wife. He then went on to tell them that, if the prosecution satisfied them of that, the defendant had to show that there were circumstances which made that killing pure accident. This put the burden of proof on the defendant to prove the defence. In the House of Lords it was held that this was not correct.

The decision in this case made several important points which the House of Lords regarded as fixed matters on English law. These were:

■ the prosecution must prove the case
■ this rule applies to all criminal cases
■ the rule must be applied in any court where there is a criminal trial (currently the Magistrates' Court and the Crown Court)
■ guilt must be proved beyond reasonable doubt and
■ a reasonable doubt can be raised by evidence from either the prosecution or the defence.

1.4.3 Raising a defence

If the defendant raises a defence then it is for the prosecution to disprove that defence. In *Woolmington v DPP* (1935) the defendant stated that the gun had gone off accidentally, thus raising the defence of accident. The prosecution was obliged to disprove this if the defendant was to be found guilty.

For all common-law defences, except insanity, the defendant only has to raise some evidence of the key points of the defence. This can be from evidence given by the defence or by the prosecution. If evidence of a defence is given at the trial then, even where the defendant has not specifically raised the defence, the prosecution must disprove at least one element of that defence. The trial judge must direct the jury to acquit unless they are satisfied that the defence has been disproved by the prosecution.

Reverse onus

For certain defences, the burden of proof is on the defendant. For example, if the defendant claims that he was insane at the time of the crime, the burden of proving this is on the defendant. This shifting of the burden of proof to the defendant is known as the 'reverse onus'. As well as applying to the common-law defence of insanity, it also applies to some defences which have been created by statute. One of these is the defence of diminished responsibility in the Homicide Act 1957 where s 2(2) states:

'On a charge of murder, it shall be for the defence to prove that the person charged is, by virtue of this section, not liable to be convicted of murder.'

Where a statute places the burden of proof on the defendant to prove a defence, the standard is the civil one of 'on the balance of probabilities'.

1.5   CRIMINAL LAW AND HUMAN RIGHTS

In 1950 the United Kingdom and 19 other European countries agreed the European Convention on Human Rights. Since then, the number of countries signing the Convention has increased so that there are now nearly 50. The Convention sets out basic human rights that people are entitled to expect.

Although the UK signed the Convention in 1950, the Convention was not part of our law until 2000. This meant that before 2000, if someone wanted to complain about a breach

of human rights, they had to take a case to the European Court of Human Rights in Strasbourg. In October 2000 the Human Rights Act 1998 incorporated the Convention into UK law. Section 1.5.4 below explains how the Act operates.

But first, we will consider what rights are given under the Convention and why they are important in the criminal justice system.

1.5.1 Right to liberty

Article 5 of the Convention gives a right to liberty. However, it does also accept that there are situations in which a person's liberty can be removed. Article 5(1) states:

'Everyone has the right to liberty and security of person. No one shall be deprived of his liberty save in the following cases and in accordance with a procedure prescribed by law:

a the lawful detention of a person after conviction by a competent court;

b the lawful arrest or detention of a person for non-compliance with the lawful order of a court … ;

c the lawful arrest or detention of a person effected for the purpose of bringing him before the competent legal authority on reasonable suspicion of having committed an offence or when it is necessary to do so to prevent his committing an offence or fleeing after having done so;

d the detention of a minor by lawful order for the purpose of educational supervision or his lawful detention for the purpose of bringing him before a competent legal authority;

e the lawful detention of persons for the prevention of the spreading of infectious diseases, of persons of unsound mind, alcoholics or drug addicts or vagrants;

f the lawful arrest or detention of a person to prevent his effecting an unauthorised entry into the country or of a person against whom action is being taken with a view to deportation or extradition.'

This prevents people from being detained unlawfully. But it does allow that people may be detained in certain situations. For example, Art 5(1)(a) does allow for judges to sentence those convicted of a crime to be detained in prison. It is judges who decide prison sentences: this makes the decision independent of the Government. It has been ruled that it is a breach of human rights for a Government Minister to decide on the length of imprisonment that should be served by a murderer. To comply with the European Convention on Human Rights, our law was changed to stop the Home Secretary setting tariffs in murder cases. Now judges do this, although they have to operate within guidelines set out by Parliament.

In September 2005 a judge decided that Ian Huntley (the 'Soham murderer'), who murdered two young girls, would have to serve a minimum of 40 years before he could be considered for parole.

Activity

Read parts b, c, d and e of Art 5(1) above and answer the following questions.

1 Explain in your own words what exceptions to the right to liberty are allowed.
2 Do you agree that all the situations set out in parts b, c, d and e of Art 5(1) should be ones where a person's liberty can be removed? Give reasons for your answer.

Article 5(2)

Article 5(2) states that:

'Everyone who is arrested shall be informed promptly, in a language which

he understands, of the reasons for his arrest and of any charge against him'.

Our law on police powers of arrest conforms to this article. An interesting case example was *Taylor v Chief Constable of Thames Valley Police* (2004). Taylor was a 10-year-old boy who had been throwing stones during an anti-vivisection demo. When he was present at a later protest he was identified by a police officer who said: 'I am arresting you on suspicion of violent disorder on April 18, 1998 at Hillgrove Farm.' The Court of Appeal held that this was a lawful arrest and that the test of whether the words of arrest were sufficient is:

'was the person arrested told in simple non-technical language that they could understand the essential legal and factual grounds for his arrest?'

You can see how this conforms to the European Convention on Human Rights. The words used had to be words which could be understood by a 10-year-old boy. It is also worth noting that, although the arrest was lawful, the Court of Appeal held that the boy had been held for an hour longer than was necessary. This was false imprisonment under our civil law and the boy was entitled to damages for this.

Article 5(3)

This states that:

'Everyone arrested or detained in accordance with the provisions of paragraph 1.c of this article shall be brought promptly before a judge … and shall be entitled to trial within a reasonable time or to release pending trial'.

In our legal system this works through the fact that any person charged with an offence must be released on police bail or brought before a Magistrates' Court as soon as possible. This is usually the next morning. The magistrates will consider whether the person charged should be given bail or remanded in custody.

Where a person is not released on bail then their trial must be held as quickly as possible. Recently, there have been efforts to speed up the criminal justice system so that defendants do not have to wait too long before trial.

1.5.2 Right to a fair trial

The right to a fair trial is set out in Art 6 of the Convention. This states:

'**6.1** *Everyone is entitled to a fair trial and public hearing within a reasonable time by an independent and impartial tribunal established by law …*
6.2 *Everyone charged with a criminal offence shall be presumed innocent until proved guilty according to the law.*
6.3 *Everyone charged with a criminal offence has the following minimum rights;*
a *to be informed promptly, in a language which he understands and in detail, of the nature and cause of the accusation against him;*
b *to have adequate time and facilities for the preparation of his defence;*
c *to defend himself in person or through legal assistance of his own choosing or, if has not sufficient means to pay for legal assistance, to be given it free when the interests of justice so require.'*

Article 6(1)

This makes it clear that judges conducting trials in criminal cases must be independent and impartial. This is the position in our legal system. A judge must not try a case where he knows someone or has an interest in the case. The article also states that there must be a hearing within a reasonable time.

Article 6(2)

This makes the same provision for the standard of proof in a criminal trial as already exists in our legal system. (see section 1.4.2) The only potential conflict with human rights is where the defendant has to prove a defence.

In the conjoined appeals of *Attorney-General's Reference No 4 of 2002* and *Sheldrake v DPP* (2004) the House of Lords considered whether defences which require the defendant to prove them on the balance of probabilities were a breach of the presumption of innocence under Art 6(2) of the European Convention on Human Rights.

The Lords came to the conclusion that in many cases the wording of the Act could be interpreted so that it did not create a legal burden to prove the defence. However, they held that even if a section did breach Art 6(2) it was permissible if it was 'justifiable, legitimate and proportionate'. This was the situation in the case of *Sheldrake v DPP* (2004).

SHELDRAKE v DPP (2004)

Sheldrake was convicted of being in charge of a motor car in a public place while over the drink–drive limit, contrary to s 5(1)(b) of the Road Traffic Act 1988. Section 5(2) of the Act allows a defence if D can prove that there was no likelihood of his driving while he was over the limit. D was convicted but the Divisional Court quashed the conviction. The prosecution then appealed to the House of Lords.

The defence argued that s 5(2) infringed the presumption of innocence guaranteed by Art 6(2) as it imposed on D a legal burden of proving innocence by proving a defence.

The House of Lords held that s 5(2) did impose on D a legal burden of proof. However, they pointed out that there is an obvious risk that a person who is in charge of a car when unfit to drive may drive and so risk causing death or serious injury. For this reason Lord Bingham said:

'It [is] much more appropriate for the defendant to prove on the balance of probabilities that he would not have been likely to drive than for the prosecutor to prove beyond reasonable doubt that he would.'

The House of Lords allowed the prosecution's appeal and reinstated the conviction.

Article 6(3)

The rights in Art 6(3)(a) and (b) are always observed in our criminal justice system. Part (c) is supported by our system of legal aid in criminal cases. At the moment, legal representation is available free to all defendants who are tried in the Crown Court. For cases in the Magistrates' Courts, where it is in the interests of justice that the defendant should be represented, the Criminal Defence Act 2006 sets out rules so that defendants who do not have sufficient means to pay for legal assistance can be represented free of charge.

1.5.3 No punishment without law

This is covered by Art 7 of the European Convention on Human Rights.

Article 7

'7.1 No one shall be held guilty of any criminal offence on account of any act or omission which did not constitute a criminal offence under national or international law at the time when it was committed …
7.2 This article shall not prejudice the trial and punishment of any person for any act or omission which, at the time when it was committed, was criminal according to the general principles of law recognised by civilised nations.'

So far as this article is concerned, any new law created by Parliament will only apply to acts or omissions *after* the Act is passed. It is very rare for an Act of Parliament to be retrospective in its effect, that is, to take effect for matters which occurred before it was passed. One of the few Acts which did this was the War Crimes Act 1991.

However, the situation is different for judge-made law. Here, the law is decided when the case is heard and applied to what the defendant allegedly did before the hearing. In *R v R* (1991), following the House of Lords' decision, the case was taken to the European Court of Human Rights as *CR v United Kingdom* (1996), claiming that there was a breach of Art 7 because marital rape was not an offence when the defendant had sexual intercourse with his wife without her consent.

The European Court of Human Rights held that there had not been any breach of Art 7, as the debasing character of rape was so obvious that to convict in these circumstances was not at variance with the object and purpose of Art 7. In fact, abandoning the idea that a husband could not be prosecuted for the rape of his wife conformed to one of the fundamental objectives of the Convention, that of respect for human dignity.

1.5.4 The Human Rights Act 1998

The 1998 Act makes it unlawful for a public authority to act in way which is incompatible with the European Convention on Human Rights. 'Public authority' includes courts and any person who has some public functions. The major limitation is that 'public authority' does not include either House of Parliament or any person exercising functions in connection with proceedings in Parliament.

The Act also states that courts in England and Wales have to interpret legislation in a way that is compatible with the Convention. If

Figure 1.2 Key facts chart on the European Convention on Human Rights

Article	Law	Comment
5(1)	Right to liberty.	Although there is a right to liberty, detention is allowed in certain circumstances, including: ■ detention after conviction ■ lawful arrest for breach of a court order ■ lawful arrest where there is reasonable suspicion that he has committed an offence ■ detention of a person with a view to deportation.
5(2)	Those arrested must be informed of the reason, promptly and in understandable language.	Our law conforms to this: *Taylor v Chief Constable of Thames Valley Police* (2004).
5(3)	Those detained to be brought before a judge promptly. Entitled to trial within a reasonable time or to be released pending trial.	Within our system, the normal rule is that those arrested must be bailed or brought before a Magistrates' Court as soon as possible. The only exception is under terrorism laws.
6(1)	Entitled to a fair hearing by an independent tribunal.	Judges must be independent and impartial.
6(2)	Presumed innocent until proven guilty.	This is the normal rule in our system: *Woolmington* (1935). But where the onus is on the defence to prove a defence, this may be a breach of human rights: *Sheldrake* (2004).
6(3)	Must be informed of the detail and nature of charges against him. Must have adequate time and facilities to prepare defence. D must be provided with free legal assistance if he cannot afford it and it is in the interests of justice.	The first two points are observed in our criminal justice system. Criminal legal aid is available in these circumstances.
7(1)	Shall not be guilty of any offence which did not exist at the time when D did the act.	In *CR v UK* (1996) the European Court of Human Rights held that there was no breach of this article, in holding that marital rape was an offence.

KEY FACTS

it is impossible for a court to do this then it will make a declaration that the legislation is incompatible with the Convention. When a court does this there is pressure on the Government to change the incompatible Act so that it does conform to the Convention.

An example of this occurring was the House of Lords' decision in *A and another v Secretary of State for the Home Department* (2004). In this case the Law Lords declared that the Anti-Terrorism Act 2001 was incompatible with the Convention. The Act had allowed foreign nationals to be detained indefinitely without trial where there was suspicion that they were involved in terrorist activity. The Law Lords held that this breached Art 5 of the Convention (the right to liberty). It was also a breach of Art 14 which states that there shall be no discrimination on the basis of nationality. This decision by the House of Lords forced the UK Government to change the law.

CHAPTER 2

Actus reus

2.1 WHAT IS *ACTUS REUS*?

As already stated in Chapter 1, the *actus reus* is the physical element of a crime. It can be:

- an act or
- a failure to act (an omission) or
- a 'state of affairs'.

In most cases the *actus reus* will be something the defendant does, but there are situations in which a failure to act is sufficient for the *actus reus*. These are set out at section 2.2. 'State of affairs' cases are very rare. These are considered at section 2.1.2.

2.1.1 Voluntary nature of *actus reus*

The act or omission must be voluntary on the part of the defendant. If the defendant has no control over his actions then he has not committed the *actus reus*. In *Hill v Baxter* (1958) the court gave examples of where a driver of a vehicle could not be said to be to doing the act of driving voluntarily. These included where a driver lost control of his vehicle because he was stung by a swarm of bees, or if he was struck on the head by a stone or had a heart attack while driving.

Other examples of an involuntary act include where the defendant hits another person because of a reflex action or a muscle spasm. Yet another is where one person pushes a second person, causing them to bump into a third person. In this situation the act of the second person who has been pushed is involuntary. Even though he has hit the third person, he has not committed the *actus reus* for any assault offence.

These examples show that the criminal law is concerned with fault on the part of the defendant. Where there is an absence of fault, then the defendant is usually not liable.

2.1.2 'State of affairs' cases

There are some rare instances in which the defendant has been convicted even though he did not act voluntarily. These situations involve what are known as 'state of affairs' cases. An example of this is the case of *Larsonneur* (1933).

LARSONNEUR (1933)

The defendant had been ordered to leave the United Kingdom. She decided to go to Eire, but the Irish police deported her and took her back to the UK. She did not wish to go back and was certainly not doing this voluntarily. When she landed in the UK she was immediately arrested and charged that being 'an alien to whom leave to land in the UK had been refused', she had been found in the UK. She was convicted because she was an alien who had been refused leave to land and she had been 'found in the UK'. It did not matter that she had been brought back by the Irish police against her will. (See also section 4.1 on strict liability).

2.1.3 Consequence of *actus reus*

For some crimes the *actus reus* must also result in a consequence. This can be seen in the offence of assault occasioning actual bodily harm (s 47 Offences Against the Person Act 1861). There must be an *actus reus* (the application or threat of unlawful force) but there must also be a consequence of 'actual bodily harm', in other words some injury to the victim. This could be just a bruise or it could be a broken nose or broken arm. It could even be psychiatric injury. Without this consequence there cannot be a s 47 offence.

2.2 OMISSIONS AS *ACTUS REUS*

The normal rule is that an omission cannot make a person guilty of an offence. This was explained by Stephen J, a nineteenth-century judge, in the following way.

'A sees B drowning and is able to save him by holding out his hand. A abstains from doing so in order that B may be drowned. A has committed no offence.'

Activity

Read the following scenario and discuss whether you think Zoe should be guilty of an offence.

Scenario

Zoe is sitting by a swimming pool in the grounds of a hotel. Jason is swimming in the pool. He is the only person in the water and there are no other people near the pool. Jason gets out of the pool and while walking around it slips and falls into the water. He is knocked unconscious. Zoe sees this happen but she does nothing. Jason drowns.

Would it make any difference to your answer if Zoe could not swim?

A 'Good Samaritan' law?

Some other countries have a law which is known as a 'Good Samaritan' law. It makes a person responsible for helping other people in an 'emergency situation', even though they are complete strangers. French law has this and an example was seen when Princess Diana's car crashed in Paris. Journalists who had been following her car took photographs of her, injured, in the car. They did not try to help her, even though she was critically injured. The French authorities threatened to charge these journalists under the French 'Good Samaritan' law.

There are problems in enforcing such a law. What if a 'rogue' pretends to be seriously hurt in order to lure a stranger to his assistance, so that the rogue can then rob the stranger? There is also the risk that an untrained person, by intervening, could do more harm to an injured person. Also, what is an 'emergency situation'? Who decides that there is an emergency so that the 'Good Samaritan' law is operating?

A problem would also arise if several people witnessed the incident. Do all of them have to help? Or is it enough if one of them helps? If one person helps, are the others still under a duty to help?

Finally, there is the question of whether would-be rescuers have to put themselves at risk in order to help. It seems unlikely that the law would require this. In the case of *Miller* (1983) (see section 2.2.1) the House of Lords thought that a defendant who has created the risk would only be expected to take reasonable steps. He would not be expected to put himself at risk. If this is the situation for the person who has caused the problem, then surely the same would have to apply to innocent passers-by?

2.2.1 Exceptions to the rule

There are exceptions to the rule that an omission cannot make a person guilty of an offence. In some cases it is possible for a failure to act (an omission) to be the *actus reus*. An Act of Parliament can create liability for an omission. Examples include the offences of failing to report a road traffic accident and of failing to provide a specimen of breath. In fact, these offences can only be committed by failing to do something.

For common-law crimes an omission is only sufficient for the *actus reus* where there is a duty to act. There are five ways in which such a duty exists.

1 A contractual duty.
2 A duty because of a relationship.
3 A duty which has been taken on voluntarily.
4 A duty through one's official position.
5 A duty which arises because the defendant has set in motion a chain of events.

A contractual duty

In *Pittwood* (1902) a railway crossing keeper omitted to shut the gates, so that a person crossing the line was struck and killed by a train. The keeper was guilty of manslaughter. A more modern example would be of a lifeguard at a beach who leaves his post unattended. His failure to do his duty could make him guilty of an offence if a swimmer were injured.

A duty because of a relationship

This is usually a parent–child relationship as a parent has a duty to care for young children. A duty can also exist the opposite way round, where a grown-up child is caring for their elderly parent. A case example involving a parent–child duty is *Gibbins and Proctor* (1918).

GIBBINS and PROCTOR (1918)
The father of a seven-year-old girl lived with a partner. The father had several children from an earlier marriage. He and his partner kept the girl separate from the father's other children and deliberately starved her to death. They were both convicted of murder.

The father had a duty to feed her because he was her parent and the mistress was held to have undertaken to look after the children, including the girl, so she was also under a duty to feed the child. The omission or failure to feed her was deliberate with the intention of killing or causing serious harm to her. In these circumstances they were guilty of murder. The failure to feed the girl was enough for the *actus reus* of murder.

A duty which has been undertaken voluntarily

In the above case of *Gibbins and Proctor* (1918) the partner had voluntarily undertaken to look after the girl. She therefore had a duty towards the child. When she failed to feed the child she was guilty of murder because of that omission.

Another example of where a duty had been undertaken voluntarily is *Stone and Dobinson* (1977).

STONE and DOBINSON (1977)
Stone's elderly sister, Fanny, came to live with the defendants. Fanny was eccentric and often stayed in her room for several days. She also failed to eat. She eventually became bedridden and incapable of caring for herself. On at least one occasion *Dobinson* helped to wash Fanny and also occasionally prepared food for her. Fanny died from malnutrition. Both defendants were found guilty of her manslaughter.

As Fanny was Stone's sister, he owed a duty of care to her. Dobinson had undertaken some care of Fanny and so also owed her a duty of care. The duty was either to help her themselves or to summon help from other sources. Their failure to do either of these meant that they were in breach of their duty.

A duty through one's official position

This is very rare but did happen in *Dytham* (1979).

DYTHAM (1979)
Dytham (D) was a police officer who was on duty. He saw a man (V) being thrown out of a nightclub about 30 yards from where he was standing. Following the throwing out, there was a fight in which three men kicked V to death. D took no steps to intervene or to summon help.

When the fight was over, D told a bystander that he was going off duty and left the scene. He was convicted of misconduct in a public office.

Because Dytham was a police officer, he was guilty of wilfully and without reasonable excuse neglecting to perform his duty.

A duty which arises because the defendant set in motion a chain of events

This concept of owing a duty and being liable through omission was created in the case of *Miller* (1983) where a squatter had accidentally started a fire.

MILLER (1983)
D was living in a squat. He fell asleep while smoking a cigarette. He awoke to find his mattress on fire. He did not attempt to put out the fire or to summon help but went into another room and went back to sleep. The house caught fire. He was convicted of arson.

In *Miller* (1983) it was not the setting of the mattress on fire which made him guilty. Instead, it was the fact that he had failed to take reasonable steps to deal with the fire when he discovered his mattress was on fire. This failure or omission meant that he had committed the *actus reus* for arson. The House of Lords pointed out that Miller was only expected to take reasonable steps. He did not have to put himself at risk. So, if, when he woke and found the fire, it was very small and could easily be put out then he was expected to do that. However, if it was too dangerous for him to deal with it personally then his duty was summon the fire brigade.

Another case where the defendant knew that there was a dangerous situation but failed to take any steps is *Santana-Bermudez* (2003).

SANTANA-BERMUDEZ (2003)
A policewoman, before searching the defendant's pockets, asked him if he had any needles or other sharp objects on him. The defendant said 'no', but when the police officer put her hand in his pocket she was injured by a needle which caused bleeding. The defendant was convicted of assault occasioning actual bodily harm under s 47 of the Offences Against the Person Act 1861.

In this case it was the failure to tell the police officer of the needle which made the defendant liable. He knew that there was danger to the police officer but failed to warn her about it. This failure was enough for the *actus reus* for the purposes of an assault causing actual bodily harm.

2.2.2 Involuntary manslaughter and omissions

Involuntary manslaughter can be committed in different ways. The two main ways are:

■ unlawful act manslaughter and
■ gross negligence manslaughter.

Unlawful act manslaughter cannot be committed by an omission. There must be an 'act'. This was decided in *Lowe* (1973).

LOWE (1973)
D was the father of a nine-week-old baby who became ill and died. D, who was of low intelligence, said he had told the baby's mother to take the child to a doctor, but he had not done anything else. The child's mother was of subnormal intelligence. D was convicted of manslaughter of the baby. The Court of Appeal quashed the conviction because there was no unlawful 'act'. A failure to do something could not be an 'act'.

Figure 2.1 Key facts chart on when omissions can be *actus reus*

KEY FACTS

Source	Explanation	Examples
Under an Act of Parliament	Parliament can word an Act so that it is an offence not to do something.	Failing to provide a specimen of breath (s 6 Road Traffic Act 1988).
A duty at common law	Under a contract, especially of employment.	*Pittwood* (1902)
	Because of a relationship such as parent and child.	*Gibbins & Proctor* (1918)
	A duty voluntarily undertaken, eg care of an elderly relative.	*Stone & Dobinson* (1977)
	Because of a public office, eg police officer.	*Dytham* (1979)
	As a result of a dangerous situation created by the defendant.	*Miller* (1983) *Santana-Bermudez* (2003)
	Other situations where a duty of care is owed.	*Khan and Khan* (1998) *Wacker* (2003)

However, gross negligence manslaughter can be committed by an omission. It could be argued that Lowe should have been convicted of this because he owed the child a duty of care and he had failed to get help. This idea was seen in *Stone and Dobinson* (1977) (above).

For gross negligence manslaughter, the defendant must owe the victim a duty of care. If a duty of care exists then the defendant can be liable if an omission or failure to act by him causes the death of the victim.

A full discussion of involuntary manslaughter is contained in Chapter 9.

2.2.3 The duty of doctors

There can be cases where doctors decide to stop treating a patient. If this discontinuance of treatment is in the best interests of the patient then it is *not* an omission which can form the *actus reus*. This was decided in *Airedale NHS Trust v Bland* (1993).

AIREDALE NHS TRUST v BLAND **(1993)**
Bland was a young man who had been crushed in crowd panic at a football stadium. This had stopped oxygen getting to his brain and left him with severe brain damage. He was in a persistent vegetative state (PVS), unable to do anything for himself and unaware of what was happening around him. He was fed artificially through tubes. He had been in this state for three years and the doctors caring for him asked the court for a ruling that they could stop feeding him.

The court ruled that the doctors could stop artificially feeding Bland even though it was known that he would die as a result. This was held to be in his best interests.

2.3   CAUSATION

Where a consequence must be proved, then the prosecution has to show that the defendant's conduct was:

- the factual cause of that consequence and
- the legal cause of that consequence and
- there was no intervening act which broke the chain of causation.

2.3.1 Factual cause

The defendant can only be guilty if the consequence would not have happened 'but for' the defendant's conduct. This 'but for' test can be seen in operation in the case of *Pagett* (1983).

> **PAGETT (1983)**
> The defendant took his pregnant girlfriend from her home by force. He then held the girl hostage. Police called on him to surrender. D came out, holding the girl in front of him and firing at the police. The police returned fire and the girl was killed by police bullets. D was convicted of manslaughter.

Pagett was guilty because the girl would not have died 'but for' him using her as a shield in the shoot-out. The opposite situation was seen in *White* (1910) where the defendant put cyanide in his mother's drink, intending to kill her. She died of a heart attack before she could drink it. The defendant was not the factual cause of her death. So, he was not guilty of murder, although he was guilty of attempted murder.

2.3.2 Legal cause

There may be more than one act contributing to the consequence. Some of these acts may be by people other than the defendant. The rule is that the defendant can be guilty if his conduct was more than a 'minimal' cause of the consequence. But the defendant's conduct need not be a substantial cause. In some cases the courts have stated that the conduct

must be more than *de minimis*. In *Kimsey* (1996) the Court of Appeal held that instead of using this Latin phrase '*de minimis*' it was acceptable to tell the jury it must be 'more than a slight or trifling link'.

> **KIMSEY (1996)**
> D was involved in a high-speed car chase with a friend. She lost control of her car and the other driver was killed in the crash. The evidence about what happened immediately before D lost control was not very clear. The trial judge directed the jury that D's driving did not have to be 'the principal, or a substantial cause of the death, as long as you are sure that it was a cause and that there something more than a slight or trifling link'. The Court of Appeal upheld D's conviction for causing death by dangerous driving.

There may be more than one person whose act contributed to the death. The defendant can be guilty even though his conduct was not the only cause of the death. In *Kimsey* both drivers were driving at high speed, but the one driver could be found guilty.

The 'thin-skull' rule

The defendant must also take the victim as he finds him. This is known as the 'thin-skull' rule. It means that if the victim has something unusual about his physical or mental state which makes an injury more serious, then the defendant is liable for the more serious injury. So, if the victim has an unusually thin skull which means that a blow to his head gives him a serious injury, then the defendant is liable for that injury. This is so even though that blow would have only caused bruising in a 'normal' person. An example is the case of *Blaue* (1975).

> ### *BLAUE* (1975)
> A young woman was stabbed by the defendant. She was told that she needed a blood transfusion to save her life but she refused to have one as she was a Jehovah's Witness and her religion forbade blood transfusions. She died and the defendant was convicted of her murder.
>
> The fact that the victim was a Jehovah's Witness made the wound fatal, but the defendant was still guilty because he had to take his victim as he found her.

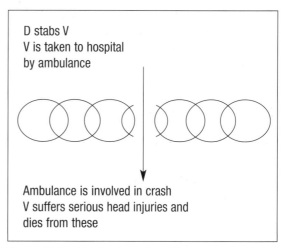

Figure 2.2 Breaking the chain of causation

2.3.3 Intervening acts

There must be a direct link from the defendant's conduct to the consequence. This is known as the *chain of causation*. In some situations something else happens after the defendant's act or omission and, if this is sufficiently separate from the defendant's conduct, it may break the chain of causation.

An example would be where the defendant has stabbed the victim who needs to be taken to hospital for treatment. On the way to hospital, the ambulance carrying the victim is involved in an accident and crashes, causing the victim fatal head injuries.

Under the 'but for' test it could be argued that the victim would not have been in the ambulance but for the defendant's act in stabbing him. However, the accident is such a major intervening act that the defendant would not be liable for the death of the victim.

The chain of causation can be broken by:

- an act of a third party or
- the victim's own act or
- a natural but unpredictable event.

In order to break the chain of causation so that the defendant is not responsible for the consequence, the intervening act must be sufficiently independent of the defendant's conduct and sufficiently serious.

Where the defendant's conduct causes a foreseeable action by a third party, then the defendant is likely to be held to have caused the consequence. This principle was applied in *Pagett* (1983) where his girlfriend was shot when he held her as a shield against police bullets (see section 2.3.1).

2.3.4 Medical treatment

Medical treatment is unlikely to break the chain of causation unless it is so independent of the defendant's acts and 'in itself so potent in causing death' that the defendant's acts are insignificant. The following three cases show this.

> ### *SMITH* (1959)
> Two soldiers had a fight and one was stabbed in the lung by the other. The victim was carried to a medical centre by other soldiers, but was dropped on the way. At the medical centre the staff gave him artificial respiration by pressing on his chest. This made the injury worse and he died. The poor treatment probably affected his chances of recovery by as much as 75 per cent. However, the original attacker was still guilty of his murder.

In this case it was held that a defendant would be guilty, provided that the injury caused by D was still an 'operating' and 'substantial' cause of death. Smith was guilty because the stab wound to the lung was still 'operating' (it obviously had not healed up) and it was a substantial cause of V's death.

CHESHIRE (1991)

D shot the victim in the thigh and the stomach. V needed major surgery. He developed breathing problems and was given a tracheotomy (ie a tube was inserted in his throat to help him breathe). Some two months after the shooting, V died from rare complications left by the tracheotomy. These complications were not diagnosed by the doctors. By the time V died, the original wounds had virtually healed and were no longer life-threatening. The defendant was still held to be liable for V's death.

In this case the Court of Appeal held that even though treatment for injuries was 'short of the standard expected of a competent medical practitioner' D could still be criminally responsible for the death. The prosecution had only to prove that D's acts contributed to the death. D's acts need not be the sole cause or even the main cause of death, provided that his acts contributed significantly to the death.

JORDAN (1956)

The victim had been stabbed in the stomach. He was treated in hospital and the wounds were healing well. He was given an antibiotic but suffered an allergic reaction to it. One doctor stopped the use of the antibiotic but the next day another doctor ordered that a large dose of it be given. The victim died from the allergic reaction to the drug. In this case the actions of the doctor were held to be an intervening act which caused the death. The defendant was not guilty of murder.

In the first two cases the doctors were carrying out treatment for the injuries in an attempt to save the victim's life. The victims would not have needed treatment if they had not been seriously injured by the defendant. In such situations the attacker is still liable even though the medical treatment was not very good. This was pointed out in *Cheshire* (1991) by Beldam LJ:

'Even though negligence in the treatment of the victim was the immediate cause of death, the jury should not regard it as excluding the responsibility of the accused unless the negligent treatment was so independent of his acts, and in itself so potent in causing death, that they regard the contribution made by his acts as insignificant.'

In the third case of *Jordan* (1956) the fact that the victim was given a large amount of a drug when the doctors knew he was allergic to it was a sufficiently independent act to break the chain of causation. However, if a normal dose of a drug is given as part of emergency treatment and the doctors do not know that the victim is allergic to it, then the giving of the drug would not break the chain of causation.

Life-support machines

The switching off a life-support machine by a doctor when it has been decided that the victim is brain-dead does not break the chain of causation. This was decided in *Malcherek* (1981).

MALCHEREK (1981)

D stabbed his wife in the stomach. At hospital she was put on a life-support machine. After a number of tests showed that she was brain dead, the machine was switched off. D was charged with her murder. The trial judge refused to allow the issue of causation to go to the jury. D was convicted and the Court of Appeal upheld his conviction.

Figure 2.3 Key cases chart on medical intervention and causation

KEY CASES

Case	Facts	Law
Smith (1959)	Soldier stabbed another soldier. V's medical treatment very poor and affected chances of recovery.	D liable if the injuries he caused are still an operating and substantial cause.
Cheshire (1991)	D shot V. V needed a tracheotomy. V died because of complications from the tracheotomy. His wounds were virtually healed.	Medical treatment would only break the chain of causation if it is 'so independent' of D's acts and 'in itself so potent in causing death'.
Jordan (1956)	V was stabbed. When his wounds were almost healed he was given a large dose of a drug to which it was known he was allergic.	The chain of causation was broken in this case.
Malcherek (1981)	D stabbed his wife. She was put on a life-support machine but when tests showed she was brain dead the machine was switched off.	Switching off a life-support machine does not break the chain of causation.

2.3.5 Victim's own act

If the defendant causes the victim to react in a foreseeable way, then any injury to the victim will be considered to have been caused by the defendant. This occurred in *Roberts* (1971).

> **ROBERTS (1971)**
> A girl jumped from a car in order to escape from Roberts' sexual advances. The car was travelling at between 20 and 40 mph and the girl was injured through jumping from it. The defendant was held to be liable for her injuries.

Another case in which it was held that D was liable if V's action were reasonably foreseeable was *Marjoram* (2000).

> **MARJORAM (2000)**
> Several people, including D, shouted abuse and kicked the door of V's hostel room. They eventually forced the door open. V then fell (or possibly jumped) from the window of the room and suffered serious injuries. D's conviction for inflicting grievous bodily harm was upheld by the Court of Appeal.
>
> In this situation it was reasonably foreseeable that V would fear that the group were going to use violence against him and that the only escape route for him was the window.

Unreasonable reaction

However, if the victim's reaction is unreasonable, then this may break the chain of causation. In *Williams* (1992) a hitch-hiker jumped from Williams' car and died from head injuries caused by his head hitting the road. The car was travelling at about 30 mph. The prosecution alleged that there had been an attempt to steal the victim's wallet and that was the reason for his jumping from the car. The Court of Appeal said that the victim's act had to be foreseeable and also had to be in proportion to the threat. The question to be asked was whether the victim's conduct was:

'within the ambit of reasonableness and not so daft as to make his own voluntary act one which amounted to a novus actus interveniens (a new intervening act) and consequently broke the chain of causation.'

This makes it necessary to consider the surrounding circumstances in deciding whether the victim's conduct has broken the chain of causation. Where the threats to the victim are serious, then it is more likely for it to be reasonable for him to jump out of a moving car (or out of a window or into a river etc.). Where the threat is very minor and the victim takes drastic action, it is more likely

that the courts will hold that it broke the chain of causation.

The main rules on causation are shown in a flowchart in Figure 2.4.

2.3.6 Problems in the law on causation

A major problem in the law on causation is: what is meant by more than a 'slight and trifling link'? This is vague and difficult to define. As a result, it could lead to juries applying different standards in different cases.

Taking your victim as you find him

Where V has a medical condition which makes the injury more serious, should D be liable for the more serious injury? It can be seen as being unjust where D does not know about the medical condition. For example, if a victim has an exceptionally thin skull, so that a blow kills him, it is justified that D should be liable for murder when the blow would not have killed a normal person. D did not intend to kill but if he intended to cause really serious injury then D is guilty of murder. (This is also a criticism of the *mens rea* for murder – see Chapter 7 for more on this.)

Also, should D be liable when V refuses treatment? This was probably justified when medical treatment was very primitive, especially when operations had to be carried out without anaesthetic. In *Holland* (1841), D deliberately cut V's finger. The cut become infected and V was advised that he should have the finger amputated. He refused to have the amputation until it was too late, and he died from the infection. D was liable for his death. In 1841 surgery was very primitive and this decision can be justified, but should D be liable on the same scenario today? D is in any event guilty of an assault causing actual bodily harm, but should he be liable for the death?

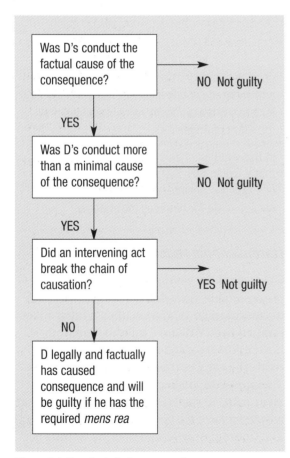

Figure 2.4 Flowchart of rules on causation

In *Blaue* (1975) the victim refused a blood transfusion because of her religious beliefs. Her life could have been saved had she had a transfusion. It can be argued that D should not be liable for her death. He could have been charged with wounding with intent to do so (s 18 Offences Against the Person Act 1861). This offence has a maximum penalty of life imprisonment, so a suitable punishment could have been imposed on D. On the other hand, it is clear that the stab wound was the cause of V's death, so on this basis it can be argued that he should be liable for her death.

What if a victim refused a blood transfusion because of a fear of becoming HIV positive through the transfusion? Is this is any different from the situation in *Blaue*? Surely the rule must apply in the same way, regardless of the reason for refusing medical treatment? An even more extreme case is *Dear* (1996).

DEAR (1996)

D slashed V several times with a Stanley knife, severing an artery. V did not bother to have the wounds attended to and, possibly, even opened the wounds further, making the bleeding worse. V died from loss of blood. D's conviction for murder was upheld by the Court of Appeal.

The court held that, provided the wounds were an operating and significant cause, the jury were entitled to convict D. Even if V had effectively decided to commit suicide by allowing the wounds to continue to bleed, the wounds were still the cause of death.

If V really had opened up the wounds further, should this be regarded as an intervening act which broke the chain of causation? Or is the court's view that as the wounds were the cause of death, then D was liable for the death?

Activity

Read the following situations and explain whether causation would be proved.

1 Aled has been threatened by Ben in the past. When Aled sees Ben approaching him in the street, Aled runs across the road without looking and is knocked down and injured by a car. Would Ben be liable for Aled's injuries?
2 Toyah stabs Steve in the arm. His injury is not serious but he needs stitches, so a neighbour takes Steve to hospital in his car. On the way to the hospital, the car crashes and Steve sustains serious head injuries. Would Toyah be liable for the head injuries?
3 Lewis has broken into Katie's third-floor flat. He threatens to rape her and in order to escape from him she jumps from the window and is seriously injured. Would Lewis be liable for her injuries?
4 Ross stabs Panjit in the chest. Panjit is taken to hospital where he is given an emergency blood transfusion. Unfortunately, he is given the wrong blood and he dies. Would Ross be liable for Panjit's death?

Negligent medical treatment

In *Smith* (1959) the court used the test of 'operating and substantial cause'. However, this test might not have led to a conviction in *Cheshire* (1991). In *Cheshire*, V's wounds were virtually healed. Were they an 'operating and substantial cause' of V's death? Probably not.

Yet, V would not have had to have a tracheotomy if he had not been shot by D. So, the medical negligence in failing to notice the complications from the tracheotomy was not 'independent of' D's acts. D's acts were a significant factor in V's death. The test developed in *Cheshire* was more suited to the situation in that case.

Examination questions

1 'English Law does not in general impose liability for a failure to act despite the fact that there may be compelling moral justification for doing so. For example, the courts have often explained that there is no legal duty upon a stranger to rescue a drowning child.'

Assess the truth of this statement and consider whether the current principles governing liability for omissions are satisfactory.

(OCR, June 2002)

2 'Liability in criminal law normally requires the prosecution to establish that the accused has caused the relevant prohibited consequences or conduct to occur. For instance, in homicide, that the accused has caused the victim's death.'

Explain, by reference to decided cases, how the courts have approached the requirement of causation.

(OCR, January 2003)

CHAPTER 3

Mens rea

Mens rea is the mental element of an offence. Each offence has its own *mens rea* or mental element. The only exceptions are offences of strict liability. These offences do not require proof of mental element in respect of at least part of the *actus reus*. In criminal cases it is for the prosecution to prove the required *mens rea*.

There are different levels of *mens rea*. To be guilty, the accused must have at least the minimum level of *mens rea* required for the offence.

The highest level of *mens rea* is intention. This is also referred to as 'specific intention'. The other main types of *mens rea* are recklessness and negligence.

3.1 INTENTION

In the case of *Mohan* (1975) the court defined 'intention' as:

'a decision to bring about, in so far as it lies within the accused's power, [the prohibited consequence], no matter whether the accused desired that consequence of his act or not'.

This makes it clear that the defendant's motive or reason for doing the act is not relevant. The important point is that the defendant decided to bring about the prohibited consequence.

This can be illustrated by looking at the offence set out in s 18 of the Offences Against the Person Act 1861. For this offence, the defendant must wound or cause grievous bodily harm. The *mens rea* is that the defendant must intend to wound or cause grievous bodily harm or intend to resist arrest.

If the defendant did not intend one of these then he cannot be guilty of this offence. For example, if a person opens a door very suddenly and hits and seriously injures someone on the other side of the door who they did not know was there, then they do not intend to 'bring about' the prohibited consequence.

Motive

Mohan (1975) also makes it clear that motive is not the same as intention and is not relevant in deciding whether the defendant had intention. For example, a person may feel very strongly that the banking system in the Western world is causing poverty in poorer nations. That person then steals millions of pounds from a bank so that he can give it to people in poorer nations. His motive is to make sure that the poor receive money. This is irrelevant in deciding whether the defendant has the *mens rea* required for theft.

3.1.1 Direct and oblique intent

In the majority of cases the defendant has what is known as *direct intent*. But there are situations where the defendant intends one thing but the actual consequence which occurs is another thing. An example of this is if the defendant intends to frighten someone so as to stop them going to work. This occurred in the case of *Hancock and Shankland* (1986). The actual consequence was that the driver of the car taking the person to work was killed. This is shown in diagram form in Figure 3.1.

Figure 3.1 Direct intent/oblique intent

3.1.2 Foresight of consequences

The main problem with proving intention is in cases where the defendant's main aim was not the prohibited consequences. He intended something else. If, in achieving the other thing, the defendant foresaw that he would also cause those consequences, then he may be found guilty. This idea is referred to as 'foresight of consequences'.

An example of this type of situation is where the defendant decides to set fire to his shop in order to claim insurance. His main aim is damaging the shop and getting the insurance. Unfortunately, he starts the fire when members of staff are still in the shop and some of them are seriously injured. Has the defendant the intention for a s 18 offence of causing grievous bodily harm?

The starting point for foresight of consequences is s 8 of the Criminal Justice Act 1967 which states that:

'A court or jury, in determining whether a person has committed an offence –

(a) *shall not be bound in law to infer that he intended or foresaw a result of his actions by reason only of its being a natural and probable consequence of those actions; but*

(b) *shall decide whether he did intend or foresee that result by reference to all the evidence, drawing such inferences from the evidence as appear proper in the circumstances.'*

This wording has been the subject of several cases over the last 20 years or so. These are mainly cases where defendants have been charged with murder. The important point is that the defendant must intend or foresee a result. In a murder case this means that the defendant must foresee that death or really serious injury will be caused. The leading case on this is now *Woollin* (1998) but to understand the law and the problems it is necessary to look at cases which came before *Woollin*. The first of these was *Moloney* (1985).

> ### *MOLONEY* (1985)
> D and his step-father had drunk a considerable amount at a family party. After the party, they were heard talking and laughing. Then there was a shot. D phoned the police, saying that he had just murdered his father. D said that they had been seeing who was the faster at loading and firing a shotgun. He had loaded his gun faster than his step-father. His step-father then said that D hadn't got 'the guts' to pull the trigger. D said 'I didn't aim the gun. I just pulled the trigger and he was dead'. D was convicted of murder but this conviction was quashed on appeal.

In this case the House of Lords ruled that foresight of consequences is only evidence of intention. It is not intention in itself. This part of the House of Lords' judgment is still law.

However, other parts of this judgment have been overruled by later cases. This was because Lord Bridge stated that jurors should be told to consider two questions:

1 was death or really serious injury a natural consequence of the defendant's act? and
2 did the defendant foresee that consequence as being a natural result of his act?

The problem with these questions (which are often referred to as the *Moloney* guidelines) is that the word 'probable' is not mentioned.

If you look back to s 8 of the Criminal Justice Act 1967, you will see that the section uses the phrase 'natural and probable consequence'. Lord Bridge referred only to a 'natural' result. This omission of the word 'probable' was held in *Hancock and Shankland* (1986) (see below) to make the guidelines defective. So they are no longer law.

HANCOCK and SHANKLAND (1986)

Ds were miners who were on strike. They tried to prevent another miner from going to work by pushing a concrete block from a bridge onto the road along which he was being driven to work in a taxi. The block struck the windscreen of the taxi and killed the driver. The trial judge used the *Moloney* guidelines to the direct the jury and Ds were convicted of murder. On appeal, the Court of Appeal quashed their convictions. This was upheld by the House of Lords.

The problem with *Moloney* (1985) was explained by Lord Scarman who stated that the guidelines in that case were unsafe and misleading. He said:

'In my judgment, therefore, the Moloney *guidelines as they stand are unsafe and misleading. They require a reference to probability. They also require an explanation that the greater the probability of a consequence the more likely it is that the consequence was foreseen and that if that consequence was foreseen the greater the probability is that that consequence was also intended.'*

The next case was *Nedrick* (1986) where the Court of Appeal thought that the judgments in the two earlier cases of *Moloney* (1985) and *Hancock and Shankland* (1986) needed to be made clearer.

NEDRICK (1986)

D had a grudge against a woman. He poured paraffin through the letter box of her house and set it alight. A child died in the fire. D was convicted of murder but the Court of Appeal quashed the conviction and substituted one of manslaughter.

To make the law decided in *Moloney*, *Hancock* and *Nedrick* easier for jurors to understand and apply in murder trials, the Court of Appeal said that it was helpful for a jury to ask themselves two questions:

1 how probable was the consequence which resulted from D's voluntary act? and
2 did D foresee that consequence?

It was necessary for the consequence to be a virtual certainty and for D to have realised that. If this was so then there was evidence from which the jury could infer that D had the necessary intention. Lord Lane CJ put it in this way:

'The jury should be directed that they are not entitled to infer the necessary intention unless they feel sure that death or serious bodily harm was a virtual certainty (barring some unforeseen intervention) as a result of the defendant's actions and that the defendant appreciated that such was the case.'

This remained the law until 1998 and the case of *Woollin* (1998). This went to the House of Lords who felt that the Court of Appeal's views in *Nedrick* (1986) were not helpful.

WOOLLIN (1998)

D threw his three-month-old baby towards his pram which was against a wall some three or four feet away. The baby suffered head injuries and died. The court ruled that the consequence must have been a virtual certainty and the defendant must have realised this. Where the jury were satisfied on both these two points, then there was evidence on which the jury could find intention.

The Law Lords thought that the two questions in *Nedrick* were not helpful. They held that the model direction from *Nedrick* should be used, but that the word 'find' should be used rather than the word 'infer'. So the model direction to be given to a jury considering foresight of consequences should now be:

'the jury should be directed that they are not entitled to <u>find</u> the necessary intention unless they feel sure that death or serious bodily harm was a virtual certainty (barring some unforeseen intervention) as a result of the defendant's actions and that the defendant appreciated that such was the case.'

This causes some problems. First of all, the word 'infer' is used in s 8 of the Criminal Justice Act 1967 and this is presumably why it was used in *Nedrick*. Does the substitution of the word 'find' improve the clarity of the direction to the jury? Another problem is whether the use of the word 'find' means that foresight of consequence is intention and not merely evidence of it.

In his judgment Lord Steyn also went on to say that the effect of the direction is that 'a result foreseen as virtually certain is an intended result'. He also pointed out that in *Moloney* the House of Lords had said that if a

person foresees the probability of a consequence as little short of overwhelming, this 'will suffice to establish the necessary intent'. Lord Steyn emphasised the word 'establish'. This seems to suggest that the House of Lords in *Woollin* regarded foresight of consequences as the same as intention, when *Moloney* had clearly stated that it was not.

In later cases there have been conflicting decisions on this point. In the civil case of *Re A* (2000), doctors asked the courts whether they could operate to separate conjoined twins when they foresaw that this would kill the weaker twin. The Court of Appeal (Civil Division) clearly thought that *Woollin* laid down the rule that foresight of consequences *is* intention.

In the criminal case of *Matthews and Alleyne* (2003) the Court of Appeal held that the judgment in *Woollin* meant that foresight of consequences is *not* intention: it is a rule of evidence. If a jury decide that the defendant foresaw the virtual certainty of death or serious injury then they are entitled to find intention but they do not have to do so.

MATTHEWS and ALLEYNE (2003)

The defendants dropped the victim 25 feet from a bridge, into the middle of a deep river. The victim had told them that he could not swim. They watched him 'dog paddle' towards the bank but left before seeing whether he reached safety. The victim drowned.

A chart of the cases on foresight of consequences is included to help keep the cases clear. (See Figure 3.2.)

Figure 3.2 Case chart on foresight of consequences

Case	Brief facts	Law	KEY CASES
Moloney (1985)	D shot step-father in 'quick on the draw' incident.	Foresight of consequences is *not* intention; it is evidence of intention.	
Hankcock and Shankland (1986)	Miners dropped lumps of concrete onto road, killing taxi driver.	The greater the probability of a consequence, the more likely it is that the consequence was foreseen and that if that consequence was foreseen the greater the probability is that that consequence was also intended.	
Nedrick (1986)	Poured paraffin through letter box, causing fire in the house in which a child died.	Jury not entitled to *infer* the necessary intention unless sure that death or serious bodily harm was a virtual certainty and that the defendant appreciated this.	
Woollin (1998)	Threw baby at pram, causing its death.	The direction in *Nedrick* should not use the word 'infer'. Instead, the jury should be told they are entitled to *find* intention.	
Re A (2000)	Doctors wanted to operate on conjoined twins but knew this would cause one of them to die.	Court thought that *Woollin* made it law that foresight of consequences is intention.	
Matthews and Alleyne (2003)	Threw V into river where he drowned.	*Woollin* meant that foresight of consequences is *not* intention. It is a rule of evidence. If a jury decide that the defendant foresaw the virtual certainty of death or serious injury then they are entitled to find intention but they do not have to do so.	

Activity

In each of the following situations, explain whether the defendant has the required intention for murder. The *mens rea* for murder is an intention to kill or an intention to cause grievous bodily harm.

1 Geraint dislikes Victor and decides to attack him. Geraint uses an iron bar to hit Victor on the head. Victor dies as a result.

2 Inderpal throws a large stone into a river to see how much of a splash it will make. Jake is swimming in the river and is hit on the head by the stone and killed.

3 Kylie throws a large stone from a bridge, onto the motorway below. It is rush hour and there is a lot of traffic on the motorway. The stone smashes through the windscreen of Ashley's car and kills his passenger.

3.1.3 Reform of the law

In 1993 the Law Commission, in its report *Offences Against the Person and General Principles*, proposed that 'intentionally' should be defined as follows:

'A person acts intentionally with respect to a result when:
i it is his purpose to cause it; or
ii although it is not his purpose to cause it, he knows that it would occur in the ordinary course of events if he were to succeed in his purpose of causing some other result.'

This was only in relation to non-fatal offences against the person, but there seems to be no reason why the definition should not be brought to apply to all offences as suggested by the Draft Criminal Code.

3.2   RECKLESSNESS

This is a lower level of *mens rea* than intention. Recklessness is where the defendant knows there is a risk of the consequence happening but takes that risk.

3.2.1 The case of *Cunningham*

The explanation of recklessness comes from the case of *Cunningham* (1957).

CUNNINGHAM (1957)
D tore a gas meter from the wall of an empty house in order to steal the money in it. This caused gas to seep into the house next door, where a woman was affected by it. Cunningham was charged with an offence under s 23 of the Offences Against the Person Act 1861, of maliciously administering a noxious thing. It was held that he was not guilty since he did not realise the risk of gas escaping into the next-door house. He had not intended to cause the harm, nor had he taken a risk he knew about.

The offence involved in *Cunningham* uses the word 'maliciously' to indicate the *mens rea* required. The court held that this word meant that to have the necessary *mens rea* the defendant must either intend the consequence or realise that there was a risk of the consequence happening and decide to take that risk. Knowing about a risk and taking it can also be referred to as 'subjective recklessness'. It is subjective because the defendant himself realised the risk.

The case of *Savage* (1992) confirmed that the same principle applies to all offences where the definition in an Act of Parliament uses the word 'maliciously'. The Law Lords said that 'maliciously' was a legal term of art. In other words, it has a special meaning when used in an Act of Parliament, not its normal dictionary definition. It means doing something intentionally or being subjectively reckless about the risk involved.

Don't forget that if the defendant has the higher level of intention he will, of course, be guilty. For example, if the defendant intends to punch the victim in the face, that defendant has the higher level of intention and is guilty of a battery. It is only when the defendant does not have the higher level that reckless has to be considered.

Offences for which recklessness is sufficient for the *mens rea* include:

- assault and battery
- assault occasioning actual bodily harm (s 47 of the Offences Against the Person Act 1861)
- malicious wounding (s 20 of the Offences Against the Person Act 1861)
- criminal damage.

3.2.2 Past problems in the law

There used to be two levels of recklessness. These were:

- subjective, where the defendant realised the risk, but decided to take it objective, where an ordinary prudent person would have realised the risk: the defendant was guilty even if he did not realise the risk.

The first type of recklessness is the only recklessness that the law now recognises as being sufficient to prove a defendant guilty where recklessness is sufficient to make the defendant guilty. However, during the period from 1982 to 2003, it was accepted that a defendant could be guilty of certain offences even though he had not realised that there was a risk. This was decided in the case of *Metropolitan Police Commissioner v Caldwell* (1981).

METROPOLITAN POLICE COMMISSIONER v CALDWELL (1981)

D had a grievance against the owner of a hotel. He got very drunk and decided to set fire to the hotel. The fire was put out quickly, without serious damage to the hotel. D was charged with arson under s 1(2) of the Criminal Damage Act 1971. This requires that D intended to endanger life or was reckless as to whether life was endangered. D claimed that he was so drunk he had not realised people's lives might be endangered. His conviction was upheld.

In *Caldwell* the House of Lords held that 'reckless' covered two situations. The first is where D had realised the risk and the second is where D had not thought about the possibility of any risk.

This second meaning of 'reckless' caused problems in cases where D was not capable of appreciating the risk involved in his conduct, even though a reasonable person would have realised there was a risk. This occurred in *Elliott v C* (1983) where D was a 14-year-old girl with learning difficulties. She did not appreciate the risk that her act might set a shed on fire. But she was found guilty because ordinary adults would have realised the risk.

This seemed very unfair. The girl was not blameworthy. If she had been judged by the standard of a 14-year-old with learning difficulties then she would not have been convicted. It was absurd to judge her against the standard of ordinary adults. This problem was eventually resolved when the House of Lords overruled *Caldwell* in the case of *G and another* (2003).

G and ANOTHER (2003)

The defendants were two boys, aged 11 and 12 years, who set fire to some bundles of newspapers in a shop yard. They threw them under a large wheelie bin. and left. They thought the fire would go out by itself. In fact, the bin caught fire and this spread to the shop and other buildings, causing about £1 million worth of damage. The judge directed the jury that they had to decide whether ordinary adults would have realised the risk. The boys were convicted under both ss 1 and 3 of the Criminal Damage Act 1971. On appeal, the House of Lords quashed their conviction.

The House of Lords held that a defendant could not be guilty unless he had realised the risk and decided to take it. The House of Lords overruled the decision in *Caldwell*, holding that in that case the Law Lords had adopted an interpretation of s 1 of the Criminal Damage Act 1971 which was 'beyond the range of feasible meanings'.

So now the law is clear. Where recklessness is sufficient for the *mens rea* of an offence, it must be subjective recklessness. The prosecution must prove that the defendant realised the risk and decided to take it.

3.3 TRANSFERRED MALICE

This is the principle that the defendant can be guilty if he intended to commit a similar crime but against a different victim. An example is aiming a blow at one person with the necessary *mens rea* for an assault causing actual bodily harm, but actually hitting another person. This occurred in *Latimer* (1886).

LATIMER (1886)
D aimed a blow with a belt at a man in a pub because that man had attacked him. The belt bounced off the man and struck a woman in the face. Latimer was guilty of an assault against the woman, although he had not meant to hit her.

However, where the *mens rea* is for a completely different type of offence, then the defendant may not be guilty. This was the situation in *Pembliton* (1874), where the defendant threw a stone, intending it to hit people with whom he had been fighting. The stone hit and broke a window. The intention to hit people could not be transferred to the window.

The doctrine of transferred malice was confirmed in an *obiter* statement by the House of Lords in the case of *Attorney-General's Reference (No. 3 of 1994)* (1997) (see section 7.2.2 for details of the case).

3.3.1 General malice

In some cases the defendant may not have a specific victim in mind: for example, a terrorist who plants a bomb in a pub, intending to kill or injure anyone who happens to be there. In this case the defendant's *mens rea* is held to apply to the actual victim.

3.4   COINCIDENCE OF *ACTUS REUS* AND *MENS REA*

In order for an offence to take place, both the *actus reus* and the *mens rea* must be present at the same time. For example, if you decide to go round to your next-door neighbour, intending to assault them, but when you get to their house you change your mind and do not actually assault them, you cannot be guilty of an assault even though you had the *mens rea*.

If, two hours later, you are driving your car out of your driveway and knock down your neighbour because you did not see them, you have now done what could be the *actus reus* for an assault. However, you are not guilty of any criminal offence since at the moment you hit your neighbour you did not have the necessary *mens rea*. The *mens rea* and the *actus reus* were not present at the same time.

In *Thabo Meli v R* (1954) the court had to decide whether the *actus reus* and *mens rea* were present together.

THABO MELI v R (1954)
Ds attacked a man and believed they had killed him. They then pushed his body over a low cliff. In fact, the man had survived the attack but died of exposure when unconscious at the foot of the cliff. It was held that Ds were guilty of murder.

The defendants in this case were guilty as the required *mens rea* and *actus reus* were combined in a series of acts. A similar situation occurred in *Church* (1965).

CHURCH (1965)
D had a fight with a woman and knocked her out. He tried, unsuccessfully, for about half an hour to bring her round. He thought she was dead and he put her in the river. She drowned. His conviction for manslaughter was upheld.

3.4.1 Continuing act

Where there is a continuing act for the *actus reus* and at some point while that act is still going on the defendant has the necessary *mens rea*, then the two do coincide and the defendant will be guilty. This is illustrated by the case of *Fagan v Metropolitan Police Commissioner* (1986).

FAGAN v METROPOLITAN POLICE COMMISSIONER (1986)

Fagan was told by a police officer to park by a kerb. In doing this Fagan drove on to the policeman's foot, without realising he had done so. Initially, Fagan refused to move the car. When the policeman pointed out what had happened, he asked Fagan several times to move the car off his foot. Eventually, Fagan did move the car. Fagan was convicted of assaulting the police officer in the execution of his duty

The Court of Appeal held that once Fagan knew the car was on the police officer's foot he had the required *mens rea*. As the *actus reus* (the car putting force on the foot) was still continuing, the two elements were then present together. The *actus reus* in this case was a continuing act and, so long as the defendant developed the *mens rea* at some time while the act was continuing, then he could be guilty.

CHAPTER 4 | Strict liability

4.1 THE CONCEPT OF STRICT LIABILITY

The previous chapter explained the different types of *mens rea*. This chapter considers those offences where *mens rea* is not required in respect of at least one aspect of the *actus reus*. Such offences are known as strict liability offences.

An example demonstrating strict liability is *Pharmaceutical Society of Great Britain v Storkwain Ltd* (1986).

PHARMACEUTICAL SOCIETY OF GREAT BRITAIN v STORKWAIN LTD (1986)
D was charged under s 58(2) of the Medicines Act 1968 which states that no one shall supply certain drugs without a doctor's prescription. D had supplied drugs on prescriptions, but the prescriptions were later found to be forged. There was no finding that D had acted dishonestly, improperly or even negligently. The forgery was sufficient to deceive the pharmacists. Despite this, the House of Lords held that the Divisional Court was right to direct the magistrates to convict D. The pharmacists had supplied the drugs without a genuine prescription and this was enough to make them guilty of the offence.

4.1.1 Requirement of *actus reus*

For nearly all strict liability offences, it must be proved that the defendant did the relevant *actus reus*. For *Storkwain*, this meant proving that the chemist had supplied drugs without a genuine prescription. It also has to be proved that the doing of the *actus reus* was voluntary. If the chemist had been forced at gun-point to provide the drug, then the act would not have been voluntary.

However, there are a few rare cases where the defendant has been found guilty even though they did not do the *actus reus* voluntarily. These are known as crimes of absolute liability.

4.2 ABSOLUTE LIABILITY

Absolute liability means that no *mens rea* at all is required for the offence. They involve 'status offences', that is offences where the *actus reus* is a 'state of affairs'. The defendant is liable because they have 'been found' in a certain situation. Such offences are very rare. To be an absolute liability offence, the following conditions must apply:

- the offence does not require any *mens rea* and
- there is no need to prove that the defendant's *actus reus* was voluntary.

The following two cases demonstrate this.

LARSONNEUR (1933)
The defendant, who was from a foreign country (and was therefore termed an 'alien', in the language of the time), had been ordered to leave the United Kingdom. She decided to go to Eire, but the Irish police deported her and took her in police custody back to the UK, where she was put in a cell in Holyhead police station. She did not want to return to the UK. She had no *mens rea*. Her act in returning was not voluntary. She was taken back to the UK. Despite this, she was found guilty under the Aliens Order 1920 of being 'an alien to whom leave to land in the United Kingdom has been refused ... found in the United Kingdom'.

The other case is *Winzar v Chief Constable of Kent* (1983).

WINZAR v CHIEF CONSTABLE OF KENT (1983)
D was taken to hospital on a stretcher, but when he was examined by doctors they found that he was not ill but was drunk. D was told to leave the hospital, but was later found slumped on a seat in a corridor. The police were called and they took D to the roadway outside the hospital. They formed the opinion that he was drunk so they put him the police car, drove him to the police station and charged him with being found drunk in a highway, contrary to s 12 of the Licensing Act 1872. The Divisional Court upheld his conviction.

As in *Larsonneur*, the defendant had not acted voluntarily. He had been taken to the highway by the police. In the Divisional Court Goff LJ justified the conviction, pointing out that the particular offence was designed to deal with the nuisance which can be caused by persons who are drunk in a public place.

It is not known how Winzar came to be taken to the hospital on a stretcher but it is possible that there may have been an element of fault in his conduct. He had become drunk (presumably voluntarily) and must have either been in a public place when the ambulance collected him and took him to hospital or he must have summoned medical assistance when he was not ill but only drunk.

4.3 STRICT LIABILITY

For all offences there is a presumption that *mens rea* is required. The courts will always start with this presumption, but if they decide that the offence does not require *mens rea* for at least part of the *actus reus* then the offence is one of strict liability. This idea of not requiring *mens rea* for part of the offence is illustrated by two cases: *Prince* (1875) and

Hibbert (1869). In both these cases the charge against the defendant was that he had taken an unmarried girl under the age of 16 out of the possession of her father, against his will, contrary to s 55 of the Offences Against the Person Act 1861.

PRINCE (1875)
Prince knew that the girl he took was in the possession of her father but believed, on reasonable grounds, that she was aged 18. He was convicted as he had the intention to remove the girl from the possession of her father. *Mens rea* was required for this part of the *actus reus* and he had the necessary intention. However, the court held that knowledge of her age was not required. On this aspect of the offence there was strict liability.

HIBBERT (1869)
The defendant met a girl aged 14 on the street. He took her to another place where they had sexual intercourse. He was acquitted of the offence as it was not proved that he knew the girl was in the custody of her father. Even though the age aspect of the offence was one of strict liability, *mens rea* was required for the removal aspect and, in this case, the necessary intention was not proved.

4.3.1 No fault

As already stated, the *actus reus* must be proved and the defendant's conduct in doing the *actus reus* must be voluntary. However, a defendant can be convicted if his voluntary act inadvertently caused a prohibited consequence. This is so even though the defendant was totally blameless in respect of the consequence. An example was the case of *Callow v Tillstone* (1900).

CALLOW v TILLSTONE (1900)

A butcher asked a vet to examine a carcass to see if it was fit for human consumption. The vet assured him that it was all right to eat and so the butcher offered it for sale. In fact, it was unfit and the butcher was convicted of the offence of exposing unsound meat for sale.

Because it was a strict liability offence the butcher was guilty, even though he had taken reasonable care not to commit the offence. The butcher was not at fault in any way.

4.3.2 No 'due diligence' defence

For some offences the statute provides a defence of 'due diligence'. In other words, the defendant will not be liable if he can show that he did all that was within his power not to commit the offence.

However, there does not seem to be any sensible pattern for when Parliament decides to include a 'due diligence' defence and when it does not. It can be argued that such a defence should always be available for strict liability offences. If it was a defence, then the butcher in *Callow v Tillstone* would not have been guilty. By asking a vet to check the meat, he had clearly done all that he could to make sure that he did not commit the offence.

Another example of where the defendants took all reasonable steps to prevent the offence but were still guilty because there was no 'due diligence' defence available is *Harrow London Borough Council v Shah and Shah* (1999).

HARROW LBC v SHAH AND SHAH (1999)

The defendants owned a newsagents' business where lottery tickets were sold. They had told their staff not to sell tickets to anyone under 16 years old. They frequently reminded their staff that if there was any doubt about a customer's age, the staff should ask for proof of age, and if still in doubt should refer the matter to the defendants. One of their staff sold a lottery ticket to a 13-year-old boy, without asking for proof of age. The salesman mistakenly believed the boy was over 16 years old. D1 was in a back room of the premises at the time: D2 was not on the premises. The defendants were charged with selling a lottery ticket to a person under 16, contrary to s 13(1)(c) of the National Lottery Act 1993. The magistrates dismissed the charges, but the prosecution appealed to the Divisional Court which held that the offence was one of strict liability. This meant that the defendants were guilty.

The Divisional Court held that the offence did not require any *mens rea*. The act of selling the ticket to someone who was actually under 16 was enough to make the defendants guilty, even though they had done their best to prevent this happening in their shop.

4.3.3 No defence of mistake

Another feature of strict liability offences is that the defence of mistake is not available. This is important as, if the defence of mistake is available, the defendant will be acquitted when he made an honest mistake. Two cases which illustrate the difference in liability are *Cundy v Le Cocq* (1884) and *Sherras v De Rutzen* (1895). Both of these involved offences under the Licensing Act 1872.

CUNDY v LE COCQ (1884)

D was charged with selling intoxicating liquor to a drunken person. The magistrate trying the case found as a fact that the defendant and his employees had not noticed that the person was drunk. The magistrate also found that while the person was on the licensed premises he had been 'quiet in his demeanour and had done nothing to indicate insobriety; and that there were no apparent indications of intoxication'. However, the magistrate held that the offence was complete on proof that a sale had taken place and that the person served was drunk, and convicted the defendant. The defendant appealed against this but the Divisional Court upheld the conviction.

SHERRAS v DE RUTZEN (1895)
D was convicted of supplying alcohol to a constable on duty. Local police, when on duty, wore an armband on their uniform. An on-duty police officer removed his armband before entering the defendant's public house. The officer was served by D's daughter in the presence of D. D thought that the constable was off duty because he was not wearing his armband. D was convicted but the Divisional Court quashed the conviction. It held that the offence was not one of strict liability and accordingly a genuine mistake provided the defendant with a defence.

The judge in the case of *Sherras* pointed out that there was nothing the publican could do to prevent the commission of the crime. Even if the publican asked the officer, it would be as easy for the constable to deny that he was on duty as for him to remove his armband before entering the public house. This explains the different decisions in the two cases. The fact of a person being drunk is an observable fact, so the publican should be put on alert and could avoid committing the offence.

4.3.4 Summary of strict liability

So, where an offence is held to be one of strict liability, the following points apply:

- the defendant must be proved to have done the *actus reus*
- this must be a voluntary act on his part
- there is no need to prove *mens rea* for at least part of the *actus reus*
- no 'due diligence' defence will be available
- the defence of mistake is not available.

These factors are well established. The problem lies in deciding which offences are ones of strict liability. For this, the courts will start with presuming that *mens rea* should apply. This is so for both common-law and statutory offences. (See Figure 4.1.)

4.4 STRICT LIABILITY AT COMMON LAW

Nearly all strict liability offences have been created by statute. Strict liability is very rare in common-law offences. Only four common-law offences have been held to be ones of strict liability. These are:

- public nuisance
- criminal libel
- blasphemous libel
- criminal contempt of court.

Public nuisance and criminal libel probably do not require *mens rea*, but there are no modern cases. There has been a relatively recent case on blasphemous libel which confirmed that it is a strict liability offence. This was *Lemon and Whitehouse v Gay News* (1979).

LEMON and WHITEHOUSE v GAY NEWS (1979)
A poem was published in *Gay News*, describing homosexual acts done to the body of Christ after his crucifixion and also describing his alleged homosexual practices during his lifetime. The editor and publishers were convicted of blasphemy. On appeal to the House of Lords, the Law Lords held that it was not necessary to prove that the defendants intended to blaspheme.

Criminal contempt of court was a strict liability offence at common law. It is now a statutory offence and Parliament has continued it as a strict liability offence.

Figure 4.1 Key facts chart on strict liability

	Law	Cases	
Absolute liability	These offences do not need proof of *mens rea* or voluntary *actus reus*.	*Larsonneur* (1933) *Winzar* (1993)	
Strict liability	*Mens rea* need not be proved.	*Storkwain* (1986)	
	Proof will not be required for one aspect of *mens rea* but may be required for another aspect of *mens rea*.	*Prince* (1875) *Hibbert* (1869)	
No fault liability	D is liable if he voluntarily did the *actus reus* (eg 'sells') even though he is not blameworthy.	*Callow v Tillstone* (1900)	
No 'due diligence' defence	If the Act of Parliament does not allow a 'due diligence' defence, then D will be guilty even though he took all possible care.	*Harrow LBC v Shah and Shah* (1999)	
No defence of mistake	D will still be guilty even though he made a genuine mistake.	*Cundy v Le Cocq* (1884)	

KEY FACTS

4.5 STRICT LIABILITY IN STATUTE LAW

The surprising fact is that about half of all statutory offences are ones of strict liability. This amounts to over 3,500 offences. Most strict liability offences are regulatory in nature. This may involve such matters as regulating the sale of food and alcohol and gaming tickets, the prevention of pollution and the safe use of vehicles.

4.5.1 Presumption of *mens rea*

In order to decide whether an offence is one of strict liability, the courts start by assuming that *mens rea* is required, but they are prepared to interpret the offence as one of strict liability if Parliament has expressly or by implication indicated this in the relevant statute.

The judges often have difficulty in deciding whether an offence is one of strict liability or not. The first rule is that where an Act of Parliament includes words indicating *mens rea* (eg 'knowingly', 'intentionally', 'maliciously' or 'permitting'), the offence requires *mens rea* and is not one of strict liability. However, if an Act of Parliament makes it clear that *mens rea* is not required, the offence will be one of strict liability.

However, in many instances a section in an Act of Parliament is silent about the need for *mens rea*. Parliament is criticised for this. If it made clear in all sections which create a criminal offence whether *mens rea* was required or not, then there would be no problem. As it is, where there are no express words indicating *mens rea* or strict liability, the courts have to decide which offences are ones of strict liability.

4.5.2 Principle in *Sweet v Parsley*

Where an Act of Parliament does not include any words indicating *mens rea*, the judges will start by presuming that all criminal offences require *mens rea*. This was made clear in the case of *Sweet v Parsley* (1969).

SWEET v PARSLEY (1969)

D rented a farmhouse and let it out to students. The police found cannabis at the farmhouse and D was charged with 'being concerned in the management of premises used for the purpose of smoking cannabis resin'. D did not know that cannabis was being smoked there. It was decided that she was not guilty as the court presumed that the offence required *mens rea*.

In giving judgment, Lord Reid said:

'*There has for centuries been a presumption that Parliament did not intend to make criminals of persons who were in no way blameworthy in what they did. That means that whenever a section is silent as to* mens rea *there is a presumption that ... we must read in words appropriate to require* mens rea.'

Although the courts start with the presumption that *mens rea* is required, they look at a variety of points to decide whether the presumption should stand or can be displaced and the offence made one of strict liability.

4.5.3 The *Gammon* tests

In *Gammon (Hong Kong) Ltd v Attorney-General of Hong Kong* (1984) the appellants had been charged with deviating from building work in a material way from the approved plan, contrary to the Hong Kong Building Ordinances. It was necessary to decide whether it had to be proved that they knew that their deviation was material or

whether the offence was one of strict liability on this point.

The Privy Council started with the presumption that *mens rea* is required before a person can be held guilty of a criminal offence, but went on to give four others factors to be considered. These were that:

■ the presumption in favour of *mens rea* applies to statutory offences
■ the presumption can only be displaced if this is clearly or by necessary implication the effect of the words of the statute
■ the presumption is particularly strong where the offence is 'truly criminal' in character
■ the presumption can only be displaced if the statute is concerned with an issue of social concern such as public safety
■ strict liability should only apply if it will help enforce the law by encouraging greater vigilance to prevent the commission of the prohibited act.

4.5.4 Looking at the wording of an Act

As already stated, where words indicating *mens rea* are used, the offence is not one of strict liability. If the particular section is silent on the point then the courts will look at other sections in the Act. Where the particular offence has no words of intention, but other sections in the Act do, then it is likely that this offence is a strict liability offence.

In *Storkwain* (1986) (see the beginning of this chapter) the relevant section, s 58(2) of the Medicines Act 1968 was silent on *mens rea*. The court looked at other sections in the Act and decided that, as there were express provisions for *mens rea* in other sections, Parliament had intended s 58(2) to be one of strict liability.

Where other sections allow for a defence of 'due diligence' but another section does not, then this is another possible indicator from within the statute that the offence is meant to be one of strict liability.

In *Harrow LBC v Shah and Shah* (1999) the defendants were charged under s 13(1)(c) of the National Lottery Act 1993. This subsection does not any words indicating either that *mens rea* is required or that it is not, nor does it contain any provision for a defence of 'due diligence'. However, another subsection, s 13(1)(a), clearly allows a defence of 'due diligence'. The inclusion of a 'due diligence' defence in part of s 13 but not in the section under which the defendants were charged was an important point in the Divisional Court coming to the decision that s 13(1)(c) was an offence of strict liability.

4.5.5 Quasi-criminal offences

In *Gammon* the Privy Council stated that the presumption that *mens rea* is required is particularly strong where the offence is 'truly criminal' in character. Offences which are regulatory in nature are not thought of as being truly criminal matters and are, therefore, more likely to be interpreted as being of strict liability.

Regulatory offences are also referred to as 'quasi-crimes'. They affect large areas of everyday life. They include offences such as breaches of regulations in a variety of fields such as:

- selling food, as in *Callow v Tillstone* (1900)
- the selling of alcohol, as in *Cundy v Le Cocq* (1884)
- building regulations, as in occurred in *Gammon* (1984)
- sales of lottery tickets to an under-age child, as in *Harrow LBC v Shah and Shah* (1999) and
- regulations preventing pollution from being caused, as in *Alphacell Ltd v Woodward* (1972).

> **ALPHACELL (1972)**
> The company was charged with causing polluted matter to enter a river, contrary to s 2(1)(a) of the Rivers (Prevention of Pollution) Act 1951, when pumps which it had installed failed and polluted effluent overflowed into a river. There was no evidence either that the company knew of the pollution or that it had been negligent. The offence was held by the House of Lords to be one of strict liability and the company was found guilty because it was of the 'utmost public importance' that rivers should not be polluted.

4.5.6 Penalty of imprisonment

Where an offence carries a penalty of imprisonment, it is more likely to be considered 'truly criminal' and so less likely to be interpreted as an offence of strict liability. This was an important factor in *B v DPP* (2000).

> **B v DPP (2000)**
> D, a 15-year-old boy, asked a 13-year-old girl on a bus to give him a 'shiner' (ie have oral sex with him). He believed she was over the age of 14. He was charged with inciting a child under the age of 14 to commit an act of gross indecency, under s 1(1) of the Indecency with Children Act 1960. The House of Lords quashed his conviction, as *mens rea* was required for the offence
>
> The offence, inciting a child under the age of 14 to commit an act of gross indecency, carried a maximum penalty of two years' imprisonment. Lord Nicholls pointed out that this was a serious offence and that:
>
> *'the more serious the offence, the greater was the weight to be attached to the presumption [of* mens rea*], because the more severe was the punishment and the graver the stigma that accompanied a conviction'.*

However, some offences carrying imprisonment have been made strict liability offences. For example in *Storkwain* (see the beginning of this chapter) the offence carried a maximum sentence of two years' imprisonment. Despite this, the House of Lords still held that the offence was one of strict liability.

It appears unjust that an individual should be liable to imprisonment even though the offence does not require proof of any fault by the defendant.

4.5.7 Issues of social concern

The type of crime and whether it is 'truly criminal' are linked to another condition laid down by the case of *Gammon*; that is the question of whether the crime involves an issue of social concern. The Privy Council ruled that the only situation in which the presumption of *mens rea* can be displaced is where the statute is concerned with an issue of social concern.

This allows strict liability to be justified in a wide range of offences, as issues of social concern can be seen to cover any activity which is a 'potential danger to public health, safety or morals'.

Regulations covering health and safety matters in relation to food, drink, pollution, building and road use are obviously issues of social concern, but other issues such as possession of guns are also regarded as matters of public safety.

Even transmitting an unlicensed broadcast has been held to be a matter of social concern. This was decided in *Blake* (1997).

BLAKE (1997)

D was a disc jockey who was convicted of using a station for wireless telegraphy without a licence, contrary to s 1(1) of the Wireless Telegraphy Act 1949. His defence was that he believed he was making a demonstration tape and did not know he was transmitting. He was convicted on the basis that the offence was one of strict liability. He appealed to the Court of Appeal but his appeal was dismissed.

4.5.8 Promoting enforcement of the law

In *Gammon* the final point in considering whether strict liability should be imposed, even where the statute is concerned with an issue of social concern, was whether it would be effective to promote the objects of the statue by encouraging greater vigilance to prevent the commission of the prohibited act. If the imposition of strict liability will not make the law more effective then there is no reason to make the offence one of strict liability.

In *Lim Chin Aik v The Queen* (1963) the appellant had been convicted under s 6(2) of the Immigration Ordinance of Singapore of remaining (having entered) in Singapore when he had been prohibited from entering by an order made by the Minister under s 9 of the same Ordinance.

The Ordinance was aimed at prevent illegal immigration. However, the appellant had no knowledge of the prohibition and there was no evidence that the authorities had even tried to bring it to his attention. The Privy Council thought that it was not enough to be sure that the statute dealt with a grave social evil in order to infer strict liability. It was also important to consider whether the imposition of strict liability would assist in the enforcement of the regulations.

If it did not, then the offence should not be one of strict liability.

Figure 4.2 Key facts chart on how the courts decide whether strict liability applies

KEY FACTS

	Law	Cases
Presumption of *mens rea*	Unless the words make it clear that *mens rea* is not required, the courts will always start with the presumption that *mens rea* is required.	*Sweet v Parsley* (1969)
Looking at the rest of the Act	If other subsections state that *mens rea* is required but the section being considered does not state this, it is likely that the offence will be held to be one of strict liability.	*Storkwain* (1986)
Quasi-criminal offences	Regulatory crimes (not truly criminal) are *more* likely to be held to be strict liability offences.	*Harrow LBC v Shah and Shah* (1999)
Penalty of imprisonment	Where an offence is punishable by imprisonment, it is *less* likely that it will be held to one of strict liability.	*B v DPP* (2000)
Issue of social concern	Where the offence involves potential danger to public health, safety or morals then it is *more* likely to be held to be a strict liability offence.	*Blake* (1997)
Would strict liability promote enforcement of the law?	If making the offence one of strict liability would *not* help law enforcement then there is no reason to make the offence a strict liability one.	*Lim Chin Aik v The Queen* (1963)

4.6 JUSTIFICATION FOR STRICT LIABILITY

4.6.1 To protect society

The main justification is that strict liability offences help protect society by regulation of activities 'involving potential danger to public health, safety or morals'. Making an offence one of strict liability promotes greater care over these matters by encouraging higher standards in such matters as hygiene in processing and selling food, or in obeying building or transport regulations. It makes sure that businesses are run properly.

As failure to comply with high standards may cause risk to the life and health of large numbers of the general public, there is good reason to support this point of view. However, some opponents of strict liability argue that there is no evidence that that strict liability leads to business taking a higher standard of care. Some even argue that strict liability may be counter-productive. If people realise that they could be prosecuted even though they have taken every possible care, they may be tempted not to take any precautions.

4.6.2 Other justifications

Other justifications for the imposition of strict liability include that:

- it is easier to enforce as there is no need to prove *mens rea*
- it saves court time as people are more likely to plead guilty
- Parliament can provide a 'due diligence' defence where this is thought to be appropriate
- lack of blameworthiness can be taken into account when sentencing.

As there is no need to prove *mens rea*, it is clear that enforcement of the law is more straightforward. In addition, rather than prosecute for minor regulatory breaches, the Health and Safety Executive and local Trading Standards officers are more likely to serve improvement notices or prohibition notices in the first instance. This can help to ensure that the law is complied with, without the need for a court hearing. When a case is taken to court, the fact that only the act has to be proved saves time and also leads to many 'guilty' pleas.

The use of a 'due diligence' defence (or a 'no negligence' defence) can soften the law on strict liability. In many instances Parliament provides such a defence in the statute creating the offence. If the inclusion of such defences was done in a consistent way, then many of the objectors to the imposition of strict liability would be satisfied.

However, the use of 'due diligence' clauses in Acts often seems haphazard. For example, in *Harrow LBC v Shah and Shah* (1999) the relevant section allowed a 'due diligence' defence for promoters of the lottery but not for those managing a business in which lottery tickets were sold. (see section 4.5.4)

The final justification for strict liability is that allowances for levels of blameworthiness can be made in sentencing. A judge can pass a very lenient sentence where he feels that the defendant's level of blameworthiness was low.

4.6.3 Arguments against strict liability

Although there are sound justifications for imposing strict liability, there are also equally persuasive arguments against its use. The main argument against strict liability is that it imposes guilt on people who are not blameworthy in any way. Even those who have taken all possible care will found guilty and can be punished.

This happened in the case of *Harrow LBC v Shah* (1999) where the defendants had done their best to prevent sales of lottery tickets to anyone under the age of 16. Another case where all possible care had been taken was *Callow v Tillstone* (1900). In this case even the use of an expert (a vet) was insufficient to avoid liability.

Although an important reason for imposition of strict liability is the maintenance of high standards so that health and safety are not put in jeopardy, there is, as already mentioned earlier, no evidence that it improves standards.

Finally, the imposition of strict liability where an offence is punishable by imprisonment is contrary to the principles of human rights.

Examination questions

1 Critically consider the circumstances in which the imposition of strict liability is justified in criminal law.
(OCR, Unit 2571, June 2004)

2 Assume that Parliament has recently passed the Inshore Waters Safety Act. This makes it an offence to 'use or permit to be used a speedboat, launch, jet-ski or similar motorised craft' without a licence from the relevant local authority.

Jet-skis Are Us Ltd, a company which specialises in the hire of jet-skis, instructs

Sharp, its area manager, to promote the hire of jet-skis at all large holiday resorts in the south of England.

Sharp telephones the local authority in Crystalwater, a southern coastal town, and is told by Jones, a clerk in the relevant department, that Jet-skis Are Us Ltd have been granted a licence but that the official confirmation may be delayed because the computer network at the local authority has crashed. In fact, Jones made a mistake and Jet-skis Are Us Ltd have been refused a licence.

Jet-skis Are Us Ltd begin hiring out jet-skis to the public from the beach at Crystalwater, believing that a licence has been granted. Hugh hires a jet-ski from Jet-skis Are Us Ltd on the opening day.

Discuss the criminal liability, including possible strict liability, if any, of Jet-skis Are Us Ltd and Sharp for permitting the use of the jet-ski without a licence, of Hugh for using the jet-ski and of Jones for aiding and abetting Sharp.

(OCR, Unit 2571, June 2002)

3 '*The law presumes that* mens rea *is always required in criminal offences, unless it is clear that Parliament intended an offence to be one of strict liability.*'
Discuss.

(WJEC, LW5, June 2005)

CHAPTER 5 | Participation

5.1 PRINCIPAL AND SECONDARY PARTIES

Sometimes more than one person is involved in committing an offence. When this happens then it depends on the involvement of each person as to whether they are:

- a principal offender or
- a secondary party.

The *principal offender* is the person who does the *actus reus* or is the immediate cause of any consequence. For example, in a burglary, one person may wait outside the house keeping watch while the other goes into the house and steals items. The person who goes into the house is the principal offender while the 'lookout' is a *secondary party* (SP) to the burglary. The SP has not entered the house so he has not committed the *actus reus* of burglary but he is still involved in the offence.

Another example is where A and B plan to kill V. The plan is that B will knock on V's door and entice V outside, where A will shoot him. Everything goes according to plan and V is killed. A is the principal offender; B is the secondary party.

5.2 PRINCIPAL OFFENDER

As already stated, this is the person who carries out the act or who is the immediate cause of the *actus reus*. However, to be guilty, the principal offender must also have the necessary *mens rea* for the offence.

It is possible for there to be two or more joint principals in a crime. Joint principals are also known as *co-principals*.

5.2.1 Joint principals

Where two or more people do the *actus reus* with the required *mens rea* then they are all principals. If, in the example of the burglary given in section 5.1, both people had entered the house, then they would both have been principal offenders.

In one unusual case it was held that there could be two principals committing the offence of driving without due care and attention. This was the case of *Tyler v Whatmore* (1976), where one man steered the car and the other changed the gears. They were both carrying out the driving of the car, so they were both principal offenders.

5.2.2 Innocent agent

An innocent agent is someone whom the principal uses to do the act. This person is a 'puppet' and so is not responsible for the offence. The principal is the person who will be charged with the offence. The agent may be innocent because:

- they do not have the capacity to commit the offence, eg where a child under the age of 10 is sent by an adult into a house to steal property or
- they do not have the necessary *mens rea* for the offence or
- they have a defence such as insanity or automatism.

In these situations, the person using the innocent agent is the principal offender.

5.3 SECONDARY PARTIES

A secondary party is also known as an *accessory* or an *accomplice*.

The secondary party will be charged with the main crime and, if found guilty, is liable to the same punishment as the principal offender. This is set out in s 8 of the Accessories and Abettors Act 1861.

A secondary party can only be convicted if there was an *actus reus* for the main offence. This was stated in *Thornton v Mitchell* (1940).

THORNTON v MITCHELL (1940)

A bus driver, H, was reversing his bus, relying on signals from Thornton who was his bus conductor. The bus knocked down two pedestrians. H was charged with driving without due care and attention but was acquitted. It was found that he had taken due care and attention. However, Thornton was convicted of aiding and abetting H. The Divisional Court quashed the conviction as there was no *actus reus* by the principal for him to aid or abet.

It had been decided that H had not driven without due care and attention so there was no offence for Thornton to aid or abet.

In other situations where the principal has carried out the act, then the secondary party can be convicted even though the principal is acquitted, if the *actus reus* was committed, but the principal:

■ lacked the required *mens rea* or
■ has a defence not available to the secondary party.

An example of this last situation would be where the principal on a charge of murder has the defence of diminished responsibility. He will then be found guilty of manslaughter because of this special defence, but any secondary party will be guilty of murder.

5.4 *ACTUS REUS* OF SECONDARY PARTICIPATION

The *actus reus* is that the secondary party must 'aid, abet, counsel or procure' the commission of an offence. (s 8 of the Accessories and Abettors Act 1861). In *Attorney-General's Reference (No. 1 of 1975)* (1975) the Court of Appeal stated that each of these four words ('aid', 'abet', 'counsel' or 'procure') has a separate meaning.

ATTORNEY-GENERAL'S REFERENCE (NO. 1 OF 1975) (1975)

D, who knew that a friend was going to drive home, laced his non-alcoholic drink with alcohol. When the friend was charged with driving while over the limit for alcohol (s 6(1) of the Road Traffic Act 1972), D was charged with aiding, abetting, counselling and procuring that offence. The trial judge ruled that there was no case to answer as there was no 'meeting of minds'. The Court of Appeal held that this was wrong.

The Court of Appeal made three points about secondary participation. These were:

1 each of the words 'aid', 'abet', 'counsel' and 'procure' has a different meaning
2 to 'procure' means to produce by endeavour
3 there must be a causal link between the procuring and the commission of the offence, ie the procuring must to some extent cause the offence to be committed.

So, as each of the four words has a different meaning, it is necessary to consider them separately. However, there can be some overlap, particularly between aiding and abetting.

5.4.1 Aiding

Aiding is giving help, support or assistance. This can be before the offence is committed; eg providing tools to carry out a burglary, as in *Bainbridge* (1959), or during the time it is being committed, eg acting as a lookout.

5.4.2 Abetting

Abetting is any conduct which instigates, incites or encourages the commission of the offence. In *Giannetto* (1997) the Court of Appeal pointed out that for abetting any involvement from 'mere encouragement upwards' is sufficient. Encouragement can be as little as patting on the back, nodding, or saying 'Oh Goody' when told of the principal's intention to commit a particular crime.

> **GIANNETTO** (1997)
> D was convicted of the murder of his wife. The prosecution relied on the fact that the wife had been murdered either by D himself or by a hired killer on D's behalf. D appealed on the basis that, as the prosecution could not prove whether he or another person had killed his wife, he should have been acquitted. The Court of Appeal held that as he had the intention to murder and the act had been carried out, it did not matter whether he was principal or secondary party.

Abetting can be immediately before the offence is committed or during its commission. An example is shouting encouragement or paying for a ticket for an illegal performance. This was decided in *Wilcox v Jeffery* (1951).

> **WILCOX v JEFFERY** (1951)
> Wilcox knew that an American saxophonist was not allowed to enter the United Kingdom. Despite this, Wilcox went to meet him at the airport and then attended (as a paying member of the audience) a concert at which the American played. D was convicted of aiding and abetting the contravention of the Aliens Order 1920.

Mere presence

So, where presence at a public performance encourages that performance, then the presence is sufficient for the defendant to be guilty of abetting the offence.

But mere presence is not usually enough for secondary participation; there must be an intention to encourage. This was shown in *Clarkson and others* (1971).

> **CLARKSON and OTHERS** (1971)
> D and another soldier entered a room within army barracks where a woman was being raped. They remained in the room while the rape continued but did nothing. Their conviction for abetting rape was quashed.

Non-interference to prevent a crime is not itself a crime. Being present but doing nothing is not sufficient to make D a secondary party unless there is a duty to control the principal offender. In this situation it has been held that passive presence may be enough, as in *Tuck v Robson* (1970).

> **TUCK v ROBSON** (1970)
> D was the landlord of a pub. He did not serve drinks after hours but he allowed customers to stay drinking after the licensing hours had ended. He was convicted of aiding and abetting breaches of the licensing laws. He was in charge of the pub and had authority to tell the people to leave. The fact that he did nothing was enough to make him guilty in the circumstances.

5.4.3 Counselling

Counselling is advising or encouraging. It takes place *before* the commission of the offence. An example is the case of *Calhaem* (1985).

CALHAEM (1985)

D was infatuated with her solicitor. She hired a 'hit man' to kill a woman with whom the solicitor had been having an affair. The hit man claimed that he had decided not to go through with the plan to kill the woman, but when he saw her he went berserk and killed her. D argued that the causal connection between her acts and the killing was broken when the 'hit man' decided of his own accord to kill V. It was held there was no need for any causal connection between the counselling and the offence. D's conviction was upheld.

In this case the Court of Appeal said that the word 'counsel' should be given its ordinary meaning, that is 'advise', 'solicit' or something of that sort. The word 'counsel' does not imply that there should be any causal connection between the counselling and the offence.

5.4.4 Procuring

Procuring means 'to produce by endeavour', that is, setting out to see that it happens and taking the appropriate steps to produce that happening. This was decided in *Attorney-General's Reference (No. 1 of 1975)* (1975) (see section 5.4 for the facts of this case).

However, subsequent cases have stated that it is not always necessary to show that D set out to produce a result by endeavour. The need for the causal link is the more important factor. Did D's act cause the offence to be committed? This was seen in *Millward* (1984).

MILLWARD (1984)

D was a farmer who gave instructions for a poorly maintained tractor and trailer to be driven on a public road. Because of the poor maintenance the trailer became detached, hit a car and killed the driver. D was convicted of procuring the offence of causing death by reckless driving, even though he certainly did not set out to produce that result through endeavour.

The case of *Millward* also illustrates that it is possible for a secondary party to be guilty, even though the principal is acquitted. In the case the driver was acquitted, as he did not know of the state of the vehicle and had not driven dangerously.

Activity

Consider whether anyone in the scenarios below has aided, abetted, counselled or procured.

1 Alvin knows that Bethany is an expert at hacking into computer sites. Alvin tells Bethany that he wants to get into secure banking sites and asks her to explain the best way to do this.
2 Carly sees Damien attacking Ella. Carly does not like Ella and so she starts shouting 'Go on, give it to her'.
3 Flint lends Greg a screwdriver which Greg uses to break into a car.
4 Hal owns a caravan. He asks Ian to tow the caravan to a new site. Hal knows that the tow bar on the caravan is poorly connected and liable to come loose. Ian tows the caravan. It comes loose and crashes into a pedestrian, killing him.

Figure 5.1 Key facts chart on the *actus reus* of participation

Type of act	Law	Cases
Aid	Giving help, support, assistance. Can be before or at the time of the commission of the offence.	*Bainbridge* (1959)
Abet	'Mere encouragement upwards' is sufficient.	*Giannetto* (1997)
	Includes paying to see an illegal performance.	*Wilcox v Jeffery* (1951)
	Passive presence is not enough unless there is a duty to control the principal's behaviour.	*Clarkson* (1971) *Tuck v Robson* (1970)
Counsel	Ordinary meaning of word, ie 'advise', 'solicit'.	*Calhaem* (1985)
	No need to prove causal link.	*Calhaem* (1985)
Procure	To produce by endeavour.	*A-G's Reference (No. 1 of 1975)* (1975)

5.5 *MENS REA* OF SECONDARY PARTICIPATION

The secondary party must have an intention to aid, abet, counsel or procure the act of the main offence. However, D can be guilty as a secondary party even if he does not care whether the offence is committed or not. This was decided in *National Coal Board v Gamble* (1958).

NATIONAL COAL BOARD v GAMBLE (1958)
A weighbridge operator employed by the National Coal Board issued a ticket to a lorry driver, although the operator knew that the lorry was overloaded. The Board was convicted as a secondary party to the offence of using a motor lorry on a road with a load weighing more than that permitted.

The *mens rea* for secondary participation is the intention to do the act which aids or abets.

Here, the weighbridge operator knew that the lorry was overloaded and still issued a ticket. This allowed the driver to commit the main offence. The fact that the weighbridge operator did not care what happened was not a defence. As Devlin J put it:

'If one man deliberately sells to another a gun to be used for murdering a third, he may be indifferent whether the third man lives or dies and interested only in the cash profit to be made out of the sale, but he can still be an aider and abettor.'

5.5.1 Knowledge

The secondary party need only have knowledge of the type of crime. He does not need to know the details of where and when it is going to take place. This was decided in *Bainbridge* (1959).

> **BAINBRIDGE (1959)**
> D bought oxygen cutting equipment on behalf of another man, E. D knew that E was going to use the equipment for criminal purposes, but D did not know the exact details. E used the equipment six weeks later, to break into the Midland Bank at Stoke Newington in north London. D's conviction for burglary was upheld.

So, a secondary party can be guilty where he knows the type of offence that the principal is going to commit. It does not matter that he does not know the details. In fact, it is sufficient that the secondary party has knowledge that one of a range of offences is going to be committed. This was decided by the House of Lords in *DPP for Northern Ireland v Maxwell* (1978).

> **DPP FOR NORTHERN IRELAND v MAXWELL (1978)**
> D was a member of a terrorist group in Northern Ireland. He guided other members of the group to a pub, where one of them threw a bomb into the pub. D knew that some sort of attack was to be carried out there, but he did not know exactly what. D was convicted of doing an act with intent to cause an explosion, and with possessing a bomb. He appealed on the basis that he did not know explosives were going to be used, but the House of Lords upheld his conviction.
>
> In *Maxwell* the House of Lords stated that *Bainbridge* was correctly decided. It was not necessary to prove that D knew details of the offence. In fact, the Lords went further than in *Bainbridge* as they said it was sufficient if the offence was one of a range which D knew was likely to take place. So, as Maxwell knew that some sort of attack was going to happen, he was a secondary party to that attack, even though he did not know that explosives were going to be used.

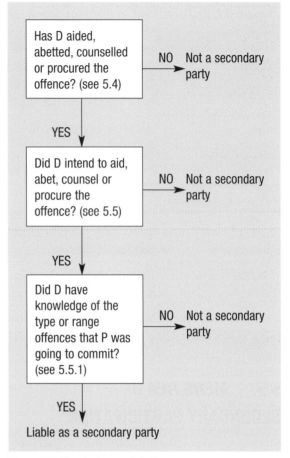

Figure 5.2 Flowchart on participation

5.5.2 Shared intention

As D must intend to aid, abet, counsel or procure the main offence, this means in most cases that the principal and the secondary party (SP) will have a shared intention. However, they do not have to agree the conduct. It is even possible, in rare cases, for a person to 'aid' an offence without the principal being aware of his help. For example, if the SP sees the principal attacking someone, the SP can decide to 'aid' this by blocking off the victim's escape route.

Another exception is where the secondary party procures the offence. Here, there is no need to prove a shared intention. This was pointed out by the Court of Appeal in

Attorney-General's Reference (No. 1 of 1975) (1975) where the court thought that it would be difficult to think of a case of aiding, abetting or counselling when the parties have not discussed the matter or at least been in some agreement. But for procuring there is no need for a similar principle to apply.

5.5.3 Joint enterprise

A joint enterprise is where two or more defendants have agreed to carrying out one crime together. Quite often this is a burglary or a robbery. But during the course of this agreed offence something goes wrong, such as the householder returning to the house during the burglary. One of the joint offenders then kills the householder. Is the other person involved in carrying out the burglary also liable for the murder as a secondary party?

This is a situation that has caused the courts problems. The rule is that if, when the SP took part in the first offence, he contemplated or foresaw that the principal might commit a certain type of other offence then the SP is guilty of this other offence. The leading cases on this are *Powell* (1997) and *English* (1997), where the two cases were heard by the House of Lords in a joined appeal. The facts of both are given below.

POWELL (1997)

D and two other men went to buy drugs at the house of a drug dealer. When the dealer opened the door, one of the other men shot him. D was prosecuted on the basis that he knew that one of the other men had a gun and that it might be used to kill or cause serious injury. D's conviction for murder was upheld.

ENGLISH (1997)

D took part with another man, W, in a joint enterprise to attack and injure a police officer with wooden posts. During the attack, W stabbed and killed the officer. D did not know that W was carrying a knife. D's conviction for murder was quashed by the House of Lords.

Foresight/contemplation

In *Powell* and *English* the House of Lords held that if the accomplice (secondary party) has foresight or contemplates that the principal may commit the offence, then this is sufficient for the *mens rea* of the accomplice.

This decision means that a lower level of intention is sufficient to convict a secondary party of murder than for a principal. This was acknowledged by the House of Lords when Lord Steyn said:

'Recklessness may suffice in the case of the secondary party but it does not in the case of the primary offender.'

The reasons for convicting an accomplice on a lower level of *mens rea* than the principal are largely based on practical and policy considerations. This was recognised by Lord Hutton in *Powell* when he said:

'The rules of common law are not based solely on logic but relate to practical concerns and, in relation to crimes committed in the course of joint enterprises, to the need to give effective protection to the public against criminals operating in gangs.'

Although this may justify the lower level of *mens rea*, there are particular problems in murder cases. This is because the judge has no discretion in sentencing: all those guilty of murder have to be sentenced to life imprisonment. Is it just that a secondary party, who did not personally carry out the killing, can be convicted on a lower level of intention and so face the same mandatory life sentence as the actual killer?

Different act

However, where the principal does a completely different act, then the secondary party is not liable. In *English* (1997), where the agreement was to assault a policeman with wooden posts, one of the defendants killed him by stabbing him with a knife. This unforeseen use of a different weapon meant that English was not a secondary party to the murder.

There can also be a situation where the principal uses a weapon that the others know he has but goes beyond what they foresaw or contemplated. This occurred in *Stewart and Schofield* (1995).

STEWART and SCHOFIELD (1995)

D1 and D2 set out with another man, L, to rob a shop. D1 went in to the shop with L, while D2 kept watch outside. They knew that L had with him a scaffolding bar and that it might be used to cause some injury. In fact, L, motivated by racial hatred, beat the shopkeeper to death. L was convicted of murder; D1 and D2 were convicted of unlawful act manslaughter.

In this case the two secondary parties had not foreseen that V would be seriously hurt or killed, so they could not be convicted of murder. However, as they knew that the scaffolding bar might be used to cause some lesser injury, they were guilty of unlawful act manslaughter. In the case of *English*, he was not liable for the death at all. This was because the death was solely due to the use of the knife which English did not know the other attacker had.

The Court of Appeal has further considered this problem of unexpected events within a joint enterprise in the case of *Uddin* (1998).

UDDIN (1998)

D was one of six men who attacked V with poles and bars. In the course of the attack, V was stabbed by one of the men and died from the stab wound. D was convicted of murder and appealed on the basis that the judge had failed to direct the jury that D could only be guilty of murder if he foresaw the possibility that a knife would be used.

In this case the Court of Appeal set out a series of principles in deciding whether D was liable as a secondary participant. The main ones are:

1 Where several persons join in a fatal attack on V, intending to inflict serious harm, they are jointly liable for murder. However, if such injury inflicted with that intent is caused solely by the actions of one person of a type entirely different from the actions which the others foresaw, only that person is guilty of murder.

2 In deciding whether the actions are of 'a type entirely different' the use of a weapon is a significant factor. If its character (eg its propensity to cause death) is different from any weapon used or contemplated by the others, then they are not responsible for the death unless it is proved that they knew or foresaw the likelihood of the use of such a weapon.

3 If some or all of the others are using weapons which could be regarded as equally likely to inflict fatal injuries, the mere fact that a different weapon was used is immaterial.

Explain whether the defendants in the scenarios below have the required *mens rea* to be a secondary party.

1 Jess sees Morag trying to lift a heavy box into a car. Jess helps her. In fact, Morag has stolen property in the box.
2 Lucy knows that Kelvin is a violent man who has attacked people in the past. Kelvin asks Lucy if she can lend him a knife. Kelvin uses the knife two days later to stab and injure Nigel.
3 Pedro and Ryan agree to burgle a shop at night when it is closed. They get into the shop but find that the store manager is still there. Pedro pulls out a gun and shoots the manager dead.
4 Sally and Tiffany agree to beat up Zara, using baseball bats. They both hit Zara, causing her to fall to the ground. Sally then stabs Zara with a knife, killing her. Tiffany did not know that Sally was carrying a knife.

5.6 WITHDRAWAL FROM A JOINT ENTERPRISE

There are some cases where the defendant has agreed to take part in an offence but then decides he does not want to go ahead. In order to be seen as 'not guilty', he must make his withdrawal from the offence clear and effective.

The more the secondary party has done towards assisting the main crime, the more effective his withdrawal must be. This was seen in *Becerra and Cooper* (1975).

BECERRA and COOPER (1975)
B and C broke into a house, to steal. B gave C a knife to use if anyone interrupted them. When they were interrupted by V, B said 'There's a bloke coming. Let's go,' and jumped out of a window. C stabbed and killed V. Both B and C were convicted of murder.

Jumping out of the window and running off was not sufficient for withdrawal at this late stage in the joint enterprise. Becerra need to do something more effective, such as take the knife back from Cooper. Merely saying 'Let's go' was not sufficient for communicating withdrawal where B had already given C the knife.

In the case of *Rook* (1993) it was held that merely not turning up at the scene to commit an agreed crime could be insufficient in some situations. The defendant had to communicate his withdrawal.

ROOK (1993)
D discussed a plan to murder V. When the others came round to collect him to go to commit the crime, D was absent. He claimed that he had absented himself because he no longer intended to take part in the crime. He did not tell the others that he was withdrawing from the offence.

The decision in *Becerra* was confirmed. D could not withdraw simply by absenting himself. There had to be 'unequivocal communication' to the others of his withdrawal.

Spontaneous offences

Where spontaneous violence has occurred then it is possible for the secondary party to withdraw effectively, by walking away. There is no need for him to communicate his withdrawal to the principal. An example of this is *Mitchell and King* (1998).

MITCHELL and KING (1999)

An unplanned fight broke out in a restaurant and continued into the street. D1 and D2 were involved in the fight during which V was badly beaten. D1 then dropped a stick, stopped fighting and walked away. D2 picked up the stick and renewed the attack on V who later died. Walking away was sufficient to withdraw effectively. D1's conviction was quashed.

So, where spontaneous violence occurs, D can withdraw without communicating his withdrawal to others involved in the attack. The position is different where there has been pre-planned violence. In these situations D must communicate his withdrawal to the others involved in the plan.

Examination question

'The criminal law deals satisfactorily with those who aid, abet, or counsel a principal offender in carrying out a crime or who procure the commission of an offence by someone else. It is vital that such participation in crime is properly dealt with.'

Assess the truth of this statement, by reference to the relevant law.

(OCR, Unit 2571, January 2005)

Activity

Decide whether in the following scenarios the defendant has sufficiently withdrawn from the offence so that he is not guilty.

1 Ahmed and Ben enter a house, intending to steal. Ahmed knows that Ben has a penknife with him, as he uses it to gain entry. The owner of the house comes back while they are still in the house. Ahmed shouts at Ben 'I'm getting out of here', pushes past the owner and runs out of the front door. Ben then stabs the owner with the penknife.

2 Zak sees a fight in the street and joins in. He punches Rob in the face several times, causing him to fall to the ground. There is a shout that the police are coming, and Zak runs off. After he leaves, another person kicks Rob in the head, causing serious injuries which lead to Rob's death.

CHAPTER 6

Inchoate offences

Inchoate offences are ones where the main offence has not been completed. There are three categories of inchoate offence:

- incitement
- conspiracy and
- attempts.

A person cannot be charged with just 'incitement' or 'conspiracy' or attempt': they must be charged with incitement etc to commit a *specific* offence. So it is possible for a person to be charged with incitement to commit murder, or conspiracy to commit murder or attempted murder. In all these situations it is not necessary for the victim to have been killed. The full offence of murder need not have taken place.

The main reason for having inchoate or incomplete crimes is that it allows defendants to be charged before the main crime is committed. It would not be sensible if, although the police knew that D1 and D2 had planed to kill V, the police had to wait until V was murdered before they could do anything.

6.1   INCITEMENT

6.1.1 What is incitement?

Incitement is a common-law crime, so far as most offences are concerned. That means that it has not been set out in an Act of Parliament. There is one main exception, and that is incitement to murder. This is covered by s 4 of the Offences Against the Person Act 1861 which states:

'Whosoever shall solicit, encourage, persuade or endeavour to persuade, or shall propose to any person, to murder any other person … shall be guilty of an offence.'

For the purposes of murder, this section defines what is meant by 'incitement' in the words 'solicit, encourage, persuade or endeavour to persuade, or shall propose to any person'.

However, for incitement to commit other offences, there is no statutory definition of 'incitement'. The type of behaviour it covers was looked at in the case of *Invicta Plastics Ltd v Clare* (1976).

INVICTA PLASTICS LTD v CLARE (1976)
The defendant company advertised in *What Car?* magazine a device which warned drivers when they were approaching a police radar speed trap. The company was convicted of inciting motorists to receive radio transmissions without a licence, contrary to s 1(1) of the Wireless Telegraphy Act 1949.

In this case it was decided that:

- incitement is normally encouragement or persuasion but can also be by threats or pressure
- the *actus reus* of incitement may be implied rather than express
- incitement is determined by looking at D's acts as a whole.

So, many different types of behaviour can be incitement. As was pointed out in *Invicta Plastics*, it is normally encouragement or persuasion. This can include persuasion by threats. If you threaten to tell about someone's secret love affair unless that person steals, then this is incitement to theft. Equally, if you pay someone £1,000 to beat up an enemy of yours, then this is incitement to commit the offence of inflicting grievous bodily harm. The payment is encouraging or persuading the other person to commit the offence.

The important point is that the offence of incitement is committed the moment the encouragement or persuasion etc takes place.

6.1.2 *Mens rea* of incitement

The inciter must intend that the other person will commit the offence. However, it does not matter that the other person never intended to carry out the offence. This was seen in *DPP v Armstrong* (2000).

DPP v ARMSTRONG (2000)

D phoned J to ask for pornography of girls 'not younger than, say, 12 years'. J was in fact an undercover police officer investigating paedophilia and did not intend to send D any pornography. D was charged with inciting J to commit the offence of distributing indecent photographs of children. The magistrates dismissed the case but the Divisional allowed the prosecution's appeal as there was no need to prove that J intended to do anything.

So, we can see that there is no need for the person incited to intend to commit the offence. So long as the inciter (the person doing the inciting) intends that the other person should commit the main offence, the inciter is guilty of incitement.

6.1.3 Inciting the impossible

If the offence incited is impossible to commit, in the sense that it can never be committed, then the inciter will not be guilty. This was decided in *Fitzmaurice* (1983).

FITZMAURICE (1983)

D's father asked D to find someone to take part in robbing a woman who was taking wages to a bank. In fact, the robbery was a fiction put forward by D's father so that he could claim reward money. D, believing that the robbery was going to take place, recruited B to take part in the supposed robbery.

Although the Court of Appeal stated that where an offence was impossible to commit then the inciter would not be guilty, it upheld D's conviction. This was because although the robbery D thought was going to happen was fictitious, there would still be women walking along the road by the bank and so it would have been possible for B to rob a woman.

An example of where it would be impossible to commit an offence is where D pays a 'hit man' to kill a specific victim (V). However, unknown to D, V died of a heart attack the day before the incitement took

---

Figure 6.1 Key facts chart on incitement

			KEY FACTS
Definition of 'incitement'	Encouraging or persuading another to commit an offence. The persuading can be by threats of pressure.	*Invicta Plastics Ltd v Clare* (1976)	
Mens rea of incitement	The inciter must intend the other person to commit the offence. There is no need for the person incited to intend to do it.	*DPP v Armstrong* (2000)	
Inciting the impossible	If the crime incited can never be committed then the inciter is not guilty.	*Fitzmaurice* (1983)	

place. The main crime is impossible to commit because a dead person cannot be murdered.

6.2   CONSPIRACY

Conspiracy is where crime is planned. The moment any plan or agreement to commit a crime is made between two or more people, then the offence of conspiracy is committed. This means that, if the plan is found out in time, criminals can be charged before they commit any main crime. Also, it is often used to charge the 'mastermind' behind crimes as they are unlikely to take part in the actual offence itself.

Conspiracy is now defined in s 1(1) of the Criminal Law Act 1977. This states:

'*… if a person agrees with any other person or persons that a course of conduct shall be pursued which, if the agreement is carried out in accordance with their intentions … will necessarily amount to or involve the commission of any offence or offences by one or more of the parties to the agreement, he is guilty of conspiracy.*'

6.2.1 Who can commit conspiracy?

The first rule is that there must be at least two people for the offence of conspiracy to be committed.

However, s 2(2) of the Criminal Law Act 1977 specifically states that it is impossible for there to be a conspiracy if the only person with whom D makes an agreement is one of the following:

- D's spouse
- a person under the age of criminal responsibility, that is under the age of 10 years or
- the intended victim.

So, there must be at least two people, not including anyone in one of these categories.

6.2.2 The *actus reus* of conspiracy

The agreement is the *actus reus*. As already stated, that agreement must be by at least two people. The other important point is that what they agree to do must 'necessarily amount to or involve the commission of any offence' by at least one of the conspirators.

This phrase 'necessarily amount to or involve the commission of any offence' was considered by the Court of Appeal in *Reed* (1982).

REED (1982)

D and another man agreed that the other man should visit individuals who were contemplating suicide and, depending on his assessment of the situation, either discourage them or actively help them to commit suicide. They were convicted of conspiracy to aid and abet suicide.

The Court of Appeal explained that, provided an offence will 'necessarily' be committed if the plan is carried out as intended, D will be guilty of statutory conspiracy. One of the judges, Donaldson LJ, used two examples to show how this works.

- The first example was where A and B agree to drive from London to Edinburgh in a time which can be achieved without exceeding the speed limit but only if the traffic is exceptionally light. So, because it is possible for the plan to be carried out without exceeding the speed limit, the agreement will not necessarily involve the commission of any offence.
- The second example was where A and B agree to rob a bank if, when they arrive at the bank if, it is safe to do so. If their agreement is carried out in accordance with their intentions, it will necessarily involve the commission of the offence of robbery. It does not matter that they may abandon the plan because they find on their arrival that there is a security guard outside the bank.

The plan can also be the other way around, ie the conspirators agree they will only commit an offence if certain circumstances occur. This is known as a 'contingency plan' and is illustrated by the case of *Jackson* (1985).

JACKSON (1985)

Three men agreed to shoot another in the leg if he was convicted, so that there would be mitigating circumstances when he was sentenced. They were convicted of conspiring to pervert the course of justice.

In this case the agreement was that the offence of perverting the course of justice would only take place if the man on trial was convicted. But if that contingency took place then the agreement necessarily involved the commission of an offence. As a result, this meant that the defendants were guilty of conspiracy.

6.2.3 *Mens rea* for conspiracy

The required *mens rea* of conspiracy is that D must have intended the agreement to be carried out. It does matter that he does not believe the plan will work. This is shown by *Anderson* (1985).

ANDERSON (1985)

D agreed to supply diamond wire to cut through bars in order to allow a prisoner to escape. D claimed that he did not believe that the plan could ever succeed. D's conviction was upheld.

D intended to play some part in the agreed course of conduct which would further the criminal purpose. In this case, he intended to supply the diamond wire. Even though he thought that the plan would not work, he was guilty of conspiring to release the prisoner.

As the offence of conspiracy involves at least two people, there must be two people

---

Figure 6.2 Key facts chart on conspiracy

			KEY FACTS
Definition of 'conspiracy'	An agreement which, if carried out in accordance with Ds' intentions, will necessarily amount to or involve the commission of an offence.	s 1(1) Criminal Law Act 1977	
What is meant by 'necessarily involve'?	If the plan is carried out as intended then an offence will be committed.	*Reed* (1982)	
	Where conspirators agree they will only commit an offence if certain circumstances occur, this is a contingency plan and they are guilty.	*Jackson* (1985)	
Mens rea of conspiracy	D must intend to play some part in the agreed course of conduct to further the commission of the criminal offence.	*Anderson* (1986)	
	There must be at least two people intending that the plan will be carried out.	*Yip Chiu-Cheung v R* (1994)	

who intend the offence to be committed. An interesting case on this is *Yip Chiu-Cheung v R* (1994).

YIP CHIU-CHEUNG v R (1994)

D conspired with N to traffic in heroin. N was in fact an undercover drugs enforcement agent. D appealed against his conviction, on the basis that N did not intend to carry out the offence and so could not be a conspirator. His conviction was upheld because N intended to take the drugs into Australia.

In this case N was intending to take the drugs into Australia and so had the intention to commit the offence, although he knew he would not be prosecuted. This meant that both D and N intended that the offence be committed and so D could be guilty of conspiracy.

6.3   ATTEMPTS

An attempt is where D tries to commit an offence but, for some reason, fails to complete it. An example of this is the case of *White* (1910) (see section 2.3.1), where D put cyanide in his mother's drink, intending to kill her. She died of a heart attack before she could drink it. He tried to commit murder but did not actually kill his mother. He was convicted of attempted murder.

'Attempt' is now defined by s 1(1) of the Criminal Attempts Act 1981. This states:

'If, with intent to commit an offence to which this section applies, a person does an act which is more than merely preparatory to the commission of the offence, he is guilty of attempting to commit the offence.'

Before 'attempt' was defined in the 1981 Act, the courts used several different tests to decide whether the defendant had actually done enough towards the commission of the main offence for him to be guilty of an attempt. The main tests were:

- the 'last act' test: had D done the last act he could do before committing the main crime?
- the 'proximity' test.

The courts have held that these common-law tests are irrelevant and the important point is whether the defendant has done an act which is 'more than merely preparatory' to the commission of the main offence.

6.3.1 More than merely preparatory

The act that the defendant does has to be more than merely preparation for the main crime. Some acts are obviously mere preparation, but other acts are more difficult to categorise.

Let's take the example where D decides to rob a bank. First, he buys himself a shotgun and converts it into a sawn-off shotgun. Both the buying and the converting are 'merely preparatory'. Next, he drives around the area, checking escape routes. Again, this is 'merely preparatory'.

On the day of the robbery, D steals a car ('merely preparatory') and drives to the bank (still 'merely preparatory'). He stands on the pavement outside the bank, carrying the sawn-off shotgun in a bag. This is getting nearer, but, according to the case of *Campbell* (1990) (see below), is still only 'merely preparatory'. Then he walks into the bank. Now he has gone beyond mere preparation and can be charged with attempted robbery.

There have been many cases on the meaning of 'merely preparatory'. It is difficult to draw any general principle from them. In *Attorney-General's Reference (No. 1 of 1992)* (1993) it was decided that D need not have performed the last act before the crime proper, nor need he have reached the 'point of no return'.

> **ATTORNEY-GENERAL'S REFERENCE (NO. 1 OF 1992) (1993)**
> D dragged a girl up some steps to a shed. He lowered his trousers and interfered with her private parts. His penis remained flaccid. He argued that he could not therefore attempt to commit rape. His conviction for attempted rape was upheld.

Looking at the whole of D's acts, this seems a sensible decision. However, if he had been stopped immediately after he had dragged the girl to the shed, and before he lowered his trousers or interfered with her, then it is unlikely that he could have been convicted. His act of dragging her was probably 'merely preparatory'.

In *Gullefer* (1987) the Court of Appeal held that 'more than merely preparatory' means the defendant must have gone beyond purely preparatory acts and be 'embarked on the crime proper'.

> **GULLEFER (1987)**
> D jumped onto a race track in order to have the race declared void and so enable him to reclaim money he had bet on the race. His conviction for attempting to steal was quashed because his action was merely preparatory to committing the offence.

Cases showing mere preparation

The case of *Gullefer* (above) illustrates a situation in which D's acts were mere preparation. Although D had tried to interfere with the race, he had several other acts to do before the theft (the point at which he would get his betting money back). He had to go to one of the betting points and ask for his money back. Even just going towards the point would not be sufficient. However, the moment he asked for the money, then this would be 'more than merely preparatory'. He

would be guilty of attempted theft. It is worth noting that the moment the money was handed to him he would be guilty of the main offence of theft.

The Court of Appeal stated that an attempt begins when 'the merely preparatory acts have come to an end and the defendant embarks upon the crime proper'. It also pointed out when this is will depend on the facts in any particular case.

The case of *Geddes* also illustrates acts which were only preparatory.

> **GEDDES (1996)**
> D was found in the boys' lavatory block of a school, in possession of a large kitchen knife, some rope and masking tape. He had no right to be in the school. He had not contacted any of the pupils. His conviction for attempted false imprisonment was quashed.

This case is difficult to justify. D had no right to be on the premises. He had entered the school with all the equipment for falsely imprisoning a student. The next step would be for him to approach one of the students. If the law of attempt is to be effective in protecting people from the main offence, then surely he should have been guilty of an attempt at that point. Is it sensible to wait until he approaches one of the students?

However, the Court of Appeal thought that attempts should be considered by asking two questions:

- had the accused moved from planning or preparation to execution or implementation?
- had the accused done an act showing that he was actually trying to commit the full offence or had he got only as far as getting ready, or putting himself in a position, or equipping himself, to do so?

Using these two questions, it can be seen that Geddes had not quite moved from planning or preparation to execution. Also, it can be argued that he had got only as far as getting ready, or putting himself in a position, to commit the full offence.

Another case which is perhaps even more difficult to justify is *Campbell* (1990).

> **CAMPBELL (1990)**
> D, who had an imitation gun, sunglasses and a threatening note in his pocket, was in the street outside a post office. His conviction for attempted robbery was quashed.

The next step in this case would have been for D to enter the post office. Again, if the law of attempt is to be effective in protecting people from the main offence, surely he should have been guilty of an attempt at that point? Is it sensible to wait until he enters the post office? If the gun had been real then customers and staff in the post office would have been put
at risk.

Cases in which there was an attempt

The following two cases show situations where the defendant had gone beyond mere preparation. In each case the defendants were held to be guilty of an attempt to commit the full offence.

> **BOYLE and BOYLE (1987)**
> The defendants were found standing by a door of which the lock and one hinge were broken. Their conviction for attempted burglary was upheld.

The Court of Appeal held that the test to use was whether the defendant was embarking on the crime proper. In this case, once the defendants had entered they would be committing burglary, so trying to gain entry was an attempt.

The difference from *Campbell* is that burglary is committed at the moment D enters as a trespasser with intent to steal (or do certain other offences). Robbery is not committed until uses force in order to steal. Walking into a building still leaves another step before the crime proper is committed.

In the next case, *Jones* (1990), the defendant had done almost everything he could before committing the full offence.

> **JONES (1990)**
> D's woman friend told him that she wanted their relationship to end and that she was seeing another man, V. D bought a shotgun and shortened the barrel. D then found V, who was in his car. D, who was wearing a crash helmet with the visor down, got into V's car and pointed the gun at V. V grabbed the gun and managed to throw it out of the car window. D's conviction for attempted murder was upheld.
>
> D tried to argue that, as the safety catch was still on, he had not done the last act before the crime proper. The Court of Appeal said that buying the gun, shortening it, loading it and disguising himself with the visor were all preparatory acts. But once D got into V's car and pointed the gun at V, then there was sufficient evidence to leave to the jury the question of whether there was an attempt.

Figure 6.3 Key cases chart on 'merely preparatory' in attempts

Case	Facts	Offence attempted	Point of law
Cases where there was sufficient for an attempt			
A-G's reference (No. 1 of 1992) (1993)	D tried to rape a girl but could not get an erection.	Rape	Need not have performed the last act.
Boyle and Boyle (1987)	Standing by door with broken lock.	Burglary	Had done part of a series of acts.
Jones (1990)		Murder	Sufficient evidence to leave the question of whether there was an attempt to the jury.
Cases which were merely preparatory			
Gullefer (1987)		Theft	Has D 'embarked upon the crime proper'?
Geddes (1996)		False imprisonment	Has D 'actually tried to commit the offence in question'?
Campbell (1990)		Robbery	Merely preparatory.

6.3.2 *Mens rea* of attempt

For an attempt, the defendant must normally have the same intention as would be required for the full offence. If the prosecution cannot prove that D had that intention then D is not guilty of the attempt. This was shown by the case of *Easom* (1971).

In this case there was no evidence that the defendant had intended to permanently deprive the owner of the bag or items in it (part of the required *mens rea* for theft). As a result, he could not be guilty of attempted theft.

A similar decision was made in the case of *Husseyn* (1977).

EASOM (1971)

D picked up a woman's handbag in a cinema, rummaged through it, then put it back on the floor without removing anything from it. His conviction for theft of the bag and its contents was quashed. The Court of Appeal also refused to substitute a conviction for attempted theft of the bag and specific contents (including a purse and a pen), as there was no evidence that D intended to steal the items.

HUSSEYN (1977)

D and another man were seen loitering near the back of a van. When the police approached, they ran off. D was convicted of attempting to steal some sub-aqua equipment that was in the van. The Court of Appeal quashed his conviction.

The decisions by the Court of Appeal in both these cases can be criticised. Surely the defendant did intend to steal something? The fact that Easom did not do so (presumably because there was nothing really worth stealing) should not make him not guilty of attempting to steal. Equally, in the case of Husseyn, the fact that he ran off because the police arrived does not mean that he was not trying to steal.

These problems were resolved in *Attorney-General's Reference (Nos 1 and 2 of 1979)* (1979) where the Court of Appeal decided that if D had a conditional intent (ie D intended stealing if there was anything worth stealing), D could be charged with an attempt to steal some or all of the contents.

So, Easom would now be charged with attempting to steal all or some of the contents of the bag, rather than the bag itself and specific items in it. Husseyn would be charged with attempting to steal some or all of the contents of the van.

Recklessness

What if it can be proved that the defendant was reckless? Is this sufficient for him to be guilty of an attempt? In *Millard and Vernon* (1987) it was decided that it was not sufficient.

MILLARD and VERNON (1987)
Ds repeatedly pushed against a wooden fence on a stand at a football ground. The prosecution alleged that they were trying to break it and they were convicted of attempted criminal damage. The Court of Appeal quashed their convictions.

Recklessness is not normally sufficient *mens rea* for an attempt. This is so even where recklessness would suffice for the completed offence. However, there is an exception in that recklessness as to one part of the offence can be sufficient. This is illustrated by

Attorney-General's Reference (No. 3 of 1992) (1994).

ATTORNEY-GENERAL'S REFERENCE (NO. 3 OF 1992) (1994)
D threw a petrol bomb towards a car containing four men. The bomb missed the car and smashed harmlessly against a wall. D was charged with attempting to commit arson with intent to endanger life. The trial judge ruled that it had to be proved that D intended to damage property *and* to endanger life. D was acquitted.

The Court of Appeal held that the trial judge was wrong. It was necessary to prove that D intended to damage property, but it was only necessary to prove that he was reckless as to whether life would be endangered.

6.3.3 Attempting the impossible

In some situations a person may intend to commit an offence and may do everything they possibly can to commit it, but in fact the offence is impossible to commit.

An example of this would be where D goes to V's room and stabs V as he lies in bed. In fact, V died of a heart attack two hours before D stabbed him. D has merely stabbed a dead body. Murdering V is physically impossible so D can not be guilt of his murder, but can D be guilty of attempting to murder V?

Another example is where D thinks that the goods he is buying very cheaply are stolen goods. He is willing to go ahead, thinking he is 'handling stolen property'. In fact, the goods are not stolen, so the offence of handling stolen property is legally impossible in this situation. Should D be guilty of attempting to handle stolen property?

Under the common law, before 1981, the House of Lords had held that where a crime was legally or physically impossible to commit, then the defendant could not be guilty of attempting to commit it. When the

Criminal Attempts Act 1981 was passed it contained a subsection (s 1(2)) which was intended to close this loophole and make defendants guilty of an attempt even though the full offence was impossible.

Section 1(2) of the Criminal Attempts Act 1981 states:

'A person may be guilty of attempting to commit an offence ... even though the facts are such that the commission of the offence is impossible.'

After the Act was passed, the House of Lords had to consider this section and the problem of attempting the impossible in the case of *Anderton v Ryan* (1985).

ANDERTON v RYAN (1985)

Mrs Ryan bought a video recorder very cheaply. She thought it was stolen. Later she admitted this to police who were investigating a burglary at her home. Her conviction was quashed because the video recorder was not in fact stolen.

The House of Lords held that even though Mrs Ryan had gone beyond merely preparatory acts, in fact all her acts were innocent. The video-recorder was not stolen. On this basis, they thought that s 1(2) did not make her guilty.

However, less than a year later, the House of Lords overruled this decision in *Shivpuri* (1986).

Figure 6.3 Key facts chart on attempts

KEY FACTS

Definition of 'attempt'	With intent to commit an offence, a person does an act which is more than merely preparatory to the commission of the offence.	s 1(1) Criminal Attempts Act 1981
'More than merely preparatory'	D must have embarked on the crime proper *or* D must be trying to commit the full offence.	*Gullefer* (1987) *Geddes* (1996)
Mens rea of attempt	D must have intention for the full offence.	*Easom* (1971)
	A conditional intention is sufficient.	*Attorney-General's Reference (Nos 1 and 2 of 1979) (1979)*
	Recklessness is not normally sufficient *but* recklessness as to part of the offence may be sufficient.	*Millard and Vernon* (1987) *Attorney-General's Reference (No. 3 of 1992) (1994)*
Attempting the impossible	ss 1(2) and 1(3) of the Criminal Attempts Act 1981 mean that D is guilty even if the full offence is legally or physically impossible.	*Shivpuri* (1986)

SHIVPURI (1986)

D agreed to receive a suitcase which he thought contained prohibited drugs. The suitcase was delivered to him, but it contained only snuff and harmless vegetable matter. D was convicted of attempting to be knowingly concerned in dealing with prohibited drugs.

This time the House of Lords said that both sub-ss 1(2) and 1(3) were relevant. Subsection 1(3) states:

'In any case where –

(a) apart from this subsection a person's intention would not be regarded as having amounted to an intent to commit an offence; but
(b) if the facts of the case had been as he believed them to be, his intention would be so regarded,

then, for the purpose of subsection (1) he shall be regarded as having an intent to commit that offence.'

The combined effect of sub-ss 1(2) and 1(3) of the Criminal Attempts Act 1981 meant that a person could be guilty of an attempt even if the commission of the full offence was impossible. In *Shivpuri* the facts as he believed them to be were that the suitcase contained prohibited drugs. He intended dealing in drugs, so his intention under s 1(3) is regarded as being an intention to commit that offence.

The House of Lords accepted that its decision in *Anderton v Ryan* had been wrong and used the Practice Statement to overrule it.

Activity

Explain whether in each of the following scenarios there is an attempt to commit an offence.

1 Amir knows his girlfriend has been going out with Blake. Amir plans to disfigure Blake. He buys some acid which he intends to throw in Blake's face and then drives to Blake's house. As he is about to get out of the car, he sees a police car nearby. Amir immediately drives off.
2 Connor puts some poison in Donna's drink, intending to kill her. The amount he puts in the drink is insufficient to kill and Donna survives.
3 Faye sees a handbag in the ladies' cloakroom. She hopes there will be some money in it, so she opens it. In fact, the bag contains only make-up and tissues. Faye closes the bag and replaces it.
4 Greg and Hans are found in the garden of a house with masks, a torch and screwdrivers in their pockets. They admit they intended to burgle the house.

6.3.4 Is the law on attempts satisfactory?

There are several points which can be argued to be unsatisfactory. These are:

■ the courts have not been very clear in deciding the dividing line between what is 'merely preparatory' and what is an attempt
■ some of the decisions in this area are not effective for protecting the public
■ the early decisions on *mens rea* left a loophole where D intended to steal if he could find anything worth stealing, but the concept of conditional intent has now clarified this
■ then there is the point of whether D should be guilty just because of intention.

What is 'more than merely preparatory'?

The cases *Gullefer, Geddes* and *Campbell* that we looked at in section 6.3.1 show that the courts are not always prepared to take a broad approach when deciding what is 'more than merely preparatory'.

Protection of the public

In considering this it is also necessary to ask why attempting an offence should make someone criminally liable. The main justification is that it can prevent the full offence from being committed. It would be ridiculous if the police had to wait until D fired the shot and killed V, instead of being able to arrest D for attempted murder. So, given that prevention of crime and protection of potential victims are important, the decisions in *Geddes* and *Campbell* in particular are hard to reconcile with this.

Should intention alone make a defendant guilty?

The opposite point of view is that a defendant should not be criminally liable for his intentions. He must do something toward the commission of the full offence. This raises the question of whether Parliament should have made defendants liable where the facts are such that the commission of the full offence is impossible. Should *Shivpuri* have been guilty? He did not actually deal in drugs or do any wrong act. Is it enough that he intended to?

Again, it can be argued that it is in the public interest to be able to convict someone like *Shivpuri*. Drug dealing causes society many problems.

Examination questions

1 Discuss whether the current law relating to attempted crimes strikes the right balance between protecting society and convicting those who deserve to be punished.

(OCR, Unit 2571, June 2004)

2 Sandra and Vincent have lived together for five years. One day, Vincent suddenly tells Sandra that he is leaving her to start a new relationship with Wendy, with whom he has been having an affair. Sandra is shocked and distressed and goes to see her friend, Ursula. Ursula has never trusted Vincent and also knows Wendy very well.

Ursula suggests to Sandra that she should take revenge by killing Vincent who is now living in Wendy's flat. They then agree that, if Sandra can obtain a gun, Ursula will trick Wendy into letting her have a key to the flat. The plan goes ahead and Ursula gives Sandra the spare key which she has obtained from Wendy. In the meantime, Sandra has bought a pistol and some ammunition from Rudi. Unknown to her, the ammunition contains only blank, imitation rounds.

One evening, Ursula invites Wendy out for a meal so that Vincent will be alone in the flat. Sandra goes round to the flat, lets herself in with the key given her by Ursula and confronts Vincent. After a brief argument, Sandra produces the pistol from her bag and fires it at Vincent while he has his back turned. Hearing the loud click, Vincent turns round and says 'What was that?'. By this time, Sandra has hastily thrust the pistol back in her bag and Vincent does not even see it.

Discuss the criminal liability, if any, of Sandra, Ursula and Rudi.

(OCR, Unit 3571, June 2003)

CHAPTER 7

Murder

Homicide is the unlawful killing of a human being. There are different offences, depending on the *mens rea* of the defendant and whether there is a special defence available to the defendant. The most serious homicide offence is murder.

7.1   DEFINITION OF 'MURDER'

Murder is a common-law offence. This means that it is not defined by any Act of Parliament. It has been defined by the decisions of judges in cases and the accepted definition is based on one given by a seventeenth-century judge, Lord Coke. This is that murder is:

'the unlawful killing of a reasonable person in being and under the King's (or Queen's) Peace with malice aforethought, express or implied'.

The different elements of this definition are considered in detail under the *actus reus* and *mens rea* of murder below at sections 7.2 and 7.3.

Jurisdiction

Obviously, a person can be charged with a murder committed anywhere in England and Wales. But murder is unusual in that jurisdiction over it also includes any murder in any country by a British citizen. This means that if the defendant is a British citizen, he may be tried in an English court for a murder he is alleged to have committed in another country.

7.2   *ACTUS REUS* OF MURDER

The *actus reus* of murder is the unlawful killing of a reasonable creature in being and under the Queen's Peace. Breaking this down, it has to be proved that:

- ▪ D killed
- ▪ a reasonable creature in being
- ▪ under the Queen's Peace and
- ▪ the killing was unlawful.

7.2.1 Killed

Act or omission

The *actus reus* of killing can be by an act or omission, but it must cause the death of the victim. Usually in murder cases, the *actus reus* is an act. But remember that we saw in Chapter 2 at section 2.2 that an omission (a failure to act) can make a person liable for an offence.

This applies to murder, as seen by the case of *Gibbins and Proctor* (1918) where the father of a seven-year-old girl and his mistress kept the girl separate from the father's other children and deliberately starved her to death. The father had a duty to feed her because he was her parent and the mistress was held to have undertaken to look after the children, including the girl, so she was also under a duty to feed the child. The omission or failure to feed her was deliberate with the intention of killing or causing serious harm to her. In these circumstances they were guilty of murder. The failure to feed the girl was enough for the *actus reus* of murder.

Causation

Murder is a *result crime*. The defendant cannot be guilty unless his act or omission caused the death. In most cases there is no problem with this. For example, D shoots V in the head and V is killed instantly. However, in some cases there may be other causes contributing to the death, such as poor medical treatment. This type of situation raises questions of causation.

The law on causation is considered fully in Chapter 2 in section 2.3 and you need to know the law stated there.

7.2.2 'Reasonable creature in being'

This phrase means 'a human being'. So, for murder, a person must be killed. Normally, this part of the definition does not cause any difficulties. The only two problem areas are:

- is a foetus in the womb a 'reasonable creature in being'?
- is a victim still considered to be alive (and so a 'reasonable creature in being') if they are 'brain-dead' but being kept alive by a life-support machine?

Foetus

A homicide offence cannot be charged in respect of the killing of a foetus. The child has to have an 'existence independent of the mother' for it to be considered a 'creature in being'. This means that it must have been expelled from her body and have an independent circulation. However, the umbilical cord connecting the child and the mother need not have been cut. Also, it is probable that the child need not have taken its first breath for it to be considered a 'reasonable creature in being'.

In addition, in *Attorney-General's Reference (No. 3 of 1994)* (1997) it was stated by the House of Lords that where the foetus is injured and the child is born alive but dies afterwards as a result of the injuries, this can be the *actus reus* for murder or manslaughter.

ATTORNEY-GENERAL'S REFERENCE (NO. 3 OF 1994) (1997)
The defendant stabbed his girlfriend who was about 23 weeks pregnant. She recovered from the stab wound but it caused her to give birth prematurely some seven weeks after the stabbing. The baby was born alive but died at the age of four months as a result of the premature birth. The defendant was charged with the murder of the child. At the trial the judge directed that a foetus was not a 'reasonable creature in being' and so the defendant could not in law be guilty of either the murder or manslaughter of the child. The defendant was acquitted.

The House of Lords agreed that this was correct where the foetus died before being born but stated *obiter* that:

'violence towards a foetus which results in harm suffered after the baby has been born alive can give rise to criminal responsibility'.

However, they held that in the circumstances the offence was manslaughter as there was no *mens rea* for murder.

Brain-dead

It is not certain whether a person who is 'brain-dead' would be considered as a 'reasonable creature in being' or not. Doctors are allowed to switch off life-support machines without being liable for homicide. This suggests that 'brain-death' is the recognised test for death, but there has been no case on this point. It is possible that the courts might decide that a defendant who switches off a life-support machine, not as a medical decision but intending to kill the victim, could be guilty of murder.

'Year and a day' rule

There used to be a rule that death must have occurred within a year and a day of the attack.

This rule was sensible in past centuries when medical knowledge was not sufficient to prove that an attack had caused the death after such a long time. However, with improvements in medical skill, the rule became out of date. In particular, it meant that, where a victim was in a coma and did not die until more than a year after the attack, the attacker could not be charged with his murder. So the 'year and a day' rule was abolished by the Law Reform (Year and a Day Rule) Act 1996. There is now no time-limit on when the death may occur after the unlawful act but, where it is more than three years after the attack, the consent of the Attorney-General is needed for the prosecution.

Activity

Read the following situations and explain whether the *actus reus* for murder is present.

1 Jane is angry because Karina is pregnant by Jane's boyfriend. When Karina is eight months pregnant, Jane stabs her in the stomach, intending to kill the foetus. Karina is rushed to hospital, where a Caesarian section is carried out. The baby is alive when it is removed from Karina's womb, but dies two hours later.

2 Anya is offered a lift home by Barnaby. After a few minutes, she realises he is driving away from her home. He then puts his hand on her thigh as he is driving and says that they can enjoy themselves. Anya is so afraid that she jumps out of the car while it is going at about 40 mph. She is hit by another car and killed.

3 Lily decides to kill Kevin. She takes his shotgun and loads it. She waits until he has gone to sleep, then she goes into his bedroom and shoots him in the head. Unknown to her, Kevin died from a drug overdose 20 minutes before she shot him.

7.2.3 Queen's Peace

'Under the Queen's Peace' means that the killing of an enemy in the course of war is not murder. However, the killing of a prisoner of war would be sufficient for the *actus reus* of murder.

7.2.4 Unlawful

The killing must be unlawful. It is not unlawful if what is done is in self-defence or in the prevention of crime and the defendant used reasonable force in the circumstances (see section 14.5 for the law on this area).

7.3 *MENS REA* OF MURDER

The *mens rea* for murder is stated as being 'malice aforethought, express or implied'. This means that there are two different intentions, either of which can be used to prove the defendant guilty of murder:

- *express* malice aforethought, which is the intention to kill or
- *implied* malice aforethought, which is the intention to cause grievous bodily harm.

A defendant has the *mens rea* for murder if he has either of these intentions. This means that a person can be guilty of murder even though they did not intend to kill. This was decided in *Vickers* (1957).

VICKERS (1957)

Vickers broke into the cellar of a local sweet shop. He knew that the old lady who ran the shop was deaf. However, the old lady came into the cellar and saw Vickers. He then hit her several blows with his fists and kicked her once in the head. She died as a result of her injuries. The Court of Appeal upheld Vickers' conviction for murder. It pointed out that where a defendant intends to inflict grievous bodily harm and the victim dies, that has always been sufficient in English law to imply malice aforethought.

The same point was considered by the House of Lords in *Cunningham* (1981) when it confirmed that an intention to cause grievous bodily harm was sufficient for the *mens rea* of murder.

CUNNINGHAM (1981)

D attacked V in a pub. He hit V repeatedly with a chair. V died from his injuries. D was convicted of murder. The House of Lords dismissed his appeal. It held that the law was firmly established. An intention to cause grievous bodily harm was sufficient for the *mens rea* of murder.

The other issue is: what is meant by 'grievous bodily harm'? In *DPP v Smith* (1961) the House of Lords decided that 'grievous bodily harm' has the natural meaning of 'really serious harm'. However, even if the judge directed the jury leaving out the word 'really' and just saying 'serious harm', this was not a misdirection.

Intention to injure a foetus

In *Attorney-General's Reference (No. 3 of 1994)* (1997) it was held that it was not possible for a defendant to have the *mens rea* to kill or seriously injure a foetus. This was because a foetus does not have a separate existence from its mother.

7.3.1 Intention

The general rules on intention apply to murder. These were discussed in Chapter 3 at

---

Figure 7.1 Key facts chart on murder

KEY FACTS

	Law	Source/case
Definition	'The unlawful killing of a reasonable person in being and under the King's (or Queen's) Peace, with malice aforethought, express or implied'	Lord Coke (17th century)
Actus reus	Must unlawfully kill a person under the Queen's Peace.	
	Can be an act or an omission.	*Gibbins and Proctor* (1918)
	A foetus is not considered a person for the purposes of murder.	*Attorney-General's Reference (No. 3 of 1994)* (1997)
Mens rea	Intention to kill *or* intention to cause grievous bodily harm.	*Vickers* (1957) *Cunningham* (1981)
	Foresight of consequences is evidence of intention.	*Moloney* (1985)
	Jury can *find* intention if death or serious injury was a virtual certainty as a result of D's actions and D appreciated this.	*Woollin* (1998)

section 3.1. The main problem with proving intention is in cases where the defendant's main aim was not to cause the death or serious injury of the victim, but something quite different, but in achieving the aim a death is caused. This is referred to as *oblique intent*. The defendant does not have the *mens rea* for murder unless he foresaw that he would also cause death or serious injury. This is known as *foresight of consequences* and was considered in detail at section 3.1.2. However, as the law in this area is complex and important, the three main cases are set out here again.

Foresight of consequences

The main rule is that foresight of consequences is not intention. In *Moloney* (1985), where the defendant shot and killed his step-father in a drunken challenge to see who was quicker on the draw, it was held that foresight of consequences is only evidence from which intention may be inferred.

In *Nedrick* (1986) the defendant poured paraffin through the letter box of a house in order to frighten the woman who lived there. A child died in the fire. The Court of Appeal suggested that juries ask themselves two questions:

■ how probable was the consequence which resulted from the defendant's voluntary act? and
■ did the defendant foresee that consequence?

The Court of Appeal also said that the jury should be directed that they are not entitled to infer the necessary intention unless they feel sure that death or serious injury was a virtual certainty as a result of the defendant's actions and that the defendant appreciated that such was the case.

In *Woollin* (1998) the House of Lords approved this direction but disapproved of the use of the two questions. The Law Lords

Activity

In each of the following situations, explain whether the defendant has the required intention for murder.

1 Jamie is annoyed because Harry has being trying to date Jamie's girlfriend. Jamie sees Harry in a local pub and goes over and punches him hard in the face, saying 'Perhaps that will make you leave my girlfriend alone'. Harry has a thin skull and the punch causes a brain haemorrhage from which he dies.

2 Diana intends to kill Edward. She fixes an explosive booby trap to the front door of his house, so that when he opens it the explosive will go off. Unknown to Diana, Edward has given Felix the keys to his house and told him to collect some papers from there. Felix opens the door and is killed by the explosion.

3 Ravinder's business has been losing a lot of money. He decides to set fire to one of the smaller buildings in the unit so that he can claim insurance on it. Ravinder knows that there is no-one in his building, so he sets it alight. Unfortunately, the fire spreads to another building on the site. Nancy, who is working in that building, is trapped by the fire and dies.

said that 'substantial risk' was not the correct test. Using this phrase blurred the line between intention and recklessness. They approved the direction given in *Nedrick*, provided that the word 'find' was used instead of 'infer'. So, the jury should be directed that they are not entitled to *find* the necessary intention unless they feel sure that death or serious injury was a virtual certainty as a result of the defendant's actions and that the defendant appreciated that such was the case.

7.4 THE NEED FOR REFORM OF THE LAW

In August 2004 the Law Commission published a report, *Partial Defences to Murder*, on diminished responsibility and provocation as defences to murder. For its proposals on diminished responsibility and provocation, this report is considered in Chapter 8. However, for the purpose of the wider law on murder it is worth noting that in its report the Law Commission described the law on murder as 'a mess'.

As a result, following the report, the Government asked the Law Commission to review the whole of the law of murder. The terms of reference for that review were:

'To review the various elements of murder, including the defences and partial defences to it, and the relationship between the law of murder and the law relating to homicide (in particular manslaughter). The review will make recommendations that:

- *take account of the continuing existence of the mandatory life sentence for murder;*
- *provide coherent and clear offences which protect individuals and society;*
- *enable those convicted to be appropriately punished; and*
- *be fair and non-discriminatory in accordance with ECHR and Human Rights Act.'*

Consultation Paper

The Law Commission started the review in 2005. In December 2005 it published a Consultation Paper considering the law on murder. This proposes splitting murder into two tiers.

1 First Tier Murder would apply only where the defendant had an intention to kill and there were no special defences.

2 Second Tier Murder would include a variety of situations where D has killed V and it is more serious than involuntary manslaughter. These are where:

- D had intention to cause serious harm
- D was recklessly indifferent to causing death
- D had the intention to kill but was under provocation
- D had the intention to kill but suffered from diminished responsibility (this would include killing in pursuance of a suicide pact)
- D had the intention to kill but was under duress.

It is proposed that the law on both diminished responsibility and provocation would also be changed.

The full report on the law of murder is expected to be published by the autumn of 2006. (Check www.lawcom.gov.uk for this.)

In the meantime it is obvious that there are several areas in which the law on murder is not satisfactory. Four main points are:

- the fact that a defendant can be convicted of murder even though he did not intend to kill
- the difficulties in deciding what is meant by 'intention'
- the fact that the only sentence for murder is life imprisonment
- the fact that the use of excessive force in a situation where some force was justified does not provide any defence.

Each of these is discussed below.

7.4.1 No intention to kill

Under the present law on murder, a defendant is guilty of murder if he had the intention to cause grievous bodily harm and actually causes the victim's death. In some of these cases the defendant may not even realise that death could occur. Yet he is just as guilty of murder as the man who deliberately sets out to kill his victim.

In *Cunningham* (1981), where this point was considered by the House of Lords, Lord Edmund Davies stated that he thought the *mens rea* for murder should be limited to an intention to kill. He said:

'[It is] strange that a person can be convicted of murder if death results from, say, his intentional breaking of another's arm, an action which, while undoubtedly involving the infliction of "really serious harm" and as such, calling for severe punishment, would in most cases be unlikely to kill.'

Although he was very critical of the law, Lord Edmund Davies felt that any change to the law had to be made by Parliament. This was because the law has been the same for over 200 years and it would therefore be wrong for judges to change such a well-established law.

There have been attempts at persuading Parliament to pass new law on murder (and indeed for all the main areas of the criminal law by having a complete code for criminal law) but Parliament has not been prepared to give the necessary time to enact such a law. The draft Criminal Code which was produced in 1989 proposed that the basic definition of murder should be:

'A person is guilty of murder if he causes the death of another:

(a) *intending to cause death; or*
(b) *intending to cause serious personal harm and being aware that he may cause death.'*

This limitation in (b) would make the law more just than at present. Under this, a defendant could still be convicted of murder where his intention was only to cause serious injury and not to kill. However, such a conviction would only occur where the jury were satisfied that the defendant was aware that his actions could cause death.

7.4.2 The meaning of 'intention'

The courts have had difficulties in deciding what is meant by 'intention'. Intention is a concept which affects all specific intent offences but most of the cases which have been heard by the House of Lords have involved murder. Section 8 of the Criminal Justice Act 1967 tried to make the law clear on this point. It states:

'A court or jury in determining whether a person has committed an offence –

(a) *shall not be bound in law to infer that he intended or foresaw a result of his actions by reason only of its being a natural and probable consequence of those actions; but*
(b) *shall decide whether he did intend or foresee that result by reference to all the evidence, drawing such inferences from the evidence as appear proper in the circumstances.'*

The main problems in the law are on foresight of consequences. The House of Lords has tried on many occasions to explain what the effect of foresight of consequences has. In *Moloney* (1985) it ruled that foresight of consequences was not intention; it was only evidence from which intention could be inferred in accordance with s 8(b) above.

However, the later decision in *Woollin* (1998), where the House of Lords speaks about intention being *found* from foresight of consequences, has made the law uncertain. It is not clear whether there is a substantive rule of criminal law that foresight of consequences is intention, or if there is only a rule of evidence that intention can be found from foresight of consequences. In *Matthews and Alleyne* (2003) the Court of Appeal even said that there was little to choose between a rule of evidence and one of substantive law, leaving it even more unclear.

7.4.3 Mandatory life sentence

If a defendant aged 18 or over is convicted of murder, the judge has to pass a sentence of life imprisonment. For offenders aged 10–17 who are found guilty of murder, the judge has to order that they be detained at Her Majesty's Pleasure. Because the judge has no discretion in what sentence to impose, this is known as a *mandatory* sentence. The judge cannot give a different sentence even if he feels that the defendant is not as blameworthy as a deliberate killer.

For other offences, including attempted murder, the judge can decide what the most appropriate sentence is for the offence and the offender. This makes it possible for a judge to give even a community sentence where the circumstances justify it. This happened in the case of *Gotts* (1992), where the father of a 16-year-old boy threatened to kill the boy unless he stabbed his mother. The boy did stab her and seriously injure her, but the injury did not kill her. He was convicted of attempted murder and because of the circumstances the judge put him on probation for three years. If the stabbing had caused the death of the mother, the judge would have had to order the boy (because of his age) to be detained at Her Majesty's Pleasure.

It is because of the mandatory life sentence for murder that the 1957 Homicide Act sets out three special defences: diminished responsibility, provocation and suicide pact (see Chapter 8), which reduce the charge to manslaughter. This allows the judge flexibility in passing sentence which he does not have when the defendant is convicted of murder.

The terms of the review of the law of murder set out by the Government in 2005 do not include a review of the sentence. The Government's intention is that the mandatory life sentence will remain.

7.4.4 No defence where excessive force is used

If a defendant can show that he used reasonable force in self-defence or prevention of crime in doing the killing, he is not guilty of murder. However, where force is necessary in self-defence or prevention of crime, but the defendant uses excessive force in the circumstances, he is guilty of murder. This 'all or nothing' effect of the defence is very harsh in murder cases, as the defendant is either acquitted or given a life sentence. He was justified in using some force and his only 'fault' is that he used more force than was reasonable. This surely does not justify a life sentence.

Two recent cases have highlighted this problem. The first was *Clegg* (1995).

> ### *CLEGG* [1995]
> D was a soldier on duty at a checkpoint in Northern Ireland when a stolen car came towards him at speed. D fired at the car. His final shot hit a passenger in the back and killed her. The evidence showed that the car had gone past D by the time this last shot was fired. It was held that he could not use self-defence or defence of another as there was no danger when he fired that shot. The force was excessive in the circumstances and his conviction for murder was upheld.

Note that in 1999 the case of *Clegg* was referred back to the Court of Appeal by the Criminal Case Review Commission. On this occasion his conviction was quashed because new forensic evidence cast doubt on whether the fatal shot had actually been fired by Clegg.

The second case was *Martin (Anthony)* (2002), where two burglars entered the defendant's house in the night. The house was in an isolated place and had been burgled before. On this occasion the noise of entry woke Martin, who got up, armed himself with a shotgun, and without warning fired three shots in the dark. One of the burglars was killed. Martin was convicted of murder. His appeal on the ground of self-defence was rejected as the force was not reasonable. However, his conviction was reduced to manslaughter because of evidence that he was suffering from diminished responsibility.

Both these decisions have been criticised. Many people believe that a person who kills where he has an honest, but unreasonable, belief as to the degree of force needed is not as blameworthy as a 'true' murderer. It is unjust that such a person is found guilty of the same crime of murder and sentenced to the same punishment.

Proposed reform

In its report, *Partial Defences and Murder*, the Law Commission did not recommend that there should be a separate special defence of excessive use of force. Instead, it thought that it could be covered as part of provocation. It recommended that fear of serious violence towards the defendant or another should be considered as provocation.

Examination questions

1 Rupert, a famous businessman, who is very heavily in debt, is being threatened with insolvency proceedings by his creditors. Without telling his family, he insures his own life to the maximum. He places a bomb in his briefcase, which is not detected at airport security, and boards a passenger plane at Heathrow, bound for New York. The bomb is set to detonate over the Atlantic, two hours into the flight. The plane develops engine trouble shortly after take-off and is forced to return to Heathrow one hour after take-off.

The passengers disembark and while they are waiting the arrival of the maintenance crew, Patrick, a cleaner, boards the aeroplane. Rupert has left his briefcase on board. The bomb explodes and Patrick is killed.

Rupert has now been charged with murder. Discuss.

(OCR, June 2000)

2 Miles and Jonas were partners in an antique shop. When Miles found out that Jonas was stealing from the shop to pay his gambling debts, he told his wife, Bella, that he was going to kill Jonas and burn down the shop, to claim the insurance money. Miles lured Jonas to the shop and struck him on the head with a brass candlestick. Jonas collapsed and, thinking that he was dead, Miles set fire to the shop and drove home. However, the shop's automatic sprinkler system went off and doused the fire. When Miles returned an hour later with Bella, they found the shop flooded and Jonas lying on the floor, apparently dead. In an attempt to dispose of the body, Miles and Bella drove Jonas to the top of a cliff and pushed him over the edge. The tide was out, and Jonas was found by the coastguard and taken to hospital, still alive but seriously injured by the fall. The consultant surgeon, Judy, decided to operate immediately, without waiting for all of Jonas's test results to come back from the lab. During the operation Judy injected Jonas with a drug to which he was allergic, and Jonas died.

Consider whether Miles, Bella or Judy may be criminally liable for Jonas's death.

(WJEC, LW4, June 2004)

CHAPTER 8 | Voluntary manslaughter

There are three special defences to a charge of murder. These are where the killing occurs when the defendant is under:

- diminished responsibility
- provocation or
- suicide pact.

All of these defences are set out in the Homicide Act 1957. These defences are available only to murder. They are also only *partial* defences, which means that the defendant is not completely acquitted. Instead, when one of these defences is successful, the charge of murder is reduced to manslaughter.

This is important because it means that the judge has discretion in what sentence he imposes. When a person is found guilty of murder, the judge has to pass a sentence of life imprisonment. However, for manslaughter the judge can choose *any* sentence which is suitable. This means that where the defendant is dangerous and his mental problems cannot be treated then the judge may pass a sentence of life imprisonment, as happened in *Byrne* (see section 8.1.1). However, if the defendant is not dangerous then he may be given a short term of imprisonment or even a community sentence. If the defendant has mental problems which can be treated, then the most suitable sentence is one which orders the defendant to have treatment, either in a hospital or in the community.

The defences of diminished responsibility and provocation are now explained in detail.

8.1   DIMINISHED RESPONSIBILITY

This defence was introduced by the Homicide Act 1957; it did not exist in English law until then. Before 1957, if a person with mental problems killed, then their only defence was insanity. The test for insanity is a very narrow one and defendants who clearly suffer from a mental illness do not always come within it. (See Chapter 14 for further information on the defence of insanity.)

Section 2(1) of the Homicide Act states that:

'Where a person kills or is party to a killing of another, he shall not be convicted of murder if he was suffering from such abnormality of mind (whether arising from a condition of arrested or retarded development of mind or any inherent causes or induced by disease or injury) as substantially impaired his mental responsibility for his acts and omission in doing or being a party to the killing.'

The burden of proving the defence is on the defendant, but the defendant need only prove it on the balance of probabilities.

This means that a defendant who pleads diminished responsibility must prove that:

- he was suffering from an abnormality of mind
- which was caused by arrested or retarded development of mind or an inherent cause or disease or injury and
- the abnormality of mind substantially impaired his mental responsibility for the killing.

8.1.1 Abnormality of mind

'Abnormality of mind' covers a wide range of situations. In *Byrne* (1960) the Court of Appeal described it as 'a state of mind so different from that of ordinary human beings that the reasonable man would term it abnormal'.

BYRNE (1960)

The defendant was a sexual psychopath who strangled a young woman and then mutilated her body. The medical evidence was that, because of his condition, he was unable to control his perverted desires. He was convicted of murder but the Court of Appeal quashed the conviction and substituted a conviction for manslaughter as it held that his condition came within the definition of diminished responsibility.

The Court of Appeal held that 'abnormality of mind' is wide enough to cover:

- the perception of physical acts and matters
- the ability to form a rational judgment as to whether an act is right or wrong and
- the ability to exercise will-power to control physical acts in accordance with that rational judgment.

This final point covers 'irresistible impulse', as in *Byrne*, where he could not resist his perverted desires. This meant that the defence of diminished responsibility was available to Byrne. However, although the Court of Appeal substituted a conviction for manslaughter, Byrne was still sentenced to life imprisonment.

In *Byrne* the medical experts had described his condition as amounting to 'partial insanity' and the Court of Criminal Appeal had approved of this. However, in *Seers* (1984), it was held that comparisons with insanity are not helpful and should be avoided.

SEERS (1984)

D, who was suffering from chronic reactive depression, killed his wife. The trial judge had directed the jury that the defence was only available to those who were 'partially insane' or 'on the borderline of insanity'. Seers was convicted of murder but the Court of Appeal quashed this conviction and substituted a conviction for manslaughter.

Diminished responsibility covers a wide range of mental conditions, including depressive illnesses, paranoia, epilepsy, pre-menstrual tension and battered wives' syndrome.

8.1.2 Causes of the abnormality of mind

The abnormality of mind must be caused by one of the matters set out in the brackets within s 2(1) of the Homicide Act 1957. These are:

- a condition of arrested or retarded development of mind or
- any inherent cause
- induced by any disease or
- induced by injury.

'Inherent cause' means one which comes from within the defendant, as opposed to an outside factor. It does not have to be permanent. A totally external factor, such as alcohol or drugs or a traumatic event or environmental influences, is not an inherent cause. However, if a traumatic event causes the defendant to suffer from post-traumatic stress disorder then this is recognised as a disease.

The important point is that there must be medical evidence given at the trial, of an abnormality of mind arising from one of the specified causes.

8.1.3 Substantially impairs

The abnormality of mind must substantially impair the defendant's mental responsibility for his acts and omissions in doing or being a party to the killing.

In *Byrne* the appeal court said that the question of whether the impairment was substantial was a one of degree and that it was for the jury to decide. In *Lloyd* (1967) it was held that 'substantial' does not mean 'total', nor does it mean 'trivial' or 'minimal'. It is something in between and it is for the jury to decide if the defendant's mental responsibility is impaired and, if so, whether it is substantially impaired. However, as it is a question of fact, the judge can withdraw the point from the jury if there is no evidence on which a reasonable jury could conclude that the defendant's mental responsibility was substantially impaired.

In *Seers* the court also considered the phrase 'substantially impaired' and held that 'substantially' means more than 'trivial' but not 'total' or 'absolute' impairment.

8.1.4 Diminished responsibility and intoxication

There are two ways in which intoxication has to be considered in the defence of diminished responsibility. These are:

- whether the effect of alcohol or drugs on the brain can be a disease
- what has to be proved where the defendant had a pre-existing mental disorder but was also intoxicated when he killed.

Intoxication and disease

In *Di Duca* (1959) the Court of Appeal held that the immediate effects of taking alcohol or drugs was not an injury, even if it did have an effect on the brain. So a 'transient' state of intoxication was not an abnormality of mind.

If the brain has been injured through alcoholism, then that injury or disease can support a finding of diminished responsibility. Also, in *Tandy* (1989) the Court of Appeal held that where the defendant is unable to resist drinking, so that it is involuntary, this may amount to diminished responsibility.

TANDY (1989)

Mrs Tandy had been an alcoholic for a number of years, usually drinking barley wine or Cinzano. One day, she drank nearly a whole bottle of vodka. That evening she told her mother that her (Tandy's) second husband had sexually interfered with her 11-year-old daughter. She then strangled her daughter. The trial judge told the jury to decide whether Tandy was suffering from an abnormality of mind as a direct result of her alcoholism or whether she was just drunk. She was convicted. The Court of Appeal dismissed her appeal because Tandy had not shown that her brain had been injured or that her drinking was involuntary.

The decision in this case has been criticised as it only looks at whether the defendant was unable to prevent themselves from drinking. It does not consider whether alcoholism is a disease. In the later case of *Inseal* (1992) where the defendant strangled his girlfriend in bed one night, medical evidence was given that he suffered from 'alcohol dependence syndrome' and that this was an abnormality of mind. Despite this, the jury were directed to focus on whether his drinking was involuntary and the Court of Appeal dismissed his appeal against his conviction, following the decision in *Tandy*.

Pre-existing mental disorder and intoxication

There are also difficulties in cases where the defendant has some abnormality of mind but, in addition, is intoxicated at the time he does the killing. This problem was considered in *Gittens* (1984).

GITTENS (1984)

D suffered from depression and had medication for this. One night he drank a lot and also took several anti-depressant pills. He then clubbed his wife to death and strangled his step-daughter. He was convicted of murder. The conviction was quashed because the trial judge had misdirected the jury on the effect of intoxication in the case. The Court of Appeal held that where there was a combination of factors, one of which was intoxication, the jury had to decide whether the combination of the factors excluding the intoxication amounted to a substantial impairment of the defendant's responsibility for his acts.

This decision was later interpreted as meaning that the defendant could only prove diminished responsibility if he could satisfy the jury that he would have killed because of the abnormality of mind even if he had not been intoxicated. However, in *Dietschmann* (2003) the House of Lords said that this was the wrong approach and was not what had been decided in *Gittens*.

DIETSCHMANN (2003)

The defendant was upset by the fact that, in his view, the victim was behaving in a way which was disrespectful to the memory of the defendant's aunt who had just died, and he killed the victim by repeatedly kicking him and stamping on him. The defendant was suffering from an adjustment disorder in the form of a depressed grief reaction to the death of his aunt. This was agreed on by the psychiatrists called by both the prosecution and the defence. However, they disagreed on whether this had substantially impaired his mental responsibility for the killing. The defendant had also drunk about a third of a bottle of whisky and two and a half pints of cider before the killing. He was convicted and appealed but the appeal was dismissed.

The Court of Appeal dismissed the appeal but certified the following questions for the House of Lords:

'1 Does a defendant seeking to prove a defence of diminished responsibility under section 2(1) of the Homicide Act 1957 in a case where he had taken drink prior to the killing of the victim, have to show (a) he would have killed as in fact he did; and (b) he would have been under diminished responsibility when he did so?

2 If not, what direction ought to be given to a jury as to the approach to be taken to self-induced intoxication which was present at the material time in conjunction with an abnormality of mind which falls within under section 2(1) of the 1957 Act?'

In the House of Lords, Lord Hutton said that the meaning of s 2(1) was reasonably clear. It meant that if the defendant satisfied the jury that, notwithstanding the alcohol he had consumed and its effect on him, his abnormality of mind substantially impaired his mental responsibility for his acts in doing the killing, the jury should not find him not guilty of murder but, instead, guilty of manslaughter under s 2(1).

Lord Hutton also pointed out that s 2(1) does not require the abnormality of mind to be the sole cause of the defendant's acts in doing the killing. Even if the defendant would not have killed if he had not taken the drink, the causative effect of the drink does not necessarily prevent an abnormality of mind from substantially impairing his mental responsibility. Lord Hutton highlighted three points from the decision in *Gittens*:

1 The abnormality of mind and the drink might each play a part in impairing the defendant's mental responsibility for the killing.

2 The jury's task was to decide whether, despite the disinhibiting effect of the drink on the defendant's mind, the abnormality of mind nevertheless substantially impaired his mental responsibility for his fatal acts.

3 It was not correct for the judge to direct the jury that unless they were satisfied that if the defendant had not taken drink he would have killed, the defence must fail. The direction was incorrect because it failed to recognise that drink and the abnormality of mind might each play a part in impairing the defendant's mental responsibility for the killing.

The House of Lords allowed the appeal and sent the case back to the Court of Appeal to decide whether to substitute a verdict of manslaughter or to order a new trial.

8.1.5 Reform of diminished responsibility

Although diminished responsibility has provided a more satisfactory defence than insanity for defendants who kill but are suffering from a mental abnormality, there are problems with the defence.

Burden of proof

A main point is that the burden of proof should not be on the defendant; in most other defences the defendant only has to raise the issue and the prosecution has to disprove it. This should also apply to diminished responsibility. At the moment, defendants pleading diminished responsibility are at a disadvantage which is not faced by those raising provocation.

There is also the possibility that putting the burden of proof on the defendant may be a breach of Art 6(2) of the European Convention on Human Rights which states that 'everyone charged with a criminal offence shall be presumed to be innocent until proven guilty according to law'. Making the defendant prove diminished responsibility could be considered a breach of this right to be presumed innocent.

Wording of s 2

There are also problems with the wording in s 2 of the Homicide Act 1957. In particular, the words in brackets in the section which state '(whether arising from a condition of arrested or retarded development of mind or any inherent causes or induced by disease or injury)' have been criticised by the Law Commission in a consultation paper published in 2003 on the partial defences to murder. It feels that these words are not clear. It points out that in different cases different doctors have classified the same conditions in different ways. Some doctors are prepared to testify that reactive depressions and dissociated states of mind are inherent causes within the Act, while other doctors do not agree.

The Law Commission also points out that there is disagreement on whether the concept of 'substantial impairment of mental responsibility' is a medical question. This means that psychiatrists are being asked to give an opinion on what many believe to be essentially a moral question.

Proposals for reform

There have been various proposals for reform in the past. In 1975, the Butler Committee considered whether the mandatory life sentence for murder should be abolished in which case there would be no need for the special defences to murder. Instead, the judge could pass an appropriate sentence, taking into account the defendant's mental abnormality. However, the Butler Committee realised that this would cause other problems. For example, juries might be unwilling to convict of murder, whereas they are at present willing to convict of manslaughter on the ground of diminished responsibility. So the Committee proposed amending the wording of s 2 to read:

'Where a person kills or is party to a killing of another he shall not be convicted of murder if there is medical evidence that he was suffering from a form of mental disorder as defined in [the mental health legislation] and if, in the opinion of the jury, the mental disorder was such as to be an extenuating circumstance which ought to reduce the offence to manslaughter.'

This would only have allowed those with a mental disorder recognised under the mental health legislation and might have been more restrictive than the wording in the 1957 Act.

In 1989 a draft Criminal Code was published by the Criminal Law Revision Committee which suggested the following:

'(1) A person who, but for this section, would be guilty of murder is not guilty of murder if, at the time of his act, he is suffering from such mental abnormality as is a substantial enough reason to reduce his offence to manslaughter...

(2) ..."mental abnormality" means mental illness, arrested or incomplete development of mind, psychopathic disorder, and any other disorder or disability of mind, except intoxication...

(3) Where a person suffering from mental abnormality is also intoxicated, this section applies only where it would apply if he were not intoxicated.'

This would have widened the causes of the mental abnormality. In addition, the burden of proof would have been on the prosecution to disprove the defence once the defendant had raised evidence of it. The problems of the intoxicated defendant were also dealt with in this draft proposal. However, the Government has not enacted either the Butler Committee's proposal or the Draft Criminal Code, so that problems remain in the law today.

Law Commission

The most recent proposal on reform to the special defences to murder is the Law Commission's report, *Partial Defences and Murder*, which was published in 2004. In this, the Law Commission did not recommend any change to the law on diminished responsibility.

Figure 8.1 Key facts chart on diminished responsibility

KEY FACTS

	Law	Act/Case
Definition	■ Suffering from an abnormality of mind. ■ Caused by arrested or retarded development of mind, an inherent cause, disease or injury. ■ The abnormality of mind substantially impaired his mental responsibility for the killing.	s 2(1) Homicide Act 1957
Abnormality of mind	A state of mind so different from that of ordinary human beings that the reasonable man would term it abnormal.	*Byrne* (1960)

Substantially impaired	A question of degree for the jury to decide.	*Byrne* (1960)
	'Substantial' does not mean 'total' nor 'trivial' or 'minimal' but something in between.	*Lloyd* (1967)
Effect of intoxication	Transient effect of drink or drugs on brain is not an injury.	*Di Duca* (1959)
	Alcoholism only defence if drinking is involuntary.	*Tandy* (1989)
	Where the defendant has a pre-existing mental disorder, intoxication does not prevent him using the defence; the abnormality of mind does not have to be the sole cause of the defendant doing the killing.	*Dietschmann* (2003)
Burden of proof	It is for the defence to prove on the balance of probabilities.	s 2(2) Homicide Acts 1957
Effect of defence	The charge of murder is reduced to manslaughter.	s 2(3) Homicide Act 1957

Activity

Read the following extract from a newspaper report by Stewart Payne in the *Daily Telegraph* of 3 November 2005 and answer the questions below.

MERCY FOR MOTHER WHO WAS DRIVEN TO KILL HER DOWN'S SYNDROME SON

'The desperate plight of a loving mother who killed her Down's Syndrome son after caring for him for 36 years led a judge to spare her a jail sentence yesterday.

Wendolyn Markcrow, 67, described as having lived a "saintly" life, finally reached her wits' end, a court heard.

During another sleepless night she "snapped" and gave her son Patrick 14 tranquillisers and suffocated him with a plastic bag.

She then slashed her neck and arm with a kitchen knife and sat down in the garden shed where she hoped to die.

She was "overwhelmed with despair" and wanted to end her life. Yet she feared for what would happen to Patrick if she were not there.

Oxford Crown Court heard that she had never thought to put her own needs before those of her son and, in the end, "spiralled into depression". Markcrow, a mother of four, who admitted manslaughter on the grounds of diminished responsibility at an earlier hearing, survived her suicide attempt. She told police: "I feel sad, desperate, defeated and ashamed."

Mr Justice Gross sentenced her to two years' prison, suspended for 18 months, and told her: "The pressures you faced were extreme."'

Questions

1 Which section of which Act allows a defence of diminished responsibility?
2 What would Mrs Markcrow's lawyers have had to prove in order to establish the defence of diminished responsibility?
3 What points in the extract support the defence?
4 The original charge against the defendant would have been murder. What effect does the defence of diminished responsibility have on that charge?
5 What sentence did the judge pass on the defendant?
6 The mandatory sentence for murder is life imprisonment. Why was the judge able to pass such a lenient sentence?

8.2   PROVOCATION

Provocation had been a common-law defence prior to the Homicide Act 1957 and the Act recognised and built on that old common-law defence. The defence of provocation is now set out in s 3 of the Homicide Act 1957 which states:

'Where, on a charge of murder, there is evidence on which the jury can find that the person charged was provoked (whether by things done or by things said or by both together) to lose his self control, the question whether the provocation was enough to make a reasonable man do as he did shall be left to be determined by the jury.'

This section does not explain what can amount to provocation, except to state that it can be 'things done or by things said or by both together'. The section also imposes a two-stage test for the jury to apply:

1 A *subjective* test – did the defendant lose his self-control?

2 An *objective* test – would a reasonable man have lost his self-control?

8.2.1 What can be provocation?

The Act states that provocation can be things done or said or both. This has been held to include a wide range of behaviour, such as:

- physical assaults, both on the defendant or on his relatives: *Pearson* (1992)
- homosexual advances
- the continual crying of a 19-day-old baby: *Doughty* (1986)
- a denial of stealing the defendant's tools: *Smith (Morgan James)* (2000)
- the actions of the wife's lover in going to meet her, where the husband was provoked into killing his wife: *Davies* (1975)
- supplying drugs to the defendant's son: *Baillie* (1995).

From these examples it can be seen that the victim does not have to deliberately aim the provocation at the defendant. In *Doughty* the defendant killed his baby son aged 19 days because the child would not stop crying. He was convicted but the Court of Appeal quashed the conviction because it should have been left to the jury to decide if the baby's crying was provocation by 'things done'. Clearly, a 19-day-old child is not deliberately trying to provoke anyone.

The acts which provoke the defendant can also be aimed at another person. This happened in *Pearson* where a father abused the defendant's younger brother. Although this behaviour was not aimed at the defendant, it was still 'things done' which caused the defendant to lose his self-control.

8.2.2 Loss of self-control

The first test is that the jury must be satisfied that the defendant lost his self-control as a result of the provocation. The accepted test comes from *Duffy* (1949) (a case which was decided under the common law before the Homicide Act was passed).

> ### DUFFY (1949)
> D, who was an abused wife, had a quarrel with her husband. She then left the room and changed her clothes. When her husband was in bed she attacked him with a hammer and a hatchet. D's conviction for murder was upheld because the court stated that there must be 'a sudden and temporary loss of self-control, rendering the accused so subject to passion as to make him or her for the moment not master of his mind'.

This concept in *Duffy* of a sudden and temporary loss of self-control has been approved by the Court of Appeal in later cases since the 1957 Act. This means that provocation is only available as a defence where D suffers a sudden loss of self-control.

Time lapse

One of the points that may be looked at to decide whether there was a 'sudden and temporary' loss of self-control is the time lapse between the provocation and the killing. The longer the time lapse between the provocation and the killing, the less likely that the defence will succeed. This was shown in the case of *Ibrams and Gregory* (1981).

> ### IBRAMS and GREGORY (1981)
> The ex-boyfriend of Ibrams' current girlfriend had been visiting the flat which Ibrams and the girlfriend shared, and had been terrorising them. On 7th October Ibrams called the police but the police did nothing. On 10th October the two defendants made a plan to attack the ex-boyfriend and they carried out this plan and killed him on 12th October. They were convicted of murder. The Court of Appeal upheld their convictions because there was no evidence of any provocation after 7th October and the gap of five days between this and the attack negatived their claims that they had lost their self-control.

This does not mean that there can never be any time lapse. Other cases have pointed out that there can still be a 'sudden and temporary loss of self-control' even after a time gap. This was seen in *Baillie* (1995).

> ### BAILLIE (1995)
> D discovered that a drug dealer had supplied his teenage sons with drugs and was now threatening the sons with violence. D armed himself with a sawn-off shotgun and a cut-throat razor and drove to the drug dealer's home and shot him. The Court of Appeal quashed his conviction for murder and ordered a re-trial. It held that even though there are factors, such as a lapse of time, which tend to equate with a desire for revenge, it is still possible for there to be a sudden and temporary loss of self-control.

It is argued that this need for a sudden loss of self-control makes the defence more available to men than women. This is because men are more likely than women to respond quickly with violence. In many cases women will take longer before they lose their self-control. This is known as 'slow burn' and was considered in *Thornton (No. 2)* (1996).

> ### THORNTON (NO. 2) (1996)
> Sara Thornton's husband was jealous and possessive and physically abused her. He also drank heavily. One night, when Sara returned home, her husband was lying on the sofa in the living room. He called her names and told her that he would kill her when she was asleep. Sara went into the kitchen and sharpened a

bread-knife. She returned to the living room and stabbed her husband in the stomach. She was convicted of murder and her first appeal failed but on the second appeal the Court of Appeal held that there could be a sudden loss of self-control triggered by a minor incident. In other words, it is the last straw which sparks the killing. The Court of Appeal also said that medical evidence that the defendant was suffering from 'Battered Woman Syndrome" could be relevant in explaining the 'slow-burn' reaction. It quashed the conviction and ordered a re-trial at which the jury acquitted the defendant.

This 'slow burn' was also seen in *Ahluwalia* (1992), where the defendant had been physically abused over many years by her husband. One night, her husband, before he went to bed, threatened her with violence the next day unless she paid a bill. Later, after the husband was asleep, the defendant poured petrol over him and set him alight. He died six days later. She was convicted of murder and appealed. The Court of Appeal did not allow her appeal on the basis of provocation. It pointed out that the defendant's reaction to the provocation had to be 'sudden' rather than 'immediate' and the longer the delay, the more likely that the act had been deliberate, so that the prosecution could negative the defence of provocation. However, the Court of Appeal did allow her appeal on the basis of diminished responsibility.

8.2.3 The 'reasonable man' test

Under s 3 of the Homicide Act 1957, the jury must take into account the effect the provocation would have on a reasonable man. This phrase 'reasonable man' has caused many problems. Before the 1957 Act, under the common law, the courts ruled that the reasonable man was an adult who was normal both mentally and physically. This ruling

often appeared unfair, as in *Bedder v DPP* (1954) where the defendant was impotent. A prostitute taunted him about this and he stabbed her to death. His conviction for murder was upheld because under the 'reasonable man' test the jury had to ignore the fact of impotence and the effect it would have on the provocation.

This was the leading case until 1978 when in *Camplin* the House of Lords held that the 1957 Act had effectively overruled *Bedder*. In *Camplin* it was held that age and sex and other relevant characteristics should be taken into account when considering how the reasonable man would have responded to the provocation.

> **CAMPLIN** (1978)
> The defendant, who was a 15-year-old boy, had been sexually abused by an older man who had then laughed at him. Camplin had reacted to this by hitting the man over the head with a chapatti pan. At the trial the judge directed the jury to ignore the boy's age and to consider what effect the provocation would have had on the reasonable adult, and he was convicted of murder. On appeal, the House of Lords overruled *Bedder* and allowed the appeal, substituting a conviction for manslaughter.

In the judgment of the House of Lords in *Camplin*, Lord Diplock said:

'... the reasonable man is a person having the power of self-control to be expected of an ordinary person of the sex and age of the accused, but in other respects sharing such of the accused's characteristics as they think would affect the gravity of the provocation to him; and that the question is not merely whether such a person would in like circumstances be provoked to lose his self-control but whether he would react to the provocation as the accused did'.

This made it clear that there were two parts to the 'reasonable man' test in s 3 of the Homicide Act 1957. These were:

1 for the purposes of self-control, the level is the power of self-control to be expected from a person of the age and sex of the defendant but
2 for the gravity of the provocation, the reasonable man shares such of the defendant's characteristics as the jury think would affect the gravity to the defendant.

Gravity of the provocation

In *Camplin* the House of Lords gave examples of a number of characteristics which could affect the gravity of the provocation where the provocation was aimed at one of those characteristics.

These included age, sex, race, colour, ethnic origin, physical deformity or infirmity, impotence (as in *Bedder*), a shameful incident in the past or even a painful abscess on the cheek where the provocation relied on was a blow to the face. Also, for female defendants they accepted that pregnancy or menstruation might be a relevant characteristic if the provocation was aimed at this.

Subsequent cases tried to set down which 'other characteristics' might be relevant. For example, in *Morhall* (1995) the fact that the defendant was a glue-sniffer was a relevant characteristic to be taken into account. Morhall had been persistently criticised by the victim about this immediately before the killling.

Power of self-control

Camplin clearly stated that age and sex could be taken into account when considering the power of self-control to be expected from the reasonable man. However, the courts were uncertain as to whether any other characteristics could be taken into account on this point. In *Thornton (No. 2)* (1996) the

Court of Appeal stated that 'Battered Woman Syndrome' might be relevant to the level of self-control.

However, in *Luc Thiet Thuan* (1997), where the defendant had suffered a previous head injury which caused him to have outbursts of temper which he could not control, the Privy Council held that mental abnormality could not be taken into account when considering the level of self-control to be expected from the defendant. The same point on level of self-control was considered by the House of Lords in *Smith (Morgan James)* (2000).

SMITH (MORGAN JAMES) (2000)
During an argument with a friend about whether the friend had stolen some tools belonging to D, D picked up a kitchen knife and stabbed the victim. There was evidence that D was suffering from a depressive illness which might have reduced his threshold for reacting to provocation. The trial judge ruled that this characteristic was not relevant to the reasonable man's loss of self-control. He was convicted of murder. The Court of Appeal allowed D's appeal against his conviction for murder. The prosecution appealed to the House of Lords and the Court of Appeal certified the following question as a point of law of general public importance:

'Are characteristics other than age and sex, attributable to a reasonable man for the purpose of s 3 of the Homicide Act 1957 relevant not only to the gravity of the provocation to him but also to the standard of self-control to be expected?'

The Lords, by a majority of three to two, rejected the prosecution's appeal.

In *Smith (Morgan James)* Lord Hoffmann pointed out that Lord Diplock's judgment in *Camplin* allows juries to take into account two characteristics (age and sex) and that age may be relevant to the power of self-control. There was no suggestion in *Camplin* that age and sex were the only factors which could be taken into account when considering self-control or that all other factors should be excluded.

The question was whether in all the circumstances the jury considered that the defendant's loss of self-control was excusable and this is judged by reference to how a person in his position, exercising ordinary powers of self-control, would have behaved. The objective element of the test for provocation was whether the jury thought that the circumstances were such as to make the loss of self-control sufficiently excusable to reduce the gravity of the offence from murder to manslaughter.

The House of Lords did, however, point out that the law expects people to exercise control over their emotions. A tendency to violent rages or childish tantrums is a defect in character rather than an excuse.

This decision in *Smith (Morgan James)* (2000) laid down general principles and left the matter to the jury, as the Homicide Act 1957 clearly set out. The general principle in the case was that the same standards of behaviour should be expected of everyone and whether the accused's loss of self-control was excusable should be judged by reference to how a person in his position, exercising ordinary powers of self-control, would have behaved.

However, the House of Lords accepted that this general principle may 'sometimes have to yield to a more important principle, which is to do justice in the particular case'. If the jury think 'that there was some characteristic of the accused, whether temporary or permanent, which affected the degree of control which society could reasonably have expected of him', they may take that into account if they think it is just to do so. This was thought to be the law but a Privy Council decision has had a major impact on this area of law.

Privy Council decision in Holley

Following the decision in *Smith*, the same point had to be considered by the Privy Council in *Attorney-General for Jersey v Holley* (2005). Unusually, a panel of nine judges was used to decide this case.

ATTORNEY-GENERAL FOR JERSEY v HOLLEY (2005)

D was an alcoholic who had been drinking heavily. He claimed that his long-standing girl-friend told him she had had sex with another man and taunted him. He struck and killed her with an axe he was using to chop wood. He was convicted of murder and his conviction was upheld by the Privy Council by a majority of six judges to three.

The conclusion of the majority of judges in the Privy Council was that only age and sex should be considered when identifying and applying the objective standard of self-control. Other characteristics of D are not relevant. So D is, for the purposes of the defence of provocation, to be judged by the standard of a person having ordinary powers of self-control. This has the merits of being a constant, objective standard in all cases.

This obviously differed from the House of Lords' decision in *Smith (Morgan James)* and the Privy Council recognised this, with Lord Nicholls stating that that decision was 'erroneous'.

However, the Privy Council did accept that other characteristics can be taken into account in assessing the gravity of the provocation to D. There is still a subjective test for the gravity of the provocation to the defendant. For this purpose the jury must 'take the defendant as they find him, "warts and all"'.

The decision in *Holley* was by the Privy Council. Normally, in the system of judicial precedent which operates in the courts in

Figure 8.2 Key facts chart on provocation

	Law	Section/case	KEY FACTS
Definition	Evidence on which the jury can find that the person charged was provoked (whether by things done or by things said or by both together) to lose his self-control.	s 3 Homicide Act 1957	
Examples of provocation	■ Physical assaults, both on the defendant or on his relatives. ■ The continual crying of a 19-day-old baby. ■ A denial of stealing the defendant's tools. ■ Supplying drugs to the defendant's son.	*Pearson* (1992) *Doughty* (1986) *Smith (Morgan James)* (2000) *Baillie* (1995)	
Loss of self-control	There must be a sudden and temporary loss of self-control, so that D is not master of his mind.	*Duffy* (1949)	
	A time lapse may negative this.	*Ibrams and Gregory* (1981)	
	It must be sudden but need not be immediate.	*Thornton (No. 2)* (1996)	
'Reasonable man' test	Was the provocation was enough to make a reasonable man do as D did?	s 3 Homicide Act 1957	
	For the gravity of the provocation the characteristics of D are taken into account.	*Morhall* (1995)	
	For the standard of self-control expected of D, the test is objective. D is judged by the standard expected of a reasonable person of the age and sex of D.	*Camplin* (1978) *Holley* (2005)	
Effect of defence	The charge of murder is reduced to manslaughter.	s 3 Homicide Act 1957	

England and Wales, decisions by the Privy Council are only persuasive. But decisions by the House of Lords are binding on all lower courts. So it was not immediately certain what influence the decision in *Holley* would have. However, in *Mohammed* (2005) the Court of Appeal followed *Holley* rather than the decision in *Smith (Morgan James)*.

It therefore appears that the law is as decided in *Holley*. There is a subjective test for the gravity of the provocation in which characteristics of the defendant can be taken into account. The test for the standard of self-control is objective: that of the reasonable person of the same age and sex as the defendant.

8.2.4 Proof of provocation

The judge decides if there is evidence of provocation for the defence to be left to the jury. If there is evidence which raises the possibility of provocation, the prosecution must then prove beyond reasonable doubt that the accused was not provoked.

In some cases the defendant may put

forward both the defence of provocation and the defence of diminished responsibility. This causes a problem over the burden of proof, as for provocation the defence only has to raise the issue but for diminished responsibility the defence has to *prove* it on the balance of probabilities. This may cause confusion to juries in such cases.

8.2.5 Reform of provocation

In 2003, when the Law Commission was reviewing the law on special defences to murder, it issued a consultation paper on the special defences to murder. In this it pointed out a number of problems with the defence of provocation, including that:

■ The defence as stated in s 3 of the Homicide Act 1957 contradicts itself; it raises the question of whether a reasonable man would ever respond to provocation.
■ The term 'reasonable man' has proved difficult for the judge to explain. The phrase has been considered by the House of Lords four times in 20 years and on the last occasion in *Smith (Morgan James) (2000)* the judges were split 3:2. (The matter has also now been considered by the Privy Council in *Holley* (2005) when the panel of nine judges were split 6:3.)
■ There is no limit to the conduct which is capable of 'provoking', so that completely innocent conduct may be regarded as provocation. This was seen in *Doughty* when the crying of a very young baby was held to be provocation.
■ It allows a defence for anger, when there is no defence if the defendant kills in fear, despair or compassion.
■ The effect of the decision in *Smith (Morgan James)* was to reduce the threshold of self-control that people are entitled to demand of all members of society. (Note that if the case of *Holley* continues to be followed by the courts in England and Wales, then this criticism disappears.)

As already pointed out in section 8.2.2, the defence is also seen as a 'male' defence, because men are more likely to suffer a sudden loss of self-control.

Abolition of the defence

If the mandatory sentence of life imprisonment for murder were to be abolished, this would then allow the defence of provocation to be abolished, as the judge would have discretion in sentencing. However, this would leave two problems. First, if the prosecution did not accept the defendant's version of what had happened, then there would still need to be an investigation of the facts before the judge could decide on a suitable sentence. Second, surely a jury is better placed than a judge to decide on the level of self-control to be expected by society from a defendant? If the defence of provocation is abolished then the matter will be entirely in the hands of a judge.

Proposals for reform

The Law Commission's report, *Partial Defences and Murder*, suggested reforming the defence of provocation in the following way.

'(1) An unlawful homicide that would otherwise be murder should instead be manslaughter if:

(a) the defendant acted in response to:
  (i) gross provocation (meaning words or conduct or a combination of words and conduct which caused the defendant to have justifiable sense of being seriously wronged): or
  (ii) fear of serious violence towards the defendant or another; or
  (iii) a combination of (i) and (ii)
(b) a person of the defendant's age

and of ordinary temperament, i.e. ordinary tolerance and self-restraint, in the circumstances of the defendant might have acted in the same or a similar way.

(2) In deciding whether a person of ordinary temperament in the circumstances of the defendant might have acted in the same or a similar way, the court should take into account the defendant's age and all the circumstances of the defendant other than matters whose only relevance to the defendant's conduct is that they bear simply on his or her general capacity for self-control.

(3) The partial defence should not apply where:

   (a) the provocation was incited by the defendant for the purpose of providing an excuse to use violence, or

   (b) the defendant acted in considered desire for revenge.'

These proposals would make several changes to the current law on provocation.

The first main difference between the proposals and the current law is that only 'gross provocation' would suffice under the proposals. This would presumably prevent such matters as the crying of a 19-day-old baby being provocation, as in *Doughty* (1986).

A second difference is that a test of whether the words and/or conduct caused the defendant to have justifiable sense of being seriously wronged would be introduced. Two words appear to be especially important in the phrase 'justifiable sense of being seriously wronged'. These are 'justifiable' and 'seriously'. The combination of the two would be likely to restrict the operation of the defence of provocation, compared with its present operation. Again, it would prevent the crying of a 19-day-old baby from being provocation.

This could scarcely give rise to a phrase 'justifiable sense of being seriously wronged'.

8.3   SUICIDE PACT

This defence is set out in s 4(1) of the Homicide Act 1957. It provides a defence to murder for the survivor of a suicide pact and reduces the offence to manslaughter.

'Suicide pact' is defined in s 4(3) of the 1957 Act as 'a common agreement between two or more persons having for its object the death of all of them'

The burden of proving that the killing was in pursuance of a suicide pact is on the defence. The standard of proof is on the balance of probabilities.

Applying the law

Explain whether any of the special defences to murder could apply in the following situations.

1   Roscoe, aged 25, has a mental age of 8. In a fit of temper, he attacks Max and kicks him to death.

2   Cameron and Jacob are working together on a building site. Cameron knows that Jacob's wife is having an affair with another man. He taunts Jacob about this. Jacob loses his temper and hits Cameron on the head with a brick, killing him.

3   Tracey and Zak are depressed after their baby daughter was born dead. They agree to end their own lives. Zak gives Tracey an injection with a lethal drug. He then swallows a large amount of painkillers. Tracey dies but Zak survives.

4   Ellie's husband, Gwyn, is an alcoholic and when drunk is often violent to her. Ellie has recently been suffering from depression for which she takes medication. One evening, Gwyn comes home drunk and hits Ellie several times. He then goes to bed. Ellie stays up and, after about four hours, in a

---

sudden burst of rage, she gets a knife and stabs Gwyn, killing him.

5 Brigid who is an immature, attention-seeking, 16-year-old, tries to commit suicide by slashing her wrists with a knife, but the cuts she makes are only superficial. Carol teases her about her inability to do anything properly. Brigid rushes at Carol and stabs her with the knife, killing her.

Examination questions

1 Critically evaluate the effectiveness of the defence of diminished responsibility. You should refer to both legislation and decided cases in your answer.

> (OCR, Unit 2571, January 2004)

2 Corinne has been in a steady relationship with David for over 10 years. They have always had arguments during which David has often hit Corinne. He has also threatened her that if she ever tries to leave him he will track her down and 'sort her out'. This has made Corinne feel depressed and trapped in the situation. She has been to her doctor who has placed her on medication to treat her depression.

One evening, Corinne and David argue again and, in the course of the dispute, David insults her, calling her 'pathetic and useless'. Corinne starts to cry, so David slaps her face and tells her to 'grow up'. David then goes to bed. Corinne sits and watches television for two hours before going to the bedroom. When she sees David asleep she is suddenly overcome with anger and picks up the bedside lamp which she smashes over David's head, killing him instantly. Corinne has now been charged with David's murder.

Discuss Corinne's potential liability, including any defences that she may have available to her under the Homicide Act 1957.

> (OCR, Unit 2571, June 2005)

3 Archie is a young man with moderately severe learning disabilities, who loves nature and is especially fond of trees. For years, Archie has been deeply attached to a beautiful silver birch tree growing in the garden of his next-door neighbour, Brian. One freezing November day, Archie saw Brian preparing to cut down the silver birch tree with a chainsaw. A heated argument developed, which ended with Archie losing his temper and hitting Brian on the head with a fallen branch. Brian slumped to the ground, unconscious. Thinking that Brian was dead, Archie gave him a woodland burial by covering him with leaves. Some time later, Brian recovered consciousness and staggered back to his house. Feeling thoroughly chilled, Brian drank several glasses of brandy before eventually calling an ambulance to take him to hospital. Chloe, the doctor who examined Brian, treated the head wound, which was minor, and kept him in hospital for further observation. However, because of the amount of alcohol that Brian had consumed, she failed to diagnose that Brian was suffering from exposure as a result of being left to lie in the damp ground. Brian's condition worsened during the night, and he died from exposure made worse by the effects of alcohol.

Consider whether Archie may be criminal liable for Brian's death, including any defences which may be available to him.

> (WJEC, LW4, June 2005)

CHAPTER 9 | Involuntary manslaughter

Involuntary manslaughter is an unlawful killing where the defendant does not have the intention, either direct or oblique, to kill or to cause grievous bodily harm. The lack of this intention is what distinguishes involuntary manslaughter from murder. It is also important not to confuse involuntary manslaughter with voluntary manslaughter. For voluntary manslaughter, the defendant has the intention to kill or cause grievous bodily harm but the charge is reduced from murder because the defendant can use one of the special defences to murder. Those special defences were explained in Chapter 8.

Involuntary manslaughter covers a wide range of circumstances. At the top end of the range, the behaviour of the defendant which caused the death can be highly blameworthy, as there was a high risk of causing death or serious injury. At the bottom end of the range, the defendant's behaviour may verge on carelessness and only just enough to be considered blameworthy. There have been criticisms that the same offence covers such a wide range of behaviour and there have been proposals for reform which are considered at section 9.4.

The maximum sentence for involuntary manslaughter is life imprisonment, so this gives the judge discretion to impose any sentence which is suitable for the particular circumstances of the offence. In some cases the judge may even pass a non-custodial sentence.

There are definitely two ways of committing involuntary manslaughter. These are:

- *unlawful act* manslaughter
- *gross negligence* manslaughter.

It is also argued that there is a third way of committing involuntary manslaughter and this is by recklessness. There has only been one case on this and it is considered in section 9.3.

9.1   UNLAWFUL ACT MANSLAUGHTER

This is also known as *constructive* manslaughter because the liability for the death is built up or constructed from the facts that the defendant has done a dangerous unlawful act which caused the death. This makes the defendant liable even though he did not realise that death or injury might occur.

The elements of unlawful act manslaughter are:

- the defendant must do an unlawful act
- that act must be dangerous on an objective test
- the act must cause the death
- the defendant must have the required *mens rea* for the unlawful act.

9.1.1 Unlawful act

The death must be caused by an unlawful act. The unlawful act must be a criminal offence. A civil wrong (tort) is not enough. In *Franklin* (1883) the defendant threw a large box into the sea from the West Pier at Brighton. The box hit and killed a swimmer. It was held that a civil wrong was not enough to create liability for unlawful act manslaughter. Another case illustrating that there must be a criminal unlawful act is *Lamb* (1967).

LAMB (1967)

Lamb and his friend were fooling around with a revolver. They both knew that it was loaded with two bullets in a five-chamber cylinder but thought that it would not fire unless one of the bullets was opposite the barrel. They knew that there was no bullet in this position, but did not realise that the cylinder turned so that a bullet from the next chamber along would be fired. Lamb pointed the gun at his friend and pulled the trigger, killing him. It was held that the defendant had not done an unlawful act. The pointing of the gun at the friend was not an assault as the friend did not fear any violence from Lamb.

There must be an act. An omission cannot not create liability for unlawful act manslaughter. In *Lowe* (1973) the defendant was convicted of wilfully neglecting his baby son and of his manslaughter. The trial judge had directed the jury that if they found the defendant guilty of wilful neglect he was also guilty of manslaughter. The Court of Appeal quashed the conviction for manslaughter because a finding of wilful neglect involved a failure to act and this could not support a conviction for unlawful act manslaughter.

In many cases the unlawful act will be some kind of assault, but any criminal offence can form the unlawful act, provided that it involves an act which is a dangerous in the sense that it is likely to cause some injury. Examples of the offences which have led to a finding of unlawful act manslaughter include arson, criminal damage and burglary.

9.1.2 Dangerous act

The unlawful act must be dangerous on an objective test. In *Church* (1966) it was held that it must be:

'*such as all sober and reasonable people would inevitably recognise must subject*

the other person to, at least, the risk of some harm resulting therefrom, albeit not serious harm'.

From this, it can be seen that the risk need only be of 'some harm'. The harm need not be serious. If a sober and reasonable person realises that the unlawful act might cause some injury, then this part of the tests for unlawful act manslaughter is satisfied. It does not matter that the defendant did not realise there was any risk of harm to another person. The case of *Larkin* (1943) illustrates both the need for an unlawful act and for there to be, on an objective viewpoint, the risk of some harm.

LARKIN (1943)

D threatened another man with an open cut-throat razor, in order to frighten him. The mistress of the other man tried to intervene and, because she was drunk, accidentally fell onto the open blade which cut her throat and killed her. On appeal, D's conviction for manslaughter was upheld. The act of threatening the other man with the razor was a technical assault. (See Chapter 10 for explanation of assaults.) It was also an act which was dangerous because it was likely to injure someone.

Humphries J explained this in the judgment when he said:

'*Where the act which a person is engaged in performing is unlawful, then, if at the same time it is a dangerous act, that is, an act which is likely to injure another person, and quite inadvertently he causes the death of that other person by that act, then he is guilty of manslaughter.'*

It is clear that the act need not be aimed at the victim. This was the situation in *Larkin* where the assault was against the man but the woman died. It is also shown by the case of *Mitchell* (1983).

MITCHELL (1983)

D tried to push his way into a queue at the post office. A 72-year-old man told him off for this. D then punched the man, causing him to stagger backwards into an 89-year-old woman. The woman was knocked over and injured and a few days later died of her injuries. D was convicted of unlawful act manslaughter. He had done an unlawful act by punching the man. This act was dangerous as it was an act which was likely to injure another person. Finally, the act caused the death of the woman.

It can be seen that all the elements set by Humphries J in the statement in *Larkin* above are present. The defendants in both *Larkin* and *Mitchell* were guilty of unlawful act manslaughter, despite the fact that in each case the person threatened (or punched) was not the one who died.

Act against property

The act need not even be aimed at a person; it can be aimed at property, provided it is 'such that all sober and reasonable people would inevitably recognise must subject another person to, at least, the risk of some harm'. This was illustrated by *Goodfellow* (1986).

GOODFELLOW (1986)

D decided to set fire to his council flat so that the council would have to re-house him. The fire got out of control and his wife, son and another woman died in the fire. He was convicted of manslaughter and appealed. The Court of Appeal upheld the conviction because all the elements of unlawful act manslaughter were present.

If you look at the facts of *Goodfellow* you can see the elements of unlawful act manslaughter. These were:

- the act was committed intentionally: *Goodfellow* intended to set the flat on fire
- it was unlawful: it was actually an offence under the Criminal Damage Act 1971 (see Chapter 13)
- reasonable people would recognise that it might cause some harm to another person: there was an obvious risk that someone in the flat might be hurt
- the act caused the death.

Physical harm

The 'risk of harm' refers to physical harm. Something which causes fear and apprehension is not sufficient. This is so even it causes the victim to have a heart attack. This meant that in the case of *Dawson* (1985) convictions for manslaughter were quashed.

DAWSON (1985)

Three defendants attempted to rob a petrol station. They were masked and armed with pick-axe handles. The petrol station attendant managed to sound the alarm but then dropped dead from a heart attack. Causing him fear through the attempted robbery was not a 'dangerous' act and did not make this manslaughter.

However, where a reasonable person would be aware of the victim's frailty and the risk of physical harm to him, then the defendant will be liable. This was stated in *Watson* (1989).

WATSON (1989)

Two defendants threw a brick through the window of a house and got into to it, intending to steal property. The occupier was a frail 87-year-old man who heard the noise and came to investigate what had happened. The two defendants physically abused him and then left. The man died of a heart attack 90 minutes later. Although the Court of Appeal quashed the convictions for manslaughter, the court stated that the act of burglary could be 'dangerous' in that it become dangerous as soon as the old man's condition would have been apparent to the reasonable man.

9.1.3 Causing the death

The unlawful act must cause the death. The rules on causation are the same as for murder and are set out in Chapter 2 at section 2.3.

Although the general rules are the same, there have been problems on causation where the defendant has supplied the victim with an illegal drug, but the victim has injected himself. There have been several cases on this. There are two points at issue. These are:

■ whether the defendant has done an unlawful act and
■ has the defendant caused the victim's death or is the self-injection is an intervening act.

The first case on this was *Dalby* (1982).

DALBY (1982)

D supplied a drug called Diconal which the victim then self-injected. The defendant's conviction for manslaughter was quashed because the Court of Appeal held that although supplying the drug was an unlawful act, it was not the act of supplying which had caused the death. The injection was the cause of the death and, as this was a voluntary act by the victim, it had broken the chain of causation.

Figure 9.1 Key cases chart on unlawful act manslaughter

KEY CASES

Case	Facts	Law
Lamb (1967)	D fired gun at a friend; both thought it was safe because there was no bullet in the firing chamber.	There must be an unlawful act. In this case there was no assault as the friend did not fear violence.
Lowe (1973)	Failed to care properly for baby.	There has to be an act – unlawful act manslaughter cannot be committed by an omission.
Larkin (1943)	Threatened a man with a razor – a woman fell on blade and died.	The unlawful act need not be aimed at V but it must be objectively dangerous in the sense that it is likely to cause harm.
Goodfellow (1986)	Set fire to flat, causing three deaths.	The unlawful act can be aimed at property. The test is whether it is objectively dangerous in the sense that it is likely to cause harm.
Dawson (1985)	Petrol station attendant died of a heart attack when his petrol station was robbed.	Causing fear is not enough. The unlawful act must put V at risk of physical harm.
Newbury and Jones (1976)	Pushed a paving stone onto a passing train, killing the guard.	D need only have the intention to do the unlawful act; there is no need for D to foresee that it might cause some harm.

However, in later cases the courts have thought that a defendant who supplies drugs could be liable for unlawful act manslaughter. An important case is *Kennedy* (1999).

> ### *KENNEDY* (1999)
> D had prepared an injection of heroin and water for the victim to inject himself. The Court of Appeal upheld his conviction for manslaughter as, by doing the acts of preparing the syringe and handing it to the victim, the defendant had encouraged and/or assisted the victim in the act of self-injecting. This distinguished the case from *Dalby* where the defendant had supplied the drug but not taken any part in its preparation.

Note that this case was referred back to the Court of Appeal by the Criminal Case Review Commission. In 2005 the Court of Appeal upheld the original conviction but certified the case for an appeal to the House of Lords. The 1999 decision in *Kennedy* was criticised in *Dias* (2002).

> ### *DIAS* (2002)
> D was a heroin addict used to injecting heroin. The victim was also a drug user but was not known to inject heroin. They were living rough and went into the stairway of a block of flats where D prepared a syringe of heroin and gave it to the victim who injected himself. D then injected himself. When D had recovered from the effects of the heroin he realised that the victim was very ill. He asked a passer-by to call an ambulance and then left the scene. The victim was taken to hospital but died. D's conviction for manslaughter was quashed.

In this case the Court of Appeal refused to follow the decision in *Kennedy*. It stated that it was not easy to see on what basis the court in *Kennedy* considered that the act of self-injection was unlawful because there was no elaboration on the point in the judgment. It also pointed out that there is no offence under the Misuse of Drugs Act 1971, or any other statute, of injecting oneself with a prohibited drug.

However, it left open the question of whether there might be a conviction in the future, on the basis that there was an unlawful act of administering a noxious substance under s 23 of the Offences Against the Person Act 1861.

In the next case, *Rogers* (2003), it was held that the act of the defendant was an offence under s 23 of the Offences Against the Person Act 1861, and that this was an unlawful act for the purposes of manslaughter.

> ### *ROGERS* (2003)
> D had participated in the injection of heroin by holding his belt round the victim's arm as a tourniquet to make it easier for the victim to find the vein to inject. The court held that the act causing death was the injection of the heroin and it was 'artificial and unreal' to separate the tourniquet from the injection. By applying and holding the tourniquet, the defendant was playing a part in the mechanics of the injection. This made him guilty of s 23 and, if death occurred as a result, he was also guilty of manslaughter.

So the effect of these cases is that:

- where the defendant supplies the drug but does nothing towards the administration of it, he has not caused the death: *Dalby*
- where the defendant prepares the syringe and hands it to the victim, he has probably not caused the death: *Dias* (but there might be a s 23 offence for the unlawful act)
- where the defendant assists in the injection in some way, he has participated in the unlawful act of administering a noxious substance, and where this act causes the death he is guilty of manslaughter: *Rogers*.

Figure 9.2 Key facts chart on unlawful act manslaughter

Elements	Comment	Cases
Unlawful act	Must be unlawful.	*Lamb* (1967)
	A civil wrong is not enough.	*Franklin* (1883)
	It must be an act; an omission is not sufficient.	*Lowe* (1973)
Dangerous act	The test for this is objective – would a sober and reasonable person realise the risk of some harm?	*Church* (1966)
	The risk need only be of some harm – not serious harm.	*Larkin* (1943)
	The act need not be aimed at the final victim.	*Mitchell* (1983)
	An act aimed at property can still be such that a sober and reasonable person would realise the risk of some harm.	*Goodfellow* (1986)
	There must be a risk of physical harm; mere fear is not enough.	*Dawson* (1985)
Causes death	Normal rules of causation apply; the act must be the physical and legal cause of death.	
	An intervening act such as the victim self-injecting a drug breaks the chain of causation.	*Dalby* (1982)
	But where D helps with the injection, the link is established.	*Rogers* (2003)
Mens rea	D must have *mens rea* for the unlawful act but it is not necessary to prove that the D foresaw any harm from his act.	*Newbury and Jones* (1976)

The matter is even more confused because in *Dias*, although the conviction on the basis of unlawful act manslaughter was quashed, the Court of Appeal suggested that in a conviction for gross negligent manslaughter might be possible where a duty of care could be established. This might possibly be through a duty not to supply and prepare drugs. (For the law on gross negligence manslaughter, see section 9.2.)

9.1.4 *Mens rea*

It must be proved that the defendant had the *mens rea* for the unlawful act, but it is not necessary for the defendant to realise that the act is unlawful or dangerous. This was made clear in the case of *Newbury and Jones* (1976).

NEWBURY and JONES (1976)
The defendants were two teenage boys who pushed a piece of paving stone from a bridge onto a railway line as a train was approaching. The stone hit the train and killed the guard. They were convicted of manslaughter and the House of Lords was asked to decide the question of whether a defendant could be convicted of unlawful act manslaughter if he did not foresee that his act might cause harm to another. The House of Lords confirmed it was not necessary to prove that the defendant foresaw any harm from his act.

So, a defendant can be convicted provided that the unlawful act was dangerous and the defendant had the necessary *mens rea* for that act.

9.2 GROSS NEGLIGENCE MANSLAUGHTER

Gross negligence manslaughter is another way of committing manslaughter. It is completely different from unlawful act manslaughter. It is committed where the defendant owes the victim a duty of care but breaches that duty in a very negligent way, causing the death of the victim. It can be committed by an act or an omission. The act or omission does not have to be unlawful. The leading case on gross negligence manslaughter is *Adomako* (1994).

ADOMAKO (1994)
D was the anaesthetist for a man who was having an operation on a detached retina. During the operation, one of the tubes supplying oxygen to the patient became disconnected. D failed to notice this until some minutes later when the patient suffered a heart attack caused by the lack of oxygen. The patient suffered brain damage and died six months later as a result. Doctors giving evidence in the trial said that a competent anaesthetist would have noticed the disconnection of the tube within 15 seconds and that D's failure to react was 'abysmal'. The trial judge directed the jury on gross negligence and they convicted. The conviction was upheld by the House of Lords.

From *Adomako* it appears that the elements of gross negligence manslaughter are:

- the existence of a duty of care towards the victim
- a breach of that duty of care which causes death
- gross negligence which the jury considers to be criminal.

Each of these elements needs to be considered.

9.2.1 Duty of care

A duty of care has been held to exist for the purposes of the criminal law in various situations. These include the duty of a doctor to his patient, as in *Adomako*. In that case Lord Mackay said that the ordinary principles of negligence in the civil law applied to ascertain whether there was a duty of care and whether that duty had been breached.

The civil principles come from the case of *Donoghue v Stevenson* (1932) where it was stated that:

'You must take reasonable care to avoid acts and omissions which you can reasonably foresee would be likely to injure your neighbour. Who then is my neighbour? The answer seems to be –

persons who are so closely and directly affected by my act that I ought reasonably to have them in contemplation as being so affected when I am directing my mind to the acts or omissions which are called into question.'

Note that an act or an omission can form the basis of negligence.

Case examples of duty of care

Since the case of *Adomako*, the criminal courts have decided that a duty of care exists in very different situations. Some of these are set out below.

> **SINGH (1999)**
> D was the landlord of property in which a faulty gas-fire caused the deaths of tenants. It was recognised that there was a duty on D to manage and maintain property properly.

> **LITCHFIELD (1998)**
> D was the owner and master of a sailing ship. He sailed, knowing that the engines might fail because of contamination to the fuel. The ship was blown onto rocks and three crew members died. It was held that D owed a duty to the crew.

In both the above cases there was a contractual duty of care. However, there does not need to be a contractual duty. Other situations can lead to a duty of care, as shown by the cases of *Khan and Khan* (1998) and *Dias* (2002).

> **KHAN and KHAN (1998)**
> The defendants had supplied heroin to a new user who took it in their presence and then collapsed. They left her alone and by the time they returned to the flat she had died. Their

conviction for unlawful act manslaughter was quashed but the Court of Appeal thought there could be a duty to summon medical assistance in certain circumstances.

> **DIAS (2002)**
> D was a heroin addict used to injecting heroin. The victim was also a drug user but was not known to inject heroin. They were living rough and went into the stairway of a block of flats where D prepared a syringe of heroin and gave it to the victim who injected himself. D then injected himself. When D had recovered from the effects of the heroin he realised that the victim was very ill. He asked a passer-by to call an ambulance and then left the scene. The victim was taken to hospital but died. Although D's conviction for manslaughter was quashed, the court suggested that it might be possible to establish a duty not to supply and prepare drugs.

Also, in *Khan and Khan* (1998) the Court of Appeal stated *obiter* that duty situations could be extended to other areas and a further extension of the type of duty recognised by the courts occurred in *Wacker* (2002).

> **WACKER (2002)**
> D agreed to bring 60 illegal immigrants into England. They were put in the back of his lorry for a cross-channel ferry crossing. The only air into the lorry was through a small vent and it was agreed that this vent should be closed at certain times to prevent the immigrants from being discovered. D closed the vent before boarding the ferry. The crossing took an hour longer than usual and at Dover the Customs officers found that 58 of the immigrants were dead. D's conviction for manslaughter was upheld by the Court of Appeal.

The defendant argued that it was impossible to determine the extent of his duty, but the Court of Appeal held it was a simple matter on the facts. The defendant knew that the safety of the immigrants depended on his own actions in relation to the vent and he clearly assumed the duty of care.

An interesting point in *Wacker* was that the victims were parties to an illegal act. In the civil law of negligence this would have meant that the victims (or their dependants) could not have made a claim against the defendant. However, the Court of Appeal held that for the criminal law, it was irrelevant that the victims were parties to an illegal act. It pointed out that the purposes of civil and criminal law were different and public policy demanded that defendants in this type of situation were liable under the criminal law.

The case of *Wacker* indicates that this area of the law may be extended in the future, and it is difficult to predict what duties may be recognised.

9.2.2 Breach of duty causing death

Once a duty of care has been shown to exist, it must be proved that the defendant was in breach of that duty of care *and* that this breach caused the death of the victim.

Whether there is a breach of duty is a factual matter. Did the defendant negligently do or fail to do something? Causation is important, as it must be proved that the breach caused the death. The general rules on causation apply. See Chapter 2 at section 2.3.

9.2.3 Gross negligence

The fact that a defendant has been negligent is not enough to convict him of gross negligence manslaughter. The negligence has to be 'gross'. This was first explained in *Bateman* (1925) which involved negligent treatment of patient by a doctor.

BATEMAN (1925)

D was a doctor who attended a woman for the birth of her child at her home. During the childbirth, part of the woman's uterus came away. D did not send V to hospital for five days, and she later died. D's conviction was quashed on the basis that he had carried out the normal procedures that any competent doctor would have done. He had not been grossly negligent.

In his judgment Lord Hewart said:

'The facts must be such that, in the opinion of the jury, the negligence of the accused went beyond a mere matter of compensation between subjects and showed such disregard for the life and safety of others as to amount to a crime against the State and conduct deserving of punishment.'

In *Adomako* (1994) the House of Lords approved this test and stressed that it was a matter for the jury. The jury had to decide whether, having regard to the risk of death involved, the conduct of the defendant was so bad in all the circumstances as to amount, in their judgment, to a criminal act or omission.

The jury have to consider the seriousness of the breach of duty in all the circumstances in which the defendant was placed when it occurred. In *Adomako* Lord Mackay said:

'The jury will have to consider whether the extent to which the defendant's conduct departed from the proper standard of care incumbent upon him, involving as it must have done a risk of death to the patient, was such that it should be judged as criminal.'

There have been criticisms of these tests because it is left to individual jury panels to decide the appropriate standard for 'gross' negligence. This may lead to inconsistent decisions in similar cases. There is also little guidance on what should be considered as 'gross' negligence.

Figure 9.3 Key facts chart on gross negligence manslaughter

KEY FACTS

Elements	Comment	Cases
Duty of care	D must owe V a duty of care.	*Adomako* (1994)
	The civil concept of negligence applies.	*Adomako* (1994)
	Covers wide range of situations, eg maintaining a gas-fire.	*Singh* (1999)
	May even cover a duty not to supply drugs.	*Rogers* (2003)
	The fact that V was party to an illegal act is not relevant.	*Wacker* (2003)
Breach of duty	This can be by an act or an omission.	
Gross negligence	Beyond a matter of mere compensation and showed such disregard for the life and safety of others as to amount to a crime.	*Bateman* (1925)
	Conduct so bad in all the circumstances as to amount to a criminal act or omission.	*Adomako* (1994)
Risk of death	There must be a risk of death from D's conduct.	*Adomako (1994)* *Misra and another* (2004)

Risk of death

In *Adomako* it was not totally clear whether there has to be a risk of death through the defendant's conduct or whether the risk need only be to 'heath and welfare' of the victim. In *Stone and Dobinson* (1977), where the defendants had undertaken the care of Stone's sister, the test was expressed as the risk being to the 'heath and welfare' of the sister who died. When Lord Mackay gave judgment in *Adomako*, he approved this way of explaining the matter. However, Lord Mackay also approved the test in *Bateman* where the test is 'disregard for the life and safety of others'. In addition, Lord Mackay specifically mentioned 'a risk of death' on two occasions in his judgment.

The matter has now been resolved in *Misra and another* (2004).

MISRA and ANOTHER (2004)

V had an operation on his knee. The two defendants were senior house doctors who were responsible for the post-operative care of V. They failed to identify and treat V for an infection which occurred after the operation. V died from the infection. The defendants were convicted and appealed on the basis that the elements of gross negligence manslaughter were uncertain and so breached Art 7 of the European Convention on Human Rights.

The Court of Appeal held that *Adomako* had clearly laid down the elements, so there was no breach of Art 7. The test in gross negligence manslaughter involves consideration of the risk of death. It is not sufficient to show a risk of bodily injury or injury to health. The defendants' conviction for manslaughter was upheld.

9.3 RECKLESS MANSLAUGHTER

After the decision in *Adomako* (1994), it was thought that reckless manslaughter no longer existed. However, in *Lidar* (2000) the Court of Appeal upheld the defendant's conviction for manslaughter even though the judge referred to recklessness (rather than gross negligence) in his directions to the jury.

LIDAR (2000)

D and others had been asked to leave a public house in Leicester. They went into the pub car park and got into a Range Rover, with D as driver. One of the passengers shouted something at V, who was the doorman of the pub. V approached the vehicle and put his arms through the open front passenger window. D then drove off, with V half in and half out of the window. After about 225 metres, V was dragged under the rear wheel of the Range Rover and suffered injuries from which he died. D was convicted of manslaughter.

Although the trial judge directed the jury on the basis of recklessness, it is obvious from the facts that the defendant could have been convicted on the basis of gross negligence manslaughter. The defendant clearly owed V a duty of care. In fact, all road users owe a duty of care to others on the road (whether as drivers, passengers or pedestrians). By driving off with V half in and half out of the window, the defendant was in breach of that duty of care. And it was open to the jury to decide that the breach was gross negligence.

In view of this, it is difficult to see why it is necessary to have a separate category of reckless manslaughter.

9.4 REFORM OF THE LAW

There have been many criticisms of manslaughter as an offence. The first general one is that the same offence covers such a wide range of behaviour. The levels of blameworthiness of individual defendants vary enormous, yet all are convicted of the same offence. There are also specific criticisms of both unlawful act manslaughter and gross negligence manslaughter.

For unlawful act manslaughter the main criticisms are:

- it covers a very wide range of conduct
- death may be an unexpected result; if the same act resulted in minor injury, the defendant would only be liable for the offence of assault occasioning actual bodily harm
- a defendant who did not realise there was risk of any injury is still guilty because of the objective nature of the test.

The Law Commission has recommended the abolition of unlawful act manslaughter. It criticises the concept of unlawful act manslaughter, pointing out:

'It ... is inappropriate to convict a defendant for an offence of homicide where the most that can be said he that he or she ought to have realised that there was the risk of some, albeit it not serious, harm to another resulting from his or her commission of an unlawful act.'

For gross negligence manslaughter, the main criticisms are:

- the test is circular, as the jury are directed to convict of a crime if they think that the conduct was criminal
- the test may lead to inconsistent verdicts, as it depends on what different juries think
- the civil test for negligence should not be used in criminal cases: the purpose of the two branches of law is quite different
- a defendant is liable even though he did not realise there was a risk of any injury; this is inconsistent with non-fatal offences against the person where serious injury is caused. In these

the defendant can only be guilty if he at least foresaw the risk of some harm.

The Law Commission has proposed that instead of gross negligence manslaughter there should be two categories of killing involving negligence. These are reckless killing and killing by gross carelessness. Reckless killing would be the more serious offence as the prosecution would have to prove that:

- the defendant is aware that his conduct will cause death or serious injury and
- it is unreasonable in the circumstances for him to take that risk, having regard to the circumstances as he believes them to be.

This would answer the criticism that a defendant can at present be liable for the very serious offence of manslaughter, without any awareness of the consequences of his act.

Killing by gross carelessness would be a lower-level offence, covering situations where the risk of death or serious injury would be obvious to a reasonable person in the position of the defendant and the defendant is capable of appreciating that risk and either:

- his conduct falls far below what can reasonably be expected of him in the circumstances or
- he intends by his conduct to cause some injury, or is aware of and unreasonably takes the risk that it may do so, and the conduct causing (or intended to cause) the injury constitutes an offence.

If these proposals were adopted then the defendant's individual level of blameworthiness would be taken into account.

Applying the law

Explain whether the following situations could be unlawful act manslaughter and/or gross negligence manslaughter.

1 Asif is throwing stones at passing cars. One of the stones goes through the open side window in Dawn's car and hits her on the side of the head. She loses control of the car and hits a pedestrian, Keith, who is killed.

2 Justine and Oliver have spent the evening at Justine's flat, drinking heavily. Oliver also knows that Justine has taken an Ecstasy tablet, although he has not taken any drugs. Justine passes out and Oliver, who is afraid he may get into trouble, decides to leave. The next morning, Justine is discovered to be dead.

3 Liam, who is very angry with Sam, kicks out at Sam. This causes Sam to trip and fall down some steps, breaking his neck and killing him.

4 Patsy has been caring for her elderly aunt who is very frail and unable to walk without assistance. Patsy goes away on a fortnight's holiday, leaving her aunt on her own. The aunt dies through lack of food and cold.

5 Brett decides to rob a local post office. He puts a mask over his face and takes an imitation gun with him. He enters the post office and tells the two members of the staff who are there, Karina and Sven, to put their hands up. Karina was so shocked that she suffered a heart attack. When her colleague, Sven, tried to go to her assistance, Brett pushed him away. Sven fell, hitting his head, and died. Karina died two hours later.

Examination questions

1 Critically consider whether the law governing involuntary manslaughter is in a satisfactory state.

(OCR, Unit 2571, June 2003)

2 Sarah was delighted when her noisy next-door neighbours left for a fortnight's holiday. However, her peace was soon shattered when her neighbour's gardener, Derek, arrived and began to lop trees with a chainsaw while listening to his portable CD player at full volume. Unable to bear the noise any longer, Sarah loaded her husband's old service revolver and fired at the CD player from an upstairs window, blasting it to fragments. Derek fainted from the shock, dropping the chainsaw and wounding himself severely in the foot.

Some time later, Sarah glanced over the fence and saw Derek lying unconscious and bleeding profusely. She put Derek in the back of his van and drove off towards the local hospital. The lock in the back door of the van was broken, and Derek fell out into the road, where he was trampled by a horse carelessly ridden by Fiona. Although suffering from multiple injuries, Derek was still alive and might have been saved by proper medical treatment. He was taken by ambulance to the hospital, where he was treated by Tim, an inexperienced young doctor who failed to recognise the full extent of his injuries. Derek died without regaining consciousness.

Discuss the potential criminal liability of Sarah, Fiona and Tim for the death of Derek.

(WJEC, LW4, June 2003)

3 Janet Jones is admitted to Dartmorton Hospital in order to remove a lump from her throat. On the morning of the operation, she is taken to the operating theatre where she is given a full general anaesthetic by Sarah, a qualified anaesthetist. During the operation the tube supplying the air and the anaesthetic becomes dislodged. The surgeon, Mr Singh, notices that Janet is turning blue and alerts Sarah, who has fallen asleep. The operation is discontinued but Janet is now in a coma, having been deprived of oxygen for several minutes. Janet is taken to the intensive care unit. She remains on a life-support system for three weeks. Two qualified doctors, Duleep and Brian, decide that she is in a persistent vegetative state and will never regain consciousness. They turn off the life-support machine and Janet dies.

Advise Sarah, Duleep and Brian as to their potential liability for the death of Janet.

(OCR, Unit 2571, January 2004)

CHAPTER 10

Non-fatal offences against the person

The main offences are set out in the Offences Against the Person Act 1861 (OAPA). They are based on whether or not the victim was injured; if there were injuries, their level of seriousness; and the intention of the defendant. The main offences are in ascending order of seriousness:

- assault – common law but charged under s 39 of the Criminal Justice Act 1988
- battery – common law but charged under s 39 of the Criminal Justice Act 1988
- assault occasioning actual bodily harm – s 47 OAPA 1861
- malicious wounding or inflicting grievous bodily harm – s 20 OAPA 1861
- wounding or causing grievous bodily harm with intent – s 18 OAPA 1861.

10.1 COMMON ASSAULT

There are two ways of committing this:

- assault
- battery.

Assault and battery are common-law offences. There is no statutory definition for either assault or for battery. However statute law recognises their existence as both of these offences are charged under s 39 Criminal Justice Act 1988 which sets out that the maximum punishment for them is six months' imprisonment or a fine of £5,000 or both.

The act involved is different for assault and battery. For assault, there is no touching, only the fear of immediate, unlawful, force. For battery, there must be actual force. There are often situations in which both occur, for example, where the defendant approaches the victim, shouting that he is going to 'get him',

then punches the victim in the face. The approaching, shouting and raising his arm prior to the punch constitute an assault, while the punch is the battery. As the act is different for each it is easier to consider assault and battery separately.

10.1.1 *Actus reus* of assault

An assault is also known as a technical assault or a psychic assault. There must be:

- an act
- which causes the victim to apprehend the infliction of immediate, unlawful, force.

An 'act'

An assault requires some act or words. An omission is not sufficient to constitute an assault. However, words are sufficient for an assault. These can be verbal or written. In *Constanza* (1997) the Court of Appeal held that letters could be an assault. The defendant had written 800 letters and made a number of phone calls to the victim. The victim interpreted the last two letters as clear threats. The Court of Appeal said there was an assault as there was a 'fear of violence at some time, not excluding the immediate future'.

In *Ireland* (1997) it was held that even silent telephone calls can be an assault. It depends on the facts of the case.

Apprehend immediate unlawful force

The important point is that the act or words must cause the victim to apprehend that immediate force is going to be used against them. There is no assault if the situation is such that it is obvious that the defendant cannot actually use force. For example, where the defendant shouts threats from a passing train there is no possibility that he can carry out the threats in the immediate future.

It was decided in *Lamb* (1967) that pointing an unloaded gun at someone who knows that it is unloaded cannot be an assault. This is because the other person does not fear immediate force. However, if the other person thought the gun was loaded then this could be an assault.

Fear of immediate force is necessary; 'immediate' does not mean 'instantaneous', but 'imminent', so an assault can be through a closed window, as in *Smith v Chief Superintendent of Woking Police Station* (1983).

SMITH v CHIEF SUPERINTENDENT OF WOKING POLICE STATION (1983)
D got into a garden and looked through V's bedroom window on the ground floor at about 11 pm one evening. V was terrified and thought that D was about to enter the room. Although D was outside the house and no attack could be made at that immediate moment, the court held that V was frightened by his conduct. The basis of the fear was that she did not know what he was going to do next, but that it was likely to be of a violent nature. Fear of what he might do next was sufficiently immediate for the purposes of the offence.

Words indicating there will be no violence may prevent an act from being an assault. This is a principle which comes from the old case of *Tuberville v Savage* (1669) where the defendant placed one hand on his sword and said, 'If it were not assize time, I would not take such language from you'. This was held not to be an assault because what he said showed he was not going to do anything.

However, it will depend on all the circumstances. For example, in *Light* (1857) the defendant raised a sword above the head of his wife and said, 'Were it not for the bloody policeman outside, I would split your head open'. It was held that this was an assault. The wife feared that force was going to be used on her and the words in the circumstances were not enough to negate that fear.

Fear of any unwanted touching is sufficient: the force or unlawful personal violence which is feared need not be serious.

There are many examples of assault; for example:

- raising a fist as though about to hit the victim
- throwing a stone at the victim which just misses
- pointing a loaded gun at someone within range
- making a threat by saying 'I am going to hit you'.

Unlawfulness of the force

The force which is threatened must be unlawful. If it is lawful, there is no offence of common assault. When force is lawful or unlawful is discussed in detail under the *actus reus* of battery in the next section.

10.1.2 *Actus reus* of battery

The *actus reus* of battery is the application of unlawful force to another person. 'Force' is a slightly misleading word as it can include the slightest touching, as shown by the case of *Collins v Wilcock* (1984).

COLLINS v WILCOCK (1984)
Two police officers saw two women apparently soliciting for the purposes of prostitution. They asked the appellant to get into the police car for questioning but she refused and walked away. As she was not known to the police, one of the officers walked after her to try to find out her

---

identity. She refused to speak to the officer and again walked away. The officer then took hold of her by the arm to prevent her leaving. She became abusive and scratched the officer's arm. She was convicted of assaulting a police officer in the execution of his duty. She appealed against that conviction on the basis that the officer was not acting in the execution of his duty, but was acting unlawfully by holding the her arm as the officer was not arresting her. The court held that the officer had committed a battery and the defendant was entitled to free herself.

In *Collins v Wilcock* the court pointed out that touching a person to get his attention was acceptable, provided that no greater degree of physical contact was used than was necessary. However, physical restraint was not acceptable.

Even touching the victim's clothing can be sufficient to form a battery. In *Thomas* (1985) the defendant touched the bottom of a woman's skirt and rubbed it. The Court of Appeal said, *obiter*, 'There could be no dispute that if you touch a person's clothes while he is wearing them that is equivalent to touching him'.

Continuing act

A battery may be committed through a continuing act, as in *Fagan v Metropolitan Police Commander* (1968) where the defendant parked his car with one of the tyres on a police officer's foot. When he parked he was unaware that he had done this, but when the police office asked him to remove it, he refused to do so for several minutes. The court said that at the start there was an act which could be a battery but the full offence of battery was not committed at that point because there was no element of intention. However, it became an offence of battery the moment the intention was formed to leave the wheel on the officer's foot.

Indirect act

A battery can also be through an indirect act such as a booby trap. In this situation the defendant causes force to be applied, even though he does not personally touch the victim. This occurred in *Martin* (1881) where the defendant placed an iron bar across the doorway of a theatre. He then switched off the lights. In the panic which followed several of the audience were injured when they were trapped and unable to open the door. Martin was convicted of an offence under s 20 of the OAPA 1861.

A more modern example is *DPP v K* (1990).

DPP v K (1990)
D was a 15-year-old schoolboy who took sulphuric acid without permission from his science lesson, to try its reaction on some toilet paper. While he was in the toilet he heard footsteps in the corridor, panicked and put the acid into a hot air hand drier to hide it. He returned to his class, intending to remove the acid later. Before he could do so another pupil used the drier and was sprayed by the acid. D was charged with assault occasioning actual bodily harm (s 47). The magistrates acquitted him because he said he had not intended to hurt anyone (see section 10.2.2 for the *mens rea* of s 47). The prosecution appealed, by way of case stated, to the Queen's Bench Divisional Court which held that a common assault (remember this includes both an assault and a battery) could be committed by an indirect act.

Another example of indirect force occurred in *Haystead v Chief Constable of Derbyshire* (2000) where the defendant caused a small child to fall to the floor by punching the woman holding the child. The defendant was found guilty because he was reckless as to whether or not his acts would injure the child. It is worth noting that, in this case, the conviction could also be justified by the principle of transferred malice.

Omissions

Criminal liability can arise by way of an omission, but only if the defendant is under a duty to act. Such a duty can arise out of a contract; a relationship; from the assumption of care for another or from the creation of a dangerous situation. As the *actus reus* of battery is the application of unlawful force it is difficult to think how examples could arise under these duty situations, but there has been one reported case, *DPP v Santana-Bermudez* (2003).

> ### DPP v SANTANA-BERMUDEZ (2003)
> In this case a police woman, before searching D's pockets asked him if he had any needles or other sharp objects on him. D said 'no', but when the police officer put her hand in his pocket she was injured by a needle which caused bleeding. The Divisional Court held that the defendant's failure to tell her of the needle could amount to the *actus reus* for the purposes of an assault causing actual bodily harm.

Other scenarios which could make a defendant liable by way of omission are where the defendant has created a dangerous situation which may lead to force being applied to the victim. This can be seen by analogy with *Miller* (1983) where D accidentally set fire to his mattress but failed to do to anything to prevent damage to the building in which he was sleeping. He was convicted of arson.

No other person was involved, but if there had been some else asleep in the room and *Miller* had failed to wake them and warn them of the danger then he could have been liable for a battery if there had been any problem. For example, if the person was hit by plaster falling from the ceiling as a result of the fire, then there appears no reason why *Miller* could not have been charged with battery of that person.

Unlawful force

For a battery to be committed the force must be unlawful. If the victim gives genuine consent to it then the force may lawful. (See section 14.9 for further information on consent as a defence.) Force may also be lawful where it is used in self-defence or prevention of crime. This can only be so if the force used is reasonable in the situation as the defendant believed it to be. (See section 14.8.) If the force is lawful, then the person using the force is not guilty of a battery.

Another situation where force may be lawful is in the correction of a child by a parent. English law recognises that moderate and reasonable physical chastisement of a child is lawful. However, in *A v UK* (1998), where a jury had acquitted a father who had beaten his son with a garden cane, the European Court of Human Rights ruled that a law allowing force to be used on children offends Art 3 of the European Convention on Human Rights. This article prohibits torture and inhuman or degrading treatment or punishment.

Despite this ruling, force used to correct a child can be lawful in the United Kingdom, provided the judge in such a case directs the jury to take account of the nature, context and duration of the force used by the parent, the physical and mental effect on the child and the reasons for the punishment. If the force is excessive then it is a criminal offence.

Battery without an assault

It is possible for there to be a battery even though there is no assault. This can occur where the victim is unaware that unlawful force is about to be used on him such as

Figure 10.1 Key cases chart on assault and battery

KEY CASES

Case	Facts	Law
Constanza (1997)	D wrote 800 letters and made phone calls to V.	Written words can be an assault if they cause V to fear immediate violence.
Smith v Chief Superintendent (Woking) (1983)	D looked through V's bedroom window late at night.	Fear of what D would do next was sufficient for the *actus reus* of assault.
Tuberville v Savage (1669)	D put hand on sword and said 'Were it not assize time, I would not take such language from you'.	Words can prevent an act from being an assault, but it depends on the circumstances.
Collins v Wilcock (1984)	A police officer held a woman's arm to prevent her walking away.	Any touching may be a battery, and always was if there was physical restraint.
Fagan V MPC (1968)	D, unknowingly, stopped his car with a wheel on a policeman's foot and refused to move when requested.	The *actus reus* of assault can be an ongoing act so that the complete offence is committed when D forms the *mens rea*.
DPP v K (1990)	D put acid in a hand drier – the next person to use it was sprayed with acid.	An indirect act can be the *actus reus* of assault.
DPP v Santana-Bermudez (2003)	D failed to tell a policewoman that he had a needle in his pocket – she was injured when she searched him.	An omission is sufficient for the *actus reus* of assault.
DPP v Majewski (1976)	D, who had taken drink and drugs, attacked the landlord of a pub and police officers	Getting drunk is a reckless course of conduct and is sufficient for the *mens rea* of assault.

where the attacker comes up unseen behind the victim's back. The first thing the victim knows is when he is struck; there has been a battery but no assault.

10.1.3 *Mens rea* of assault and battery

The *mens rea* for an assault is either an intention to cause another to fear immediate unlawful personal violence or recklessness as to whether such fear is caused. The *mens rea* for battery is either an intention to apply unlawful physical force to another or recklessness as to whether unlawful force is applied. So intention or recklessness is sufficient for both assault and battery.

The test for recklessness is subjective. For an assault, the defendant must realise there is a risk that his acts/words could cause another to fear unlawful personal violence. For a battery the defendant must realise there is a risk that his act (or omission) could cause unlawful force to be applied to another.

Assault and battery are as classed as offences of basic intent. This means that if the defendant is intoxicated when he does the relevant *actus reus* he is considered as doing it recklessly. This was stated by the House of Lords in *DPP v Majewski* (1976).

DPP v MAJEWSKI (1976)

D had consumed large quantities of alcohol and drugs and then attacked the landlord of the public house where he was drinking. The landlord called the police and D also attacked the police officers who tried to arrest him. The Law Lords held that getting himself intoxicated by drink and drugs was a reckless course of conduct and recklessness is enough to constitute the necessary *mens rea* in assault cases.

This ruling can be criticised as the point at which the drink or drugs is taken is a quite separate time to the point when the *actus reus* for the offence is committed. It is difficult to see how there is coincidence of the two. It is reasonable to say that the defendant is reckless when he takes drink or other intoxicating substances but this does not necessarily mean that when he commits an assault or battery three or four hours later he is reckless for the purposes of the offence. The decision can be viewed as a public policy decision.

Activity

Explain whether there is an assault and/or battery in the following situations.

1 At a party Tanya sneaks up behind Wilhelm, whom she knows well, and slaps him on the back.
2 Vince throws a stone at Delyth, but misses. He picks up another stone and this time hits the edge of Delyth's coat.
3 Imram turns round quickly without realising

---

that Harry is standing just behind him and bumps into Harry. Harry shouts at him 'If you were not wearing glasses, I would hit you in the face.'
4 Ramsey and Sue are having an argument. During the argument, Ramsey says 'If you don't shut up, I'll thump you'. Sue is so annoyed at this that she gets out a penknife and waves in front of Ramsey's face. Ramsay pushes her away.

10.2 ASSAULT OCCASIONING ACTUAL BODILY HARM

We now look at assaults where an injury is caused. The lowest level of injury is referred to the 1861 Act as 'actual bodily harm' and the offence is under s 47 of the Offences Against the Person Act 1861. It is a triable either way offence. The section states:

'Whosoever shall be convicted of any assault occasioning actual bodily harm shall be liable … to imprisonment for five years.'

As can be seen from this very brief section, there is no definition of 'assault' or 'actual bodily harm'. Nor is there any reference to the level of *mens rea* required. For all these points it is necessary to look at case law.

10.2.1 *Actus reus* of s 47

It is necessary to prove that there was an assault or battery and that this caused actual bodily harm.

Actual bodily harm

In *Miller* (1954) it was said that actual bodily harm is 'any hurt or injury calculated to interfere with the health or comfort of the victim'. In *R(T) v DPP* (2003) loss of consciousness, even momentarily, was held to be actual bodily harm.

R(T) v DPP (2003) — D and a group of other youths chased V. V fell to the ground and saw D coming towards him. V covered his head with his arms and was kicked. He momentarily lost consciousness and remembered nothing until being woken by a police officer. D was convicted of assault occasioning actual bodily harm.

> ### R(T) v DPP (2003)
> D and a group of other youths chased V. V fell to the ground and saw D coming towards him. V covered his head with his arms and was kicked. He momentarily lost consciousness and remembered nothing until being woken by a police officer. D was convicted of assault occasioning actual bodily harm.

So, s 47 can be charged where there is any injury. Bruising, grazes and scratches all come within this.

Psychiatric injury is also classed as 'actual bodily harm'. This was decided by the Court of Appeal in *Chan Fook* (1994). However, they pointed out that actual bodily harm does not include 'mere emotions such as fear, distress or panic' nor does it include 'states of mind that are not themselves evidence of some identifiable clinical condition'.

This decision was approved by the House of Lords in *Burstow* (1997) where it was said that 'bodily harm' in ss 18, 20 and 47 of the Offences Against the Person Act 1861 must be interpreted so as to include recognisable psychiatric illness.

10.2.2 *Mens rea* of s 47

The section in the Act makes no reference to *mens rea* but, as the essential element is a common assault, the courts have held that the *mens rea* for a common assault is sufficient for the *mens rea* of a s 47 offence.

This means the defendant must intend or be subjectively recklessness as to whether the victim fears or is subjected to unlawful force. This is the same *mens rea* as for an assault or a battery. It is important to note that there is no need for the defendant to intend or be reckless as to whether actual bodily harm is caused. This is demonstrated by the case of *Roberts* (1971).

> ### ROBERTS (1971)
> D, who was driving a car, made advances to the girl in the passenger seat and tried to take her coat off. She feared that he was going to commit a more serious assault and jumped from the car while it was travelling at about 30 miles per hour. As a result of this she was slightly injured. D was found guilty of assault occasioning actual bodily harm even though he had not intended any injury or realised there was a risk of injury. He had intended to apply unlawful force when he touched her as he tried to take her coat off. This satisfied the *mens rea* for a common assault and so he was guilty of an offence under s 47.

This decision was confirmed by the House of Lords in the combined appeals of *Savage* and *Parmenter* (1991).

> ### SAVAGE (1991)
> D threw beer over another woman in a pub. In doing this the glass slipped from D's hand and V's hand was cut by the glass. D said that she had only intended to throw beer over the woman. D had not intended her to be injured, nor had she realised that there was a risk of injury. She was convicted of a s 20 offence but the Court of Appeal quashed that and substituted a conviction under s 47 (assault occasioning actual bodily harm). She appealed against this to the House of Lords. The Law Lords dismissed her appeal.
>
> The fact that she intended to throw the beer over the other woman meant she had the intention to apply unlawful force and this was sufficient for the *mens rea* of the s 47 offence.

Figure 10.2 Key facts chart on assault, battery and s 47

KEY FACTS

Offence	*Actus reus*	Consequence (injury) required	*Mens rea*
Assault	Causing V to fear immediate unlawful violence. Requires an act but can be by silent telephone calls. *Ireland* (1997) or letters *Constanza* (1997)	None needed.	Intention of, or subjective reckless as to, causing V to fear immediate unlawful violence.
Battery	Application of unlawful violence even the slightest touching. *Collins v Wilcock* (1984)	None needed.	Intention of, or subjective reckless as to, applying unlawful force. *DPP v Majewski* (1976)

NB Assault and battery are both charged under s 39 Criminal Justice Act 1988 and are known as common assault.

| Assault occasioning actual bodily harm. s 47 OAPA 1861 | Assault, ie an assault or battery. | Actual bodily harm (eg bruising). This includes:
■ momentary loss of consciousness *R(T) v DPP* (2003)
■ psychiatric harm *Chan Fook* (1994) | Intention or subjective recklessness as to causing fear of unlawful violence or of applying unlawful force, ie the *mens rea* for an assault or battery. |

10.3 MALICIOUS WOUNDING/ INFLICTING GRIEVOUS BODILY HARM

This is the next offence in seriousness. It is an offence under s 20 of the Offences Against the Person Act 1861 which states:

'Whosoever shall unlawfully and maliciously wound or inflict any grievous bodily harm upon any other person, either with or without a weapon or instrument,

shall be guilty of an offence and shall be liable ... to imprisonment for not more than five years.'

The offence is commonly known as 'malicious wounding'. It is triable either way and the maximum sentence is five years. This is the same maximum sentence as for s 47 offence, despite the fact that s 20 is seen as a more serious offence and requires both a higher degree of injury and *mens rea* as to an injury.

For the offence to be proved it must be shown that the defendant:

■ wounded or
■ inflicted grievous bodily harm

and that he did this:

■ intending some injury (but not serious injury) be caused or
■ being reckless as to whether any injury was inflicted.

10.3.1 'Wound'

'Wound' means a cut or a break in the continuity of the whole skin. A cut of internal skin, such as in the cheek, is sufficient, but internal bleeding where there is no cut of the skin is not sufficient. In *JCC v Eisenhower* (1983) the victim was hit in the eye by a shotgun pellet. This did not penetrate the eye but did cause severe bleeding under the surface. As there was no cut, it was held that this was not a wound. The cut must be of the whole skin, so that a scratch is not considered a wound.

Even a broken bone is not considered a wound, unless the skin is broken as well. In the old case of *Wood* (1830) where the victim's collar bone was broken but, as skin was intact, it was held there was no wound.

10.3.2 Grievous bodily harm

It was held in *DPP v Smith* (1961) that grievous bodily harm means 'really serious harm'. The harm does not have to be life-threatening and in *Saunders* (1985) it was held that it was alright to direct a jury that there need be 'serious harm' not including the word 'really'.

In *Bollom* (2004) it was held that the severity of the injuries should be assessed according to the victim's age and health.

BOLLOM (2004)

A 17-month-old child had bruising to her abdomen, both arms and left leg. D was convicted of causing grievous bodily harm. The Court of Appeal quashed his conviction and substituted a conviction for assault occasioning actual bodily harm. However, the court stated that bruising could amount to grievous bodily harm. Bruising of this severity would be less serious on an adult in full health, than on a very young child.

In *Burstow* (1997) where the victim of a stalker suffered a severe depressive illness as a result of his conduct, it was decided that serious psychiatric injury can be grievous bodily harm.

In *Dica* (2004) there was the first conviction for causing grievous bodily harm through infecting the victims with HIV. The defendant had unprotected sex with two women without telling them he was HIV positive, infecting them. Although on appeal the defendant's conviction was quashed on the question of consent and the case sent for re-trial, there was no doubt that infecting someone with HIV was inflicting grievous bodily harm. At his re-trial the defendant was convicted.

10.3.3 Inflicting grievous bodily harm

Section 20 uses the word 'inflict'. Originally, this was taken as meaning that there had to be a technical assault or battery. Even so it allowed the section to be interpreted quite widely as shown in *Lewis* (1974) where D shouted threats at his wife through a closed door in a second floor flat and tried to break his way through the door. The wife was so frightened that she jumped from the window and broke both her legs. *Lewis* was convicted of a s 20 offence. The threats could be considered as a technical assault.

In *Burstow* (1997) it was decided that 'inflict' does not require a technical assault or a battery.

> **BURSTOW (1997)**
> D carried out an eight-month campaign of harassment against a woman with whom he had had a brief relationship some three years earlier. The harassment consisted of both silent and abusive telephone calls, hate mail and stalking. This caused V to suffer from severe depression. D's conviction under s 20 OAPA 1861 was upheld by the House of Lords.

This means that it need only be shown that the defendant's actions have led to the consequence of the victim suffering grievous bodily harm. The decision also means that there now appears to be little, if any, difference in the *actus reus* of the offences under s 20 and s 18 which uses the word 'cause'. In fact, in *Burstow* Lord Hope said that for all practical purposes there was no difference between the two words.

10.3.4 *Mens rea* of s 20

The word used in the section is 'maliciously'. In *Cunningham* (1957) it was held that 'maliciously' did not require any ill-will towards the person injured. It simply meant either:

- an intention to do the particular kind of harm that was in fact done or
- recklessness as to whether such harm should occur or not (ie the accused has foreseen that the particular kind of harm might be done, and yet gone on to take the risk of it).

> **CUNNINGHAM (1957)**
> The defendant tore a gas meter from the wall of an empty house in order to steal the money in it. This caused gas to seep into the house next door where a woman was affected by it. Cunningham was not guilty of an offence against s 23 of the Offences Against the Person Act 1861 of maliciously administering a noxious thing, as he did not realise the risk of gas escaping into the next-door house. He had not intended to cause the harm, nor had he been subjectively reckless about it.

In *Parmenter* (1991) the House of Lords confirmed that the *Cunningham* meaning of recklessness applies to all offences in which the statutory definition uses the word 'maliciously'.

So, for the *mens rea* of s 20 the prosecution can prove either that the defendant intended to cause another person some harm or that he was subjectively recklessness as to whether another person suffered some harm.

This left another point which the courts had to resolve. What was meant by the particular kind of harm? Does the defendant need to realise the risk of a wound or grievous bodily harm? It was decided by the House of Lords in *Parmenter* that, although the *actus* reus of s 20 requires a wound or grievous bodily harm, there is no need for the defendant to foresee this level of serious injury.

> **PARMENTER (1991)**
> D injured his three-month-old baby when he threw the child in the air and caught him. D said that he often done this with slightly older children and did not realise that there was risk of any injury. He was convicted of an offence under s 20. The House of Lords quashed this conviction as there was no evidence that he foresaw any injury but substituted a conviction for assault occasioning actual bodily harm under s 47.

This decision means that, although there are four offences which appear to be on a ladder in terms of seriousness, there is overlap in terms of the *mens rea*.

Figure 10.3 Different levels of *mens rea* and injury for assault cases

Offence	Mens rea	Injury
s 18	Specific intent to wound or cause GBH or resist arrest etc.	Wound or grievous bodily harm.
s 20	Intention or recklessness as to some harm.	
s 47	Intention or recklessness as to put V in fear of unlawful force or applying unlawful force assault.	Actual bodily harm.
Common assault		No injury.

10.4 WOUNDING OR CAUSING GRIEVOUS BODILY HARM WITH INTENT

This offence under s 18 of the Offences Against the Person Act 1861 is often referred to as 'wounding with intent'. In fact, it covers a much wider range of than this implies.

It is considered a much more serious offence than s 20, as can be seen from the difference in the maximum punishments. Section 20 has a maximum of five years' imprisonment whereas the maximum for s 18 is life imprisonment. Also, s 20 is triable either way but s 18 must be tried on indictment at the Crown Court. The definition in the Offences Against the Person Act 1861 states:

'Whosoever shall unlawfully and maliciously by any means whatsoever wound or cause any grievous bodily harm to any person, with intent to do some grievous bodily harm to any person, or with intent to resist or prevent the lawful apprehension or detainer of any person, shall be guilty of ... an offence.'

10.4.1 *Actus reus* of s 18

This can be committed in two ways:

- wounding or
- causing grievous bodily harm.

The meanings of 'wound' and 'grievous bodily harm' are the same as for s 20. The word 'cause' is very wide so that it is only necessary to prove that the defendant's act was a substantial cause of the wound or grievous bodily harm.

10.4.2 *Mens rea* of s 18

This is a specific intent offence. The defendant must be proved to have intended to:

- do some grievous bodily harm or
- resist or prevent the lawful apprehension or detainer of any person.

Intent to do some grievous bodily harm

Although the word 'maliciously' appears in s 18, it has been held that this adds nothing to the *mens rea* of this section where grievous bodily harm is intended. The important point is that s 18 is a specific intent crime. Intention must be proved; recklessness is not enough for the *mens rea* of s 18. 'Intention' has the same meaning as shown in the leading cases on murder.

So, as decided in *Moloney* (1985), foresight of consequences is not intention; it is only evidence from which intention can be inferred or found. And following the cases of *Nedrick* (1986) and *Woollin* (1998), intention cannot be found unless the harm caused was a virtual certainty as a result of the defendant's actions and the defendant realised that this was so. (See section 3.1.2 for a fuller discussion on these cases and the meaning of intention.)

Where the defendant is trying to resist or prevent arrest or detention then the level of intention regarding the injury is lower. The prosecution must prove that he had specific intention to resist prevent arrest but so far as the injury is concerned they need only prove that he was reckless as to whether his actions would cause a wound or injury. This was decided in *Morrison* (1989).

> **MORRISON (1989)**
> A police officer seized hold of D and told him that she was arresting him. He dived through a window, dragging her with him as far as the window so that her face was badly cut by the glass. The Court of Appeal held that as the word 'maliciously' is used in respect of this part of the section it must have same meaning as in *Cunningham* (1957). This means that the prosecution must prove that the defendant either intended injury or realised there was a risk of injury and took that risk.

Figure 10.4 Key facts chart on s 20 and s 18

KEY FACTS

Offence	*Actus reus*	Consequence (injury) required	*Mens rea*
Maliciously wounding or inflicting grievous bodily harm s 20 OAPA 1861	A direct or indirect act or omission: *Martin* (1881) No need to prove an assault: *Burstow* (1998)	Either a wound – a cutting of the whole skin: *JCC v Eisenhower* (1984) or Grievous bodily harm (really serious harm) which includes psychiatric harm: *Burstow* (1998)	Intention or subjective recklessness as to causing some injury (though not serious): *Parmenter* (1991)
Wounding or causing grievous bodily harm with intent s 18 OAPA 1861	A direct or indirect act or omission which causes V's injury.	A wound or grievous bodily harm (as above).	Specific intention to wound or to cause grievous bodily harm or Specific intention to resist or prevent arrest plus recklessness as to causing injury: *Morrison* (1989).

Activity

Read the following newspaper article and answer the questions below.

THUG JAILED FOR STAMPING ON POLICEMAN'S FACE

A thug has been jailed for two-and-a-half years for a vicious attack on a police officer after New Year's Eve celebrations erupted in violence.

Kevin Vidler assaulted the PC and then stamped on his face, fracturing his cheekbone, and kicked him in the head.

His brother Neil was given 240 hours' community punishment order for assaulting another man. He was ordered to pay his victim £250 compensation.

Maidstone Crown Court heard in October how the party at a working men's club in Southborough was in full swing when the victim, a club member, intervened in a couple's heated argument. There was a 'verbal tirade' and he asked one of the men to leave.

Soon afterwards he was punched in the face by 37-year-old Neil Vidler. The police were called but the trouble continued outside.

When the PC and a fellow officer arrived, a teenager hit out at them. Kevin Vidler, aged 36, tried to help the youth, grabbing the constable by the throat and punching him in the head.

Kevin Vidler was convicted of causing grievous bodily harm with intent. Neil Vidler was convicted of assault causing actual bodily harm.

(*Kent Messenger*, 5th December 2003)

Questions

1 What offence was Kevin Vidler convicted of?
2 Which section of the Offences Against the Person Act 1861 would this come under?
3 What are the elements which have to be proved for this section?
4 Explain what Kevin had done to make him guilty of this offence.
5 What offence was Neil Vidler convicted of?
6 Which section of the Offences Against the Person Act 1861 would this come under?
7 What are the elements which have to be proved for this section?
8 What Neil had done to make him guilty of this offence?
9 What sentences were the two brothers given?
10 Explain why they received different sentences.

10.5 THE CROWN PROSECUTION CHARGING STANDARDS

When Crown Prosecutors decide on which level of offence to charge, they refer to a document called 'Charging Standards' which is issued to all Crown Prosecutors. This document sets out the matters they should consider in deciding the level to be charged. This document is not the law on the subject and it can be argued that on some occasions prosecutors choose a lower level of offence than might be strictly available under the law.

However, the Charging Standards do give some useful examples. For example in deciding whether to charge the defendant with a common assault or with a s 47 offence, it states:

'Where battery results in injury, a choice of charge is available. The Code for Crown Prosecutors recognises that there will be

factors which may properly lead to a decision not to prefer or continue with the gravest possible charge. Thus, although any injury that is more than transient or trifling can be classified as actual bodily harm, the appropriate charge ... will be contrary to section 39 [common assault] where the injuries amount to no more that the following:

- *Grazes;*
- *Scratches;*
- *Abrasions;*
- *Minor bruising;*
- *Swellings;*
- *Reddening of the skin;*
- *Superficial cuts;*
- *A "black eye".*

Aggravating features

It is also recognised that there are features which make an assault more serious when it is appropriate to charge the highest possible level of offence. For example, the following features make it more appropriate to charge a s 47 offence even though the level of injury is within the list above:

- the nature of the assault, such as the use of a weapon, biting or kicking a victim who is on the ground
- the vulnerability of the victim, such as when the victim is elderly, disabled or a child.

The full charging standards can be found on the Internet at www.cps.gov.uk/legal

10.6   CONSENT AS A DEFENCE

Consent may be a defence to battery and other offences against the person. However, it is never a defence to murder or to situations where serious injury is caused.

Consent is strictly speaking not a defence, as where the other person consents, there is no offence. For example where the other person consents to being touched then there is no battery as there is no unlawful force. This is illustrated by *Donovan* {1934).

> **DONOVAN (1934)**
> D caned a 17-year-old girl for the purpose of sexual gratification. This caused bruising and he was convicted of indecent assault and a common assault. D appealed on the basis that V had consented to the act. His conviction was quashed.

A more extreme case illustrating the same point is *Slingsby* (1995) where the defendant was charged with manslaughter.

> **SLINGSBY (1995)**
> D was charged with involuntary manslaughter by an unlawful act. D and the victim had taken part in sexual activity which was described as 'vigorous' but which had taken place with the victim's consent. During this a signet ring which D was wearing caused small cuts to the victim and this led to blood poisoning from which she died. The victim's consent meant that there was no battery or other form of assault and so D was held to be not guilty of manslaughter as there was no unlawful act.

There must, however, be true consent. In *Tabassum* (2000) the defendant had persuaded women to allow him to measure their breasts for the purpose of preparing a database for sale to doctors. The women were fully aware of the nature of the acts he proposed to do, but they said they consented only because they thought that D had either medical qualifications or medical training. The Court of Appeal approved the trial judge's direction when he said:

'I should prefer myself to say that consent in such cases does not exist at all, because the act consented to is not the act done.

Consent to a surgical operation or examination is not consent to sexual connection or indecent behaviour.'

In *Dica* (2004), where consent was given to sexual intercourse without knowledge of the fact that the defendant was HIV positive, the Court of Appeal held that there was no consent to the risk of infection.

DICA (2004)

D, who knew he was HIV positive, had relationships with two women. They had unprotected sex with him and both became infected. They claimed that they did not know he was HIV positive and that if they had they would not have agreed to unprotected sex. D was charged with an offence under s 20 of the Offences Against the Person Act 1861. At his trial, the judge did not allow the issue of consent to go to the jury, so the Court of Appeal quashed the conviction but ordered a re-trial.

The decision in *Dica* makes it clear that even though V has consented to sexual intercourse, D can be guilty of an offence under s 20 of the Offences Against the Person Act 1861. This overruled the decision in *Clarence* (1888) where, unknown to the wife, the husband was suffering from a venereal disease and the wife became infected when they had sexual intercourse. It was held that a wife's consent to sexual intercourse with her husband meant that there was no assault.

10.6.1 Implied consent

There are situations in which the courts imply consent to minor touchings, which would otherwise be a battery. These are the everyday situations where there is a crowd of people and it is impossible not to have some contact. In *Wilson v Pringle* (1987) it was held that the ordinary 'jostlings' of everyday life were not battery. Nobody can complain of the jostling which is inevitable from his presence in, for example, a supermarket, an underground station or a busy street; nor can a person who attends a party complain if his hand is seized in friendship, or even if his back is (within reason) slapped.

This also applies to contact sports. When a person takes part in sport such as rugby or judo he is agreeing to the contact which is part of that sport. However, if the contact goes beyond what is allowed within the rules then it is possible for an offence to be committed. For example, a rugby player consents to a tackle within the rules of the game, but he does not consent to an opposition player stamping on his head.

The breach of the rules of the sport must be a serious one. The Court of Appeal said in *Barnes* (2004) that where an injury is caused during a match, then a criminal prosecution should be reserved for those situations where the conduct was sufficiently grave to be properly categorised as criminal.

BARNES (2004)

D made a late tackle on V during an amateur football match. V suffered a serious leg injury. D's conviction of an offence under s 20 of the Offences Against the Person Act 1861 was quashed.

10.6.2 Consent to minor injuries

There have been arguments as to whether consent could be a defence to an offence under s 47 of the Offences Against the Person Act 1861. It used to be thought that consent could be a defence where the injuries were not serious. However, in *Attorney-General's Reference (No. 6 of 1980)* (1981) where two young men agreed to fight in the street to settle their differences following a quarrel, the Court of Appeal held that consent could not be a defence to such an action as it was not in the public interest. They said:

'It is not in the public interest that people should try to cause, or should cause, each other bodily harm for no good reason. Minor struggles are another matter. So, in our judgment, it is immaterial whether the act occurs in private or public; it is an assault if actual bodily harm is intended and/or caused. This means that most fights will unlawful regardless of consent.'

So it is now accepted that consent is not a defence to a s 47 offence, unless the situation is one of the exceptions which have been recognised by the courts. In *Attorney-General's Reference (No. 6 of 1980)* the Court of Appeal gave the following list of exceptions:

'properly conduct games and sports, lawful chastisement or correction, reasonable surgical interference, dangerous exhibitions, etc.'

The court added 'etc' to the end of the list to show that there may be other situations where consent would be permitted to be a defence. It is a question of whether it is in the public interest or not.

In deciding what was in the public interest the courts have come to decisions which are difficult to reconcile. In *Brown* (1993) the House of Lords held that consent was not a defence to sado-masochistic acts done by homosexuals, even though all the participants were adult and the injuries inflicted were transitory and trifling.

BROWN (1993)
Five men in a group of consenting adult sado-masochists were convicted of offences of assault causing actual bodily harm (s 47 Offences Against the Person Act 1861) and malicious wounding (s 20 Offences Against the Person Act 1861). They had carried out acts which included applying stinging nettles to the genital area and inserting map pins or fish hooks into the penises of each other. All the victims had consented and

none had needed medical attention. Their convictions were upheld by the House of Lords.

The Law Lords clearly made this decision as a matter of public policy. Lord Templeman actually said:

'The question whether the defence of consent should be extended to the consequences of sado-masochistic encounters can only be decided by consideration of policy and public interest … Society is entitled and bound to protect itself against a cult of violence.'

However, in *Wilson* (1996), the Court of Appeal held that where a defendant branded his initials on his wife's buttocks with a hot knife, at her request, this was not an unlawful act, even though she had to seek medical attention for the burns which were caused. It held it was not in the public interest that such consensual behaviour should be criminalised. This was a situation of 'personal adornment' like having a tattoo.

10.6.3 Mistaken belief in consent

Where the defendant genuinely, but mistakenly, believes that the victim is consenting then there is a defence to an assault.

In this area the decisions of the courts are even more difficult to reconcile with the general principle that 'it is not in the public interest that people should try to cause, or should cause, each other bodily harm for no good reason'. In the following two cases the courts held that mistaken belief in consent was a defence to the offences charged.

JONES (1986)
Two schoolboys aged 14 and 15 were tossed into the air by older youths. One victim suffered a broken arm and the other a ruptured spleen. The defendants claimed they believed that the two victims consented to the activity. The Court

Figure 10.5 Key facts chart on consent as a defence

Offence	Can consent be a defence?	Comment/case
Murder s 18 OAPA 1861	Never a defence to these crimes.	Not in the public interest.
s 20 OAPA 1861 s 47 OAPA 1861	Generally not a defence.	Not in public interest, eg fighting (*Attorney-General's Reference (No. 6 of 1980)* (1981)) or sado-masochistic acts (*Brown* (1993)).
	BUT there are exceptions where consent is a defence.	Properly conducted sports, surgery, dangerous exhibitions (*Jones* (1986)) or personal adornment such as tattoos (*Wilson* (1996)).
Battery	Always allowed as a defence.	Consent can also be implied to the 'jostlings' of everyday life (*Wilson v Pringle* (1986)).

of Appeal quashed their convictions for offences under s 20 of the Offences Against the Person Act 1861 because the judge had not allowed the issue of mistaken belief in consent to go to the jury. The court held that a genuine mistaken belief in consent to 'rough and undisciplined horseplay' could be a defence, even if that belief was unreasonable.

A similar decision was reached in *Aitken* (1992) where RAF officers poured white spirit over a colleague who was wearing a fire-resistant flying suit, but who was asleep and drunk at the time this was done. He suffered 35 per cent burns. Their convictions under s 20 were quashed as the mistaken belief in the victim's consent should have been left to the jury.

10.7 THE NEED FOR REFORM OF THE LAW

This area of the law is in need of reform and recommendations have been made by both the Criminal Law Revision Committee and the Law Commission. The Law Commission pointed out that there are three main problems with the Offences Against the Person Act 1861. These are:

- it uses complicated, obscure and old-fashioned language; eg the words 'maliciously' and 'grievous'
- the structure of the Act is complicated
- non-lawyers find the Act completely unintelligible.

In fact some of the difficulties have been resolved by the judges in case decisions. For example there was considerable debate as to whether the word 'inflict' in s 20 meant that a technical assault had to take place. This was resolved by the case of *Burstow* (see section

10.3.3) in which the House of Lords ruled that it did not.

Also, the courts have extended the meaning of 'bodily harm' to include injury to mental health so that defendants causing such injury can also be convicted.

10.7.1 Inconsistency between offences

There are inconsistencies in the Act, especially with regard to the *mens rea* required for each offence. In particular, s 47 has the same *mens* rea as for an assault or battery. It does not require the defendant to intend or even realise that there is a risk of any injury. This appears unjust.

It is also unjust that a person who causes a small cut can be charged with the more serious offence of s 20 instead of the offence of 'occasioning actual bodily harm' under s 47. This is because s 20 refers to 'wound or grievous bodily harm'. Yet clearly there are different levels of wound and many of them do not equate with grievous bodily harm.

It is also inconsistent that a defendant who intends or foresees the risk of minor injury can be convicted of the very serious offence of s 18 if serious injury then occurs when he intends to resist arrest. This is the effect of the decision in *Morrison* (see section 10.4.2). Is it right that the fact the defendant intends to resist arrest makes him liable for the same offence as someone who has intended to cause very serious injuries?

10.7.2 Law Commission's proposals

In 1993 the Law Commission proposed new law to take its place, but the Government did nothing about this until 1998 when the Home Office issued a Consultation Document, *Violence: Reforming the Offences against the Person Act 1861*. This included a draft Bill which set out four main offences. These were

intended to replace s 18, s 20, s 47, and assault and battery. In order, starting with the most serious (which is in clause 1 of the draft Bill), they are:

1 Intentional serious injury where a person would be guilty if he intentionally caused serious injury to another.
2 Reckless serious injury where a person would be guilty if he recklessly caused serious injury to another.
3 Intentional or reckless injury where a person would be guilty if he intentionally or recklessly caused injury to another.
4 Assault: a person would be guilty if he intentionally or recklessly
   a applied force to or caused an impact on the body of another, or
   b caused the other to believe that any such force or impact is imminent.

In each of these the level of injury and the required *mens rea* are made clear by the wording. In addition, the draft Bill also defined the word' injury', making it clear that both physical and mental injury were included. The word 'wounding' is not used. So this would mean that a serious cut would be considered to be a serious injury, while a small cut would be considered to be merely an injury. This would have cleared up most of the problems in the present law. Unfortunately, although the Bill was sent out for consultation in 1988, the Government has done nothing more, so the law still remains in an unsatisfactory state.

In the draft Bill, the Law Commission defined 'injury'. It said that it included both physical and mental illness and it gave a definition for both of these:

■ *physical* injury was defined as including pain, unconsciousness and any other impairment of a person's physical health
■ *mental* injury was defined as any impairment of person's mental health.

They also included disease as a physical injury for the purposes of the most serious offence. However, this would meant that it would be almost impossible to convict a defendant of infecting another person with HIV since the proposed most serious offence (no.1 in the list above) can only be committed where the defendant has intentionally caused serious injury. This would mean that convictions for recklessly transmitting HIV, as in the case of *Dica* (see section 10.3.2) would not be possible.

Activity

Explain, in each of the situations below, what type of offence may have been committed.

1 In a football match Billy is kicked by Rio as Rio tries to get control of the ball. This causes bruising to Billy's leg. Billy is annoyed at this and punches Rio in the face, causing a cut to his lip.
2 Anish is walking along a canal bank. Carol, who is in a hurry, pushes past him, knocking him into the canal. Anish hits his head on the side and suffers a fractured skull.
3 A police officer sees Jason damaging a parked car. The officer puts his hand on Jason's shoulder and says 'I am arresting you for criminal damage'. Jason punches the officer hard in the face, breaking his jaw. Jason then runs off.
4 Karl waves a knife at Lily, saying 'I am going to cut that silly smile off'. Lily is very frightened and faints. She falls against Mary, who is knocked to the ground and suffers bruising.
5 Nick plays rugby for his college team. During one match Nick is tackled very hard by Dave. Nick is angry about this and makes sure that every time Dave has the ball, he (Nick) tackles Dave hard. When they are leaving the pitch at the end of the match Nick pushes Dave. What defence(s) might be available to Nick if he is charged with battery in respect of the tackles and the push?

Examination questions

1 Kate and Mark are partners. Kate reluctantly allows him to brand the letter 'M' on her right thigh with a piece of hot wire, as a token of their love. The pain is so great that Kate lashes out uncontrollably and strikes Mark in the face, breaking his glasses and cutting his eyebrow. Mark is now so annoyed that he retaliates by hitting out at Kate, catching her in the face and causing her nose to bleed. Kate storms out, saying she will never forgive him for hitting her.

For the next three months Mark telephones Kate at her parents' house as many as ten times a day. Each time he threatens her that she will 'regret it' if she ever decides to go out with another man. Kate becomes so frightened and depressed that she cannot leave the house and gives up her job.

Consider what offences, if any, have been committed by Kate and Mark and whether any defences are available to either of them.
(OCR, Unit 2572, January 2004)

2 After drinking rather a lot of beer at a Halloween party, Eric felt the need for a curry and went into an Indian takeaway, still wearing his gruesome Halloween mask. The proprietor's wife was behind the counter and was terrified by the sight of him. The proprietor, Sanjay, thought that Eric had come to rob the till, and rushed at Eric brandishing a baseball bat. Eric fled towards

the door and reached it just as two other customers, Roger and Nicola, were coming in from the street. Finding his escape route blocked, Eric panicked and punched Roger in the face, breaking his nose. Nicola screamed in terror at the sight of so much blood and ran out into the road, where she was knocked down and injured by a passing car. Sanjay wrestled Eric to the ground and struck him several blows with the baseball bat, causing him serious internal injuries.

Consider the potential criminal liability of Eric and Sanjay, including any defences which may be available to them.

(WJEC, LW4, June 2004)

3 *'Where offences against the person are concerned, there are very few circumstances in which the courts are willing to accept that consent on the part of the victim can amount to a defence.'*
Discuss.

(WJEC, LW5, June 2005)

CHAPTER 11

Theft

Theft is defined in s 1 of the Theft Act 1968 which states that:

'A person is guilty of theft if he dishonestly appropriates property belonging to another with the intention of permanently depriving the other of it.'

The Act then goes on in the next five sections to give some help with the meaning of the words or phrases in the definition. This is done in the order that the words or phrases appear in the definition, making it easy to remember the section numbers. They are:

- ■ s 2 – dishonestly (part of the *mens rea*)
- ■ s 3 – appropriates (part of the *actus reus*)
- ■ s 4 – property (part of the *actus reus*)
- ■ s 5 – belonging to another (part of the *actus reus*)
- ■ s 6 – with the intention of permanently depriving the other of it (part of the *mens rea*).

Remember that the offence is in s 1. A person charged with theft is always charged with stealing 'contrary to s 1 of the Theft Act 1968'. Sections 2–6 are definition sections explaining s 1. They do not themselves create any offence.

The *actus reus* of theft is made up of the three elements in the phrase 'appropriates property belonging to another'. So, to prove the *actus reus* it has to be shown that there was appropriation by the defendant of something which is property within the definition of the Act and which, at the time of the appropriation, belonged to another.

There are two elements which must be proved for the *mens rea* of theft. These are that the appropriation of the property must be done 'dishonestly' and there must be the intention of permanently depriving the other person of it.

11.1 APPROPRIATION

The more obvious situations of theft involve a physical taking, for example a pickpocket taking a wallet from someone's pocket. But appropriation is much wider than this.

Section 3(1) states that:

'Any assumption by a person of the rights of an owner amounts to an appropriation, and this includes, where he has come by the property (innocently or not) without stealing it, any later assumption of a right to it by keeping or dealing with it as owner.'

The important words are 'any assumption by a person of the rights of an owner amounts to appropriation'. The rights of the owner include selling the property or destroying it as well such things as possessing it, consuming it, using it, lending it or hiring it out. So for there to be appropriation, the thief must do something which assumes (takes over) one of the owner's rights.

The rights of an owner also include the right to sell property. An appropriation by assuming the right to sell is demonstrated by the case of *Pitham and Hehl* (1977).

> **PITHAM and HEHL (1977)**
> D had sold furniture belonging to another person. This was held to be an appropriation. The offer to sell was an assumption of the rights of an owner and the appropriation took place at that point. It did not matter whether the furniture was removed from the house or not. Even if the owner was never deprived of the property D had still appropriated it by assuming the rights of the owner to offer the furniture for sale.

The right to destroy property is also an owner's right. This means that if D destroys property belonging to another D can be charged with theft, although it is also, of course, the offence of criminal damage.

Theft can also be charged where D does not destroy the other's property but throws it away. For example, if D threw a water-proof watch belonging to another into the sea, this could be theft. Again, only the owner has the right to this to the property.

The wording in s 3(1) is '*any* assumption by a person of *the* rights of an owner'. One question which the courts have had to deal with is whether the assumption has to be of *all* of the rights or whether it can just be of *any* of the rights. This was considered in *Morris* (1983).

> **MORRIS (1983)**
> D had switched the price labels of two items on the shelf in a supermarket. He had then put one of the items, which now had a lower price on it, into a basket provided by the store for shoppers and taken the item to the checkout, but had not gone through the checkout when he was arrested. His conviction for theft was upheld.
>
> Lord Roskill in the House of Lords stated that:
>
> '*It is enough for the prosecution if they have proved ... the assumption of <u>any</u> of the rights of the owner of the goods in question.*'

So it is clear that there does not have to be an assumption of all the rights. This is a sensible decision since in many cases the defendant will not have assumed all of the rights. Quite often, only one right will have been assumed, usually the right of possession. In *Morris* the right was the owner's right to put a price label on the goods.

Morris did stress that there had to be adverse interference with the owner's right.

11.1.1 Consent to the appropriation

Can a defendant appropriate an item when it has been given to them by the owner? This is an area which has caused major problems. The Theft Act does not state that the appropriation has to be without the consent of the owner. So, what is the position where the owner has allowed the defendant to take something because the owner thought that the defendant was paying for it with a genuine cheque? This point was considered in *Lawrence* (1971).

> **LAWRENCE (1971)**
> An Italian student, who spoke very little English, arrived at Victoria Station and showed an address to Lawrence who was a taxi driver. The journey should have cost 50p, but Lawrence told him it was expensive. The student got out a £1 note and offered it to the driver. Lawrence said it was not enough and so the student opened his wallet and allowed Lawrence to help himself to another £6. Lawrence put forward the argument that he had not appropriated the money as the student had consented to him taking it. Both the Court of Appeal and the House of Lords rejected this argument and held that there was appropriation in this situation.

The point as to whether the appropriation had to be without the consent of the owner was considered again by the House of Lords in *Gomez* (1993).

> **GOMEZ (1993)**
> D was the assistant manager of a shop. He persuaded the manager to sell electrical goods worth over £17,000 to an accomplice and to accept payment by two cheques, telling the manager they were as good as cash. The cheques were stolen and had no value. D was

charged with and convicted of theft of the goods.

The Court of Appeal quashed the conviction relying on the judgment in *Morris* that there had to be 'adverse interference' for there to be appropriation. They decided that the manager's consent to and authorisation of the transaction meant there was no appropriation at the moment of taking the goods.

The case was appealed to the House of Lords with the Court of Appeal certifying, as a point of law of general public importance, the following question:

'When theft is alleged and that which is alleged to be stolen passes to the defendant with the consent of the owner, but that has been obtained by a false representation, has:

(a) *an appropriation within the meaning of section 1(1) of the Theft Act 1968 taken place, or*
(b) *must such a passing of property necessarily involve an element of adverse interference with or usurpation of some right of the owner?'*

The House of Lords, by a majority of four to one, answered (a) 'yes'. An appropriation has taken place. They answered (b) 'no'. There was no need for adverse interference with or usurpation some right of the owner. In other words, to be guilty of theft, the defendant need not do anything contrary to the owner's wishes. They pointed out that the decision in the case of *Lawrence* (1971) ruled that an act may be an appropriation even if it is done with the consent of the owner.

> ### *HINKS* (2000)
>
> D was a 38-year-old woman who had befriended a man who had a low IQ and was very naïve. He was, however, mentally capable of understanding the concept of ownership and of making a valid gift. Over a period of about eight months D accompanied the man on numerous occasions to his building society where he withdrew money. The total was about £60,000 and this money was deposited in D's account. The man also gave D a television set. The judge directed the jury to consider whether the man was so mentally incapable that D herself realised that ordinary and decent people would regard it as dishonest to accept a gift from him. D was convicted of theft of the money and the TV set.
>
> On appeal, it was argued that if the gift was valid, the acceptance of it could not be theft. The House of Lords dismissed the appeal by a majority of three judges to two. Four of the judges decided that, even though the property was a valid gift, there was an appropriation. Lord Hobhouse dissented, ruling that there could not be an appropriation in these circumstances. Lord Hutton, although agreeing with the majority on the point of law, dissented on whether the conduct showed dishonesty.

A major argument against the ruling in *Hinks* is that in civil law the gift was valid and the £60,000 and the TV set belonged to the defendant. Lord Steyn, in the leading judgment, accepted that this was the situation but he considered it was irrelevant to the decision.

11.1.2 Consent without deception

So does the decision in *Gomez* extend to situations where a person has given property to another without any deception being made? This was the problem raised in the case of *Hinks* (2000).

11.1.3 A later assumption of a right

Section 3(1) makes it clear that there can also be an appropriation where the defendant acquires property without stealing it, but then later decides to keep or deal with the property as owner. The appropriation in this type of situation takes place at the point of 'keeping' or 'dealing'.

This could occur where the defendant hires a video from a shop, but instead of returning it decides to keep it. He is acting as though he is the owner with the right to keep the video.

Dealing in the property could occur where the defendant borrows a cycle (or other property) but then sells it or gives it away. This can also happen where a hires a car. If he sells it instead of returning it, then he has dealt with it as an owner.

Applying the law

Discuss whether there has been an appropriation in each of the following situations.

1 Jake has an argument with his neighbour. When his neighbour is out, Jake holds an auction of the neighbour's garden tools. The neighbour returns before any of the tools are taken away.
2 Saskia goes shopping at the local supermarket and takes her five-year-old son, Tom, with her. While at the checkout Tom takes some bars of chocolate and puts them in his pocket. Saskia does not realise Tom has done this until she finds the chocolate when they get home. Saskia decides that she will not take the chocolate back to the supermarket.
3 The owner of a shop asks Parvati, who is a lorry driver, to pick up a load of computer equipment and take it to a warehouse. Parvati agrees to do this but, after collecting the equipment, she decides that she will not take it to the warehouse but will instead sell it.
4 Otto, aged 18, is infatuated with Harriet, a married woman aged 32. Otto uses his student loan to buy expensive presents for Harriet. She knows he is a student and has very little money but she accepts the gifts from him.

11.2 PROPERTY S4 AR

For there to be theft the defendant must have appropriated 'property'. Section 4 gives a very comprehensive definition of property which means that almost anything can be stolen. The definition is in s 4(1) of the Theft Act 1968:

"Property" includes money and all other property real or personal, including things in action and other intangible property.'

This section lists five types of items which are included in the definition of 'property'. These are:

- money
- real property
- personal property
- things in action
- other intangible property.

In this list money is self-explanatory. It means coins and banknotes of any currency. Personal property is also straightforward as it covers all moveable items. Books, CDs, jewellery, clothes, cars are obvious examples, but it also includes very large items such as aeroplanes or tanks. It also includes very small trivial items such as a sheet of paper. It has even been held in *Kelly and Lindsay* (1998) that dead bodies and body parts can be personal property for the purposes of theft.

KELLY and LINDSAY (1998)
Kelly was a sculptor who asked Lindsay to take body parts from the Royal College of Surgeons where he worked as a laboratory assistant. Kelly made casts of the parts. They were convicted of theft and appealed on the point of law that body parts were not property. The Court of Appeal held that, though a dead body was not normally property within the definition of the Theft Act, the body parts were property as they had acquired 'different attributes by virtue of the application of skill, such as dissection or preservation techniques, for exhibition or teaching purposes.'

11.2.1 Real property

Real property is the legal term for land and buildings. Under s 4(1) land can be stolen, but s 4(2) states that this can only be done in three circumstances. These are where:

- a trustee or personal representative takes land in breach of his duties as a trustee or personal representative;
- someone not in possession of the land severs anything forming part of the land from the land;
- a tenant takes a fixture or structure from the land let to him.

Under the second point, it is theft to dig up turf from someone's lawn or to dismantle a wall and take the bricks. In 1972 a man was prosecuted for stealing Cleckheaton railway station by dismantling it and removing it. He was in fact acquitted by the jury as he said he was acting under a claim of right, but there was no doubt that the station could be property under the Theft Act definition.

11.2.2 Things in action

A thing in action is a right which can be enforced against another person by an action in law. The right itself is property under the definition in s 4. An example is a bank account. The bank does not keep coins or banknotes for each customer's account in a separate box! Instead the customer has a right to the payment of amount in his account. So, if D causes the bank to debit another person's account he has appropriated a thing in action. If he does this dishonestly and with the intention to permanently deprive the other of it, then D is guilty of theft.

A cheque itself is a thing in action, but it is also a piece of paper which is property which can be stolen, and it is a 'valuable security' which can also be stolen under the definition of property.

11.2.3 Other intangible property

This refers to other rights which have no physical presence but can be stolen under the Theft Act. In *Attorney-General for Hong Kong v Chan Nai-Keung* (1987) an export quota for textiles was intangible property which could be stolen. A patent is also intangible property which can be stolen.

However, there are some types of intangible property which have been held not to be property within the Theft Act definition. In *Oxford v Moss* (1979) knowledge of the questions on an examination paper was held not to be property.

OXFORD v MOSS (1979)
D was a university student who acquired a proof of an examination paper he was due to sit. It was accepted that D did not intend to permanently deprive the university of the piece of paper on which the questions were printed. But he was charged with theft of confidential information (ie the knowledge of the questions). He was found not guilty.

11.2.4 Things which cannot be stolen

There are some things which cannot be stolen. These are set out in s 4(3) and s 4(4) of the Theft Act 1968. The first of these concerns plants and fungi growing wild.

'*A person who picks mushrooms growing wild on any land, or who picks flowers, fruit or foliage from a plant growing wild on any land, does not (although not in possession of the land) steal what he picks, unless he does it for reward or sale or other commercial purpose.*

For the purposes of this subsection "mushroom" includes any fungus, and "plant" includes any shrub or tree.'

This only applies to plants etc growing wild, so it is possible to steal cultivated plants. Taking apples from trees in a farmer's orchard would be theft, but picking blackberries growing wild in the hedgerow around the field would not be theft unless it was done for sale or reward or other commercial purpose. Similarly, picking roses from someone's garden would be theft, but picking wild flowers in a field would not (unless for sale or reward). Though it should be noted that it is an offence to pick, uproot or destroy certain wild plants under the Wildlife and Countryside Act 1981.

Where picking fungi, flowers, fruit or foliage is done with the intention of selling them or for reward or any commercial purpose then they are considered property which can be stolen. An example of this is picking holly to sell at Christmas time.

The other exception of personal property which is not 'property' for the purpose of theft concerns wild creatures. Section 4(4) states:

'Wild creatures, tamed or untamed, shall be regarded as property; but a person cannot steal a wild creature not tamed nor ordinarily kept in captivity, or the carcase of any such creature, unless it has been reduced into possession by or on behalf of another person and possession of it has not since been lost or abandoned, or another person is in course of reducing it into possession.'

The effect of this subsection is that it is not theft if a wild creature such as a deer is taken from the grounds of a large estate (though there is an offence of poaching) but it is theft if a deer is taken from a zoo, as in this case it is ordinarily kept in captivity.

Electricity

Electricity is another sort of intangible property which cannot be stolen, but there is a separate offence under s 11 of the Theft Act 1968 of dishonestly using electricity without due authority, or dishonestly causing it to be wasted or diverted.

Activity

Explain whether the items in each of the following situations would be property for the purposes of theft.

1 Arnie runs a market stall selling flowers. Just before Christmas, he picks a lot of holly from a wood, intending to sell it on his stall. He then digs up a small fir tree for his own use. On his way home, he sees some late flowering roses in a garden and picks them to give to his girlfriend.

2 Della finds the examination papers she is to sit next week in the next-door office. She writes out the questions from the first paper on to a note pad of her own. The second paper is very long, so she uses the office photocopier to take a copy, using paper already in the machine.

11.3   BELONGING TO ANOTHER

In order for there to be a theft of the property, that property must 'belong to another'. However, s 5(1) of the Theft Act 1968 gives a very wide definition of what is meant by 'belonging to another'.

'Property shall be regarded as belonging to any person having possession or control of it, or having in it any proprietary right or interest (not being an equitable interest arising only from an agreement to transfer or grant an interest).'

From this it can be seen that possession or control of the property or any proprietary interest in it is sufficient. One reason for making it wide is so that the prosecution does not have to prove who is the legal owner.

11.3.1 Possession or control

Obviously, the owner of property normally has possession and control of it, but there are many other situations in which a person can have either possession or control of property. Someone who hires a car has both possession and control during the period of hire. If the car is stolen during this time then the thief can be charged with stealing it from the hirer. Equally, as the car hire firm still own the car (a proprietary right), the thief could be charged with stealing it from them.

The possession or control of the item does not have to be lawful. Where B has stolen jewellery from A and subsequently C steals it from B, B is in possession or control of that jewellery and C can be charged with stealing it from B. This is useful where it is not known who the original owner is, as C can still be guilty of theft. This wide definition of 'belonging to' has led to the situation in which an owner was convicted of stealing his own car.

> ### TURNER (NO. 2) (1971)
> D left his car at a garage for repairs. It was agreed that he would pay for the repairs when he collected the car after the repairs had been completed. When the repairs were almost finished the garage left the car parked on the roadway outside their premises. D used a spare key to take the car during the night without paying for the repairs. The Court of Appeal held that the garage was in possession or control of the car and so D could be guilty of stealing his own car.

It is possible for someone to be in possession or control of property even though they do not know it is there. This happened in *Woodman* (1974).

> ### WOODMAN (1974)
> A company, English China Clays, had sold all the scrap metal on its site to another company which arranged for it to be removed. Unknown to English China Clays, a small amount had been left on the site. There was no doubt that they were in control of the site itself as they had put a barbed wire fence round it and had notices warning trespassers to keep out. D took the remaining scrap metal. He was convicted of theft and the Court of Appeal upheld the conviction.

Section 5 goes on to make it clear that in certain situations a defendant can be guilty of theft even though the property may not 'belong to another'. These are situations in which the defendant is acting dishonestly and has caused a loss to another or has made a gain. These are:

- trust property, where a trustee can steal it
- property received under an obligation
- property received by another's mistake.

11.3.2 Property received under an obligation

There are many situations in which property (usually money) is handed over to D on the basis that D will keep it for the owner or will deal with it in a particular way. Subsection 5(3) of the Theft Act 1968 tries to make sure that such property is still considered as 'belonging to the other' for the purposes of the law of theft. It states:

'Where a person receives property from or on account of another, and is under an obligation to the other to retain and deal with that property or its proceeds in a particular way, the property shall be regarded (as against him) as belonging to the other.'

Under this subsection there must be an obligation to retain and deal with the property in a particular way. So, where money is paid as a deposit to a business, the prosecution must prove that there was an obligation to retain and deal with those deposits in a particular way. If the person paying the deposit only expects it to be paid into a bank account of the business, then if that is what happens there cannot be theft, even if all the money from the account is used for other business expenses and the client does not get the goods or service for which he paid the deposit. This is what happened in *Hall* (1972).

HALL (1972)
D was a travel agent who received deposits from clients for air trips to America. D paid these deposits into the firm's general account but never organised any tickets and was unable to return the money. He was convicted of theft but on appeal his conviction was quashed because when D received the deposits he was not under an obligation to deal with it in a particular way. The Court of Appeal stressed that each case depended on its facts.

In *Klineberg and Marsden* (1999) there was a clear obligation to deal with deposits in a particular way.

KLINEBERG and MARSDEN (1999)
The two defendants operated a company which sold timeshare apartments in Lanzarote to customers in England. Each purchaser paid the purchase price on the understanding that the money would be held by an independent trust company until the apartment was ready for the purchase to occupy. Over £500,000 was paid to the defendants' company but only £233 was actually paid into the trust company's account. The defendants were guilty of theft as it was clear that they were under an obligation to the

---

purchasers 'to retain and deal with that property or its proceeds in a particular way' and that they had not done this.

There can be an obligation in less formal situations In *Davidge v Bunnett* (1984) it was held that D was guilty of theft when she was given money by her flatmates to pay the gas bill but instead used it to buy Christmas presents. There was a legal obligation in this situation as there was an intention to create legal relations under contract law. It is not clear whether there would be a legal obligation (and so theft) if the situation happened between members of the same family or whether this would be a domestic arrangement without the intention to create legal relations.

11.3.3 Property got by a mistake

Section 5 also provides for situations where property has been handed over to D by another's mistake and so has become D's property. If there were no special provision in the Act then this could not be 'property belonging to another' for the purposes of the law of theft. The section states, in s 5(4):

'Where a person gets property by another's mistake, and is under an obligation to make restoration (in whole or in part) of the property or its proceeds or of the value thereof, then to the extent of that obligation the property or proceeds shall be regarded (as against him) as belonging to the person entitled to restoration, and an intention not to make restoration shall be regarded accordingly as an intention to deprive that person of the property or proceeds.'

This section was considered in *Attorney-General's Reference (No. 1 of 1983)* (1985).

ATTORNEY-GENERAL'S REFERENCE (NO. 1 OF 1983) (1985)

D's salary was paid into her bank account by transfer. On one occasion her employers mistakenly overpaid her by £74.74. She was acquitted but the prosecution asked the Court of Appeal to rule on whether a person in this situation who dishonestly decided not to repay the £74.74 would be guilty of theft. The Court of Appeal held that s 5(4) clearly provided for exactly this type of situation. The defendant was under an 'obligation to make restoration' and if there was a dishonest intention not to make restoration then all the elements of theft were present.

There must be a legal obligation to restore the property. In *Gilks* (1972) the defendant had placed a bet on a horse race. The bookmaker made a mistake about which horse D had backed and overpaid D on the bets he had placed. D realised the error and decided not to return the money. The ownership of the money had passed to D, so the only way he could be guilty of theft was if s 5(4) applied. It was held that as betting transactions are not enforceable at law s 5(4) did not apply and D was not guilty.

11.4 DISHONESTLY S2 MR

The first point which needs to be proved for the *mens rea* of theft is that when the defendant appropriated the property he did it dishonestly. There is no definition of what is meant by this in the Act but s 1(1) states that it is immaterial whether the appropriation is made with a view to gain, or is made for the thief's own benefit. In other words, if all the elements of theft are present, the motive of the defendant is not relevant.

This means that a modern-day Robin Hood stealing to give to the poor could be guilty of theft. The defendant does not have to gain anything from the theft.

11.4.1 Behaviour which is not dishonest

The 1968 Theft Act does not define dishonesty, though it does give three situations in which D's behaviour is not considered dishonest. These are in s 2 of the 1968 Act which provides that a person's appropriation of property belonging to another is not to be regarded as dishonest if he appropriates the property in the belief that:

- he has in law the right to deprive the other of it, on behalf of himself or of a third person or
- he would have the other's consent if the other knew of the appropriation and the circumstances of it or
- the person to whom the property belongs cannot be discovered by taking reasonable steps.

All these three situations depend on D's belief. It does not matter whether it is a correct belief or even whether it is reasonable belief. If D has a genuine belief in one of these three then he is not guilty of theft.

11.4.2 Willing to pay

In some situations D may say that he is willing to pay for the property or may, on taking property, leave money to pay for it. This does not prevent D's conduct from being dishonest as s 2(2) states that 'a person's appropriation of property belonging to another may be dishonest notwithstanding that he is willing to pay for the property'.

At first this may seem severe, but it prevents D taking what he likes, regardless of the owner's wishes. For example, D likes a painting which is hanging in a friend's home. He asks the friend how much it is worth and is told that it is only a copy, worth less than £100, but it was painted by the friend's grandmother and is of sentimental value. A few days later D takes the painting without the friend's consent but leaves £200 in cash to pay for it. D's taking of the painting may be considered dishonest even though he left more than the cash value of it.

11.4.3 The *Ghosh* test

The case of *Ghosh* (1982) is the leading case on what is meant by dishonesty. In this case the Court of Appeal set out the tests to be used.

> **GHOSH (1982)**
> Ghosh was a doctor acting as a locum consultant in a hospital. He claimed fees for an operation he had not carried out. He said that he was not dishonest as he was owed the same amount for consultation fees. The trial judge directed the jury that they must apply their own standards to decide if what he did was dishonest. He was convicted and appealed against the conviction.
>
> The Court of Appeal decided that the test for dishonesty has both an objective and a subjective element to it. These are:
>
> ■ was what was done dishonest according to the ordinary standards of reasonable and honest people?
> ■ did the defendant realise that what he was doing was dishonest by those standards?

The *Ghosh* test means that the jury have to start with an objective test. Was what was done was dishonest by the ordinary standards of reasonable and honest people? If it was not dishonest by those standards, that is the end of the matter and the prosecution fails. The defendant is not guilty. However, if the jury decide that it was dishonest by those standards then they must consider the more subjective test of whether the defendant knew it was dishonest by those standards.

This second test is not totally subjective as the defendant is judged by what he realised ordinary standards were. This prevents a

defendant from saying that, although he knew that ordinary people would regard his actions as dishonest, he did not think that those standards applied to him.

In a trial the judge will use the *Ghosh* test to direct the jury only where there is an issue about dishonesty.

11.5 INTENTION OF PERMANENTLY DEPRIVING

The final element which has to be proved for theft is that the defendant had the intention permanently to deprive the other of the property. In many situations there is no doubt that the defendant had such an intention. For example, where an item is taken and sold to another person or where cash is taken and spent by the defendant. This last example is true even if the defendant intends to replace the money later, as was shown in *Velumyl* (1989).

> **VELUMYL (1989)**
> D, a company manager, took £1,050 from the office safe. He said that he was owed money by a friend and he was going to replace the money when that friend repaid him. The Court of Appeal upheld his conviction for theft as he had the intention of permanently depriving the company of the banknotes which he had taken from the safe, even if he intended replacing them with other banknotes to the same value later.

Another situation where there is a clear intention permanently to deprive is where the defendant destroys property belonging to another. This can be charged as theft, although it is also criminal damage.

There are, however, situations where it is not so clear and, to help in these, s 6 of the Theft Act 1968 explains and expands the meaning of the phrase. It provides that, even though a person appropriating property belonging to another does not mean the other permanently to lose the thing itself, he can be regarded as having the intention permanently to deprive the other of it if his intention is to treat the thing as his own to dispose of, regardless of the other's rights.

The Court of Appeal has stated that the meaning of 'dispose of' should be that given by the *Shorter Oxford Dictionary*. This is: 'To deal with definitely: to get rid of; to get done with, finish. To make over by way of sale or bargain or sell.'

However, in *DPP v Lavender* (1994) the Divisional Court ruled that the dictionary definition of 'dispose of' was too narrow as a disposal could include 'dealing with' property.

> **DPP v LAVENDER (1994)**
> D took doors from a council property which was being repaired and used them to replace damaged doors in his girlfriend's council flat. The doors were still in the possession of the council but had been transferred without permission from one council property to another. The Divisional Court held that the question was whether he intended to treat the doors as his own, regardless of the rights of the council. The answer to this was yes, so the defendant was guilty of theft.

11.5.1 Borrowing or lending

Another difficulty with s 6 is the point at which 'borrowing or lending' comes within the definition. Normally borrowing would not be an intention to permanently deprive. Take the situation of a student taking a textbook from a fellow student's bag in order to read one small section and then replace the book. This is clearly outside the scope of s 6 and cannot be considered as an intention permanently to deprive. But what if that student also took a photocopying card, which had a limit placed on its use, used it, then returned it? The photocopy card has been returned but it is no longer as valuable as it was. So is there an intention permanently to deprive so far as the card is concerned?

Section 6 states that borrowing is not theft unless it is for a period and in circumstances making it equivalent to an outright taking or disposal. In *Lloyd* (1985) it was held that this meant borrowing the property and keeping it until 'the goodness, the virtue, the practical value . . . has gone out of the article'.

> **LLOYD (1985)**
> The projectionist at a local cinema gave D a film that was showing at the cinema so that D could make an illegal copy. D returned the film in time for the next screening at the cinema. His conviction for theft was quashed because, by returning the film in its original state, it was not possible to prove an intention permanently to deprive.

From this it appears that, in the example of the photocopy card, there would be an intention permanently to deprive if all the value of the card had been used up, but if it still had value then there is no intention permanently to deprive.

Another difficulty is where the defendant picks up property to see if there is anything worth stealing. What is the position if he decides it is not worth stealing and returns it? This is what happened in *Easom* (1971). The defendant picked up a handbag in a cinema, rummaged through the contents and then replaced the handbag without having taken anything. His conviction for theft of the handbag and its contents was quashed. There was no evidence that the defendant had intended permanently to deprive the owner of the bag or items in it so he could not be guilty of theft. (See section 6.3.2 on the point of whether a defendant in this situation can be guilty of attempted theft.)

Figure 11.1 Key facts chart on theft

Section of Theft Act 1968	Definition	Comment/Case
s 1	A person is guilty of theft if he dishonestly appropriates property belonging to another with the intention of permanently depriving the other of it.	Full definition of 'theft'. D is charged under this section.
s 2	**Dishonesty** (1) Not dishonest if believes: ■ has right in law ■ would have the other's consent ■ owner cannot be discovered. (2) Can be dishonest even if intends paying for property.	No definition of 'dishonesty' in the Act. *Ghosh* (1982): two-part test: ■ is it dishonest by ordinary standards? ■ if so, did D know it was dishonest by those standards?
s 3	**Appropriation** (1) 'any assumption of the rights of an owner' Includes a later assumption of rights	Held to be assumption of *any* of the rights of an owner: *Gomez* (1993) Given 'neutral' meaning, so consent irrelevant: *Lawrence* (1971), *Hinks* (2000)
s 4	**Property** Includes money and all other property real or personal, including things in action and other intangible property. Land cannot be stolen except by trustee or tenant or by severing property from land. Wild mushrooms, fruit, flowers and foliage cannot be stolen unless done for commercial purpose. Wild animals cannot be stolen unless tamed or in captivity.	
s 5	**Belonging to another** Property is regarded as belonging to any person having possession or control or any proprietary right.	Not limited to owner: *Turner (No. 2)* (1972) stole own car.

KEY FACTS

Property belongs to the other where it is received under an obligation to retain and deal with it in a particular way.	Must be a particular way: *Hall* (1972), *Klineberg and Marsden* (1999).
Property received by a mistake where there is a legal obligation to make restoration belongs to the other.	*A-G's Reference (No. 1 of 1983)* (1985). Must be a legal obligation: *Gilks* (1972)

s 6	**Intention permanently to deprive**
Treat the thing as his own to dispose of regardless of the other's rights.	The 'goodness' or practical value must have gone from the property: *Lloyd* (1985).
Dispose of includes 'dealing with' property.	*DPP v Lavender* (1994).

Activity

In each of the following situations, explain whether all the elements of theft are present.

1 Roland works in a small factory where there are only 20 employees. One day he finds a small purse in the washroom. He opens it. It contains a £10 note and some coins. There is no name or other identification in it. Roland decides to keep the money as he does not think he can find the owner.

2 Venus comes from a country where property placed outside a shop is meant for people to take free of charge. She sees a rack of clothes on the pavement outside a shop and takes a pair of jeans from it.

3 Natalie is given a Christmas cash bonus in a sealed envelope. She has been told by her boss that the bonus would be £50. When she gets home and opens the envelope she finds there is £60 in it. She thinks her employer decided to be more generous and so keeps the money. Would your answer be different if:

 a Natalie realised there had been a mistake but did not return the money or

 b the amount in the envelope was £200?

4 Errol is given permission by his employer to borrow some decorative lights for use at a party. Errol also takes some candles without asking permission. When putting up the lights Errol smashes one of them. He lights two of the candles so that by the end of the evening they are partly burnt down. One of the guests admires the remaining lights and asks if he can have them to use at a disco at the weekend. Errol agrees to let him take the lights.

5 Arnie is late for work one day so he takes his neighbour's bicycle to get to work on time. His neighbour is away, but Arnie has used the bicycle on previous occasions. He intends returning it that evening when he comes home from work. Arnie parks the bicycle at the back of the shop where he works. When he leaves work in the evening he finds that the lamp and the pump have been taken from the bicycle and it has been damaged. He is frightened to return the bicycle in this state so he throws it into the local canal.

11.6 PROBLEMS IN THE LAW OF THEFT

When the Theft Act 1968 was passed the definition of 'theft' was meant to be in simple everyday language that ordinary people could understand. However, there have been some case decisions on the elements of theft which make it more difficult to understand the law. The main problems with each element are discussed below.

11.6.1 Appropriation

The decision in *Gomez* (1993) (see section 11.1.1) that there could be appropriation even though the owner consented to the appropriation has meant that virtually all cases of obtaining property by deception under s 15 of the Theft Act 1968 could be charged as theft. This overlap makes the law on theft more complex, although at least in *Gomez* the consent was only given because the defendant falsely told the manager that the cheques were as good as cash. The manager would not have consented to the taking of the goods if he had known the truth.

The problem has become even greater since the House of Lords in *Hinks* (2000) (see section 11.1.2) ruled that even where the consent to the appropriation was genuine, the appropriation could still amount to theft. As the items were gifts to the defendant, it is very difficult to see what the defendant did as appropriation.

Lord Hobhouse, one of the judges in the case, stated that in his opinion there was no appropriation. This was because the civil law on gifts involves conduct by the owner who transfers the ownership of the gift to donee (the person receiving the gift). Once this is done the gift is the property of the donee. The donee does not have to do anything for the gift to become their property. It is not even necessary that the donee should know of the gift. For example, money could be transferred to the donee's bank account without the donee's knowledge. In view of this Lord Hobhouse thought that it was impossible to say that there was any appropriation by the defendant.

Remember that appropriation on its own is not enough for theft. All the other elements of theft must be present; in particular there must be dishonesty. There are many situation where there is appropriation but there is no dishonesty so that there cannot be theft. For example, all honest shoppers who place items in a basket or trolley provided by the store are appropriating the items, but because they intend to pay for them, they are not dishonest and so there is no offence of theft.

11.6.2 Property belonging to another

The word 'property' has not caused any real problems. The definition in the Act is so very wide. It includes almost everything. The Act itself sets out detailed rules on when land, animals and plants can or cannot be stolen. The decision in *Oxford v Moss* (1979), where information on examination questions was obtained, that knowledge cannot be stolen does not normally cause any problems as most instances are covered by other offences such as copyright laws.

'Belonging to another'

The Act states that 'belonging to another' includes situations where property is in the possession or control of another, or where another person had any proprietary right or interest in the property. This wide definition of 'belonging to another' is needed since in many cases it might be difficult for the prosecution to prove that the victim was the legal owner. However, this phrase has caused some surprising decisions, in particular the decision in *Turner (No. 2)* (1971).

In this case the owner of a car took it from a

garage without paying for repairs. The garage clearly had a lien (a legal right to retain the car until payment was made) and it could have been held that this gave the garage control of the car. However the judge at the trial had directed the jury to ignore any question of a lien. On appeal to the Court of Appeal the judges simply based their decision to uphold the conviction on the fact that the garage had possession and control. In fact, if the question of lien is ignored, the garage were legally bailees of the car and under the law of bailment Turner had the right to end the bailment at any time and take the car back.

11.6.3 Dishonesty

There are criticisms of the *Ghosh* test (1982) for dishonesty. The main criticism is that it leaves too much to the jury, so that there is a risk of inconsistent decisions with different juries coming to different decisions in similar situations. It has been argued that it would be better for the judge to rule on whether there was dishonesty as a point of law rather than leave it as a matter of fact for the jury. However, this overlooks that fact that the jury still need to decide whether they believe what the defendant says.

Another criticism of the test is that it places too much emphasis on objective views of what is dishonest rather than the defendant's intentions. The first stage of the test requires the jury to consider whether what was done was dishonest according to the ordinary standards of reasonable and honest people. This has the odd effect that if the jury think it is not dishonest, then the defendant will be found not guilty even though he may have thought he was being (and intended to be) dishonest.

Whether the defendant is being dishonest has become much more important in view of the ruling in *Hinks* (2000) that 'appropriation' is a neutral word. This means that whether a theft has occurred or not is dependent on whether the appropriation was dishonest. The whole of the illegality of the act is based on the *mens rea* of the defendant.

11.6.4 Intention permanently to deprive

The first point that can be made on this part of the definition of theft is whether it is necessary to include it as part of the law of theft. If someone dishonestly takes property belonging to another does it matter whether they intend permanently to deprive that person of the property? This would make it possible to convict of theft in situations such as *Lloyd* (1985) where a film was copied and then returned. On the present law *Lloyd* was not guilty, yet he had appropriated property belonging to another, was being dishonest as the only reason for the appropriation was to take an illegal copy. He temporarily deprived the other of the property. Abolishing the need for an intention *permanently* to deprive would include this behaviour within the law of theft.

It is because of this need to prove an intention permanently to deprive another of property that the Theft Act 1968 includes a separate offence of taking vehicles without consent. It is recognised that in many cases where a car or other vehicle is taken there is no intention permanently to deprive. The taker merely wants to drive the vehicle, but will then abandon it, often not far from where it was originally parked.

The other problem is what can be called 'conditional' intention to deprive. This is where the defendant picks property to see if is worth stealing. If he then decides it is not worth stealing and returns it there is no theft. This happened in *Easom* (1971) where the defendant picked up a handbag looked in it, could not find anything worth stealing and put the bag back. *Easom* was not guilty of theft because a conditional intention to deprive is not enough to convict the defendant of theft. Again, if in the definition of theft, the word 'permanent' were replaced with the word 'temporary' defendants behaving in this way could be convicted.

This would also bring the law into line with the law on burglary where the courts have ruled that a conditional intention to steal anything worth stealing in the building which the defendant is entering is sufficient for the defendant to be guilty of burglary under s 9(1)(a) of the Theft Act 1968.

Activity

Read the following extract adapted from an article in *The Kent and Sussex Courier*, 9th January 2004, and answer the question below.

£2,000 STOLEN IN CASH SCAM

A commuter became the latest victim of a cashpoint scam when she had nearly £2,000 stolen from her bank account after using a Paddock Wood cash machine on her way to work on December 19.

When she checked her balance on the internet on December 27 she found that the money, which included her entire December salary, was missing from her account.

She said: 'I was shocked. I thought, "I could have sworn I had been paid," then I saw withdrawals of £150, £200 and £250 two or three times a day.

'It didn't say the location of the banks but different ones had been used including Barclays, Alliance and Leicester, NatWest and HSBC.'

She is not Paddock Wood's only victim of card 'skimming', where a removable scanner is placed in the machine to copy the card details.

As reported last week a 50-year-old man from the town had money stolen from his account between December 19 and December 22 after using the NatWest machine.

Question

The article states that the money has been stolen from the victim's account. Define 'theft' and explain the different elements of theft in relation to this situation.

Examination questions

1 The *actus reus* of theft as defined in the Theft Act 1968 is 'appropriating property belonging to another'.

Discuss the difficulties that the courts have encountered in interpreting and applying these words.

(OCR, Unit 2572, June 2002)

2 Graham goes to his favourite corner store. In the shop he places some items of food in the wire shopping basket that is provided for shoppers. He also hides a small bottle of whisky in his coat pocket. He then takes a label from the case of a high priced CD that is in the charts and switches it with the label from a specially reduced CD on the shelf below and places it in the basket. He then goes to the checkout and only pays for the items in the basket.

Outside the shop, Graham see a mountain bike that was there when he went in and which he also remembers seeing there at the same time the previous week. He rides home on it alongside a canal. On the way, he notices a personal CD player on a table on board a canal longboat that is moored to the towpath. He climbs aboard and takes the CD player. He leaves the bike leaning against a fence at the end of his road and goes home.

Discuss Graham's criminal liability.

(OCR, Unit 2572, June 2003)

CHAPTER 12 | Robbery and burglary

12.1 ROBBERY

Robbery is an offence under s 8 of the Theft Act 1968. In effect it is a theft which is aggravated by the use or threat of force. Section 8 states:

'A person is guilty of robbery if he steals, and immediately before or at the time of doing so, and in order to do so, he uses force on any person or puts or seeks to put any person in fear of being then and there subjected to force.'

So the elements which must be proved for robbery are for the *actus reus*:

- theft AR
- force or putting or seeking to put any person in fear of force. hc

In addition, there are two conditions on the force and these are that it must be immediately before or at the time of the theft and it must be in order to steal.

For the *mens rea* of robbery it must be proved that the defendant:

- had the *mens rea* for theft and
- intended to use force to steal.

12.1.1 Completed theft

There must be a completed theft for a robbery to have been committed. This means that all the elements of theft have to be present. If any one of them is missing then, just as there would be no theft, there is no robbery. For example, there is no theft in the situation where D takes a car, drives it a mile and abandons it, because D has no intention permanently to deprive. Equally there is no robbery where D uses force to take that car.

There is no offence of theft, so using force cannot make it into robbery.

The case of *Robinson* (1977) demonstrates that if the elements of theft are not complete then there cannot be robbery.

ROBINSON (1977)
D ran a clothing club and was owed £7 by V's wife. D approached V and threatened him. During a struggle the man dropped a £5 note and D took it, claiming he was still owed £2. D's conviction for robbery was quashed because the trial judge had wrongly directed the jury that D had honestly to believe he was entitled to get the money in that way. In fact If D had a genuine belief that he had a right in law to the money, then his actions were not dishonest under s 2(1)(a) of the Theft Act 1968.

Where force is used to steal, then the moment the theft is complete there is a robbery. This is demonstrated by the case of *Corcoran v Anderton* (1980).

CORCORAN v ANDERTON (1980)
One of the defendants hit a woman in the back and tugged at her bag. She let go of the bag and it fell to the ground. The defendants ran off without the bag (because the woman was screaming and attracting attention). It was held that the theft was complete so the defendants were guilty of robbery.

However, if the theft is not completed, for instance if the woman in the case of *Corcoran v Anderton* had not let go of the bag, then there is an attempted theft and the defendant could be charged with attempted robbery.

12.1.2 Force or threat of force

As well as theft the prosecution must prove force or the threat of force. The amount of force can be small. This is clearly shown by the case of *Dawson and James* (1976).

DAWSON and JAMES (1976)
One of the defendants pushed the victim causing him to lose his balance which enabled the other defendant to take his wallet. They were convicted of robbery. The Court of Appeal held that 'force' was an ordinary word and it was for the jury to decide if there had been force.

This decision was confirmed in *Clouden* (1987) where the Court of Appeal held that D was guilty of robbery when he had wrenched a shopping basket from the victim's hand. The Court of Appeal held that the trial judge was right to leave the question of whether D had used force on a person to the jury.

It can be argued that using force on the bag was effectively using force on the victim as the bag was wrenched from her hand. However, if a thief pulls a shoulder bag so that it slides off the victim's shoulder, would this be considered force? Probably not. And it would certainly not be force if a thief snatched a bag which was resting (not being held) on the lap of someone sitting on a park bench.

The definition of 'robbery' makes clear that robbery is committed if D puts or seeks to put a person in fear of force. It is not necessary that the force be applied. Putting V 'in fear being there and then subjected to force' is sufficient for robbery. This covers threatening words, such as 'I have a knife and I'll use it unless you give me your wallet', and threatening gestures, such as holding a knife in front of V.

Robbery is also committed even if the victim is not actually frightened by D's actions or words. If D seeks to put V in fear of being then and there subjected to force, this element of robbery is present. So if V is a plain clothes policeman put there to trap D and is not frightened, the fact that D sought to put V in fear is enough.

On any person

This means that the person threatened does not have to be the person from whom the theft occurs. An obvious example is an armed robber who enters a bank, seizes a customer and threatens to shoot that customer unless a bank official gets money out of the safe. This is putting a person in fear of being then and there subjected to force. The fact that it is not the customer's property which is being stolen does not matter.

12.1.3 Force immediately before or at the time of the theft

The force must be immediately before or at the time of stealing. This raises two problems. First, how immediate does 'immediately before' have to be? What about the situation where a bank official is attacked at his home by a gang in order to get keys and security codes from him? The gang then drive to the bank and steal money. The theft has taken place an hour after the use of force. Is this 'immediately before'? It would seem sense that the gang should be convicted of robbery. But what if the time delay were longer, as could happen if the attack on the manager was on Saturday evening and the theft of the money not until 24 hours later? Does this still come within 'immediately before'? There have been no decided cases on this point.

The second problem has come in deciding the point at which a theft is completed, so that the force is not 'at the time of stealing'. This was considered in *Hale* (1979).

> ### HALE (1979)
>
> The two defendants knocked on the door of a house. When a woman opened the door they forced their way into the house. One defendant put his hand over her mouth to stop her screaming while the other defendant went upstairs to see what he could find to take. He took a jewellery box. Before they left the house they tied up the householder.
>
> On appeal the defendants argued that the theft was complete as soon as the second defendant picked up the jewellery box, so the use of force in tying up the householder was not at the time of stealing. However, the Court of Appeal upheld their convictions. The Court of Appeal thought that the jury could have come to the decision that there was force immediately before the theft when one of the defendants put his hand over the householder's mouth. In addition, the Court of Appeal thought that the tying up of the householder could also be force for the purpose of robbery as they held the theft was still ongoing.

The decision in *Hale* was followed in *Lockley* (1995). In this case the defendant was caught shoplifting cans of beer from an off-licence. He used force on the shopkeeper who tried to stop him from escaping. Lockley appealed on the basis that the theft was complete when he used the force, but the Court of Appeal followed the decision in *Hale* and held that he was guilty.

But there must be a point when the theft is complete and so any force used after this point does not make it robbery. What if in *Lockley* the defendant had left the shop and was running down the road when a passer-by (alerted by the shouts of the shopkeeper) tried to stop him? The defendant then uses force on the passer-by to escape. Surely the theft is completed before this use of force? The force used is a separate act to the theft and does not make the theft a robbery. The force will, of course, be a separate offence of assault.

12.1.4 Force in order to steal

The force must be used in order to steal. So if the force was not used for this purpose, then any later theft will not make it into robbery. Take the situation where D has an argument with V and punches him, knocking him out. D then sees that some money has fallen out of V's pocket and decides to take it. The force was not used for the purpose of that theft and D is not guilty of robbery, but guilty of two separate offences: an assault and theft.

12.1.5 *Mens rea* for robbery

D must have the *mens rea* for theft, that is, he must be dishonest and he must intend permanently to deprive the other of the property. He must also intend to use force to steal.

> ## Activity
>
> Read the following extract from an article in *Sevenoaks Chronicle* on 15th January 2004 and answer the questions below.
>
> ### ARMED RAID AT OFF-LICENCE
>
> An armed raider burst into a village off-licence and demanded cash.
>
> The man entered Unwins in The Square, Riverhead at about 6.30 pm on Sunday, and produced what appeared to be a pistol.
>
> He threatened staff with the weapon and demanded money, which the employees handed over from the till.
>
> The raider then fled on foot along London Road, towards Dunton Green.
>
> None of the staff, who have not been identified, were hurt in the attack.

The incident comes less than six months after two men used knives to intimidate employees into giving them cash and cigarettes at the store.'

Questions

1 Identify the offence which was committed at the off-licence.
2 Explain what is required for the *actus reus* of that offence and identify the acts which form the *actus reus* in this particular raid.
3 Explain what has to be proved for the *mens rea* of the offence.

Activity

Explain whether or not a robbery has occurred in each of the following situations.

1 Albert holds a knife to the throat of a three-year-old girl and orders the child's mother to hand over her purse or he will 'slit the child's throat'. The mother hands over her purse.

2 Brendan threatens staff in a post office with an imitation gun. He demands that they hand over the money in the till. One of the staff presses a security button and a grille comes down in front of the counter so that

---

Figure 12.1 Key facts chart on robbery

KEY FACTS

Element	Law	Case
Theft	There must be a completed theft if any element is missing there is no theft and therefore no robbery.	*Robinson* (1977)
	The moment the theft is completed (with the relevant force) there is robbery.	*Corcoran v Anderton* (1980)
Force or threat of force	The jury decide whether the acts were force, using the ordinary meaning of the word.	*Dawson and James* (1976)
	It includes wrenching a bag from V's hand.	*Clouden* (1987)
On any person	The force can be against *any* person. It does not have to be against the victim of the theft.	
Immediately before or at the time of the theft	For robbery, theft has been held to be a continuing act.	*Hale* (1979)
	Using force to escape can still be at the time of the theft.	*Lockley* (1995)
In order to steal	The force must be in order to steal. Force used for another purpose does not become robbery if D later decides to steal.	
Mens rea	*Mens rea* for theft plus an intention to use force to steal.	

the staff are safe and Brendan cannot reach the till. He leaves without taking anything.

3 Carla snatches a handbag from Delia. Delia is so surprised that she leaves go of the bag and Carla runs off with it.

4 Ellie breaks into a car in a car park and takes a briefcase out of it. As she is walking away from the car, the owner arrives, realises what has happened and starts to chase after Ellie. The owner catches hold of Ellie, but Ellie pushes him over and makes her escape.

5 Freya tells Harmid to hand over his Rolex watch and, that if he does not, Freya will send her boyfriend, Grant, round to beat Harmid up. Harmid knows that Grant is a very violent man. Harmid takes his watch off and gives it to Freya.

12.2 BURGLARY

This is an offence under s 9 of the Theft Act 1968. Section 9 provides two different ways in which burglary can be committed. Under s 9(1)(a) person is guilty of burglary if he enters any building or part of a building as a trespasser with intent to steal, inflict grievous bodily harm, or do unlawful damage to the building or anything in it.

Under s 9(1)(b) a person is guilty of burglary if, having entered a building or part of a building as a trespasser, he steals or attempts to steal anything in the building or inflicts or attempts to inflict grievous bodily harm on any person in the building.

Figure 12.2 shows these different ways of committing burglary.

Although sub-ss 9(1)(a) and 9(1)(b) create different ways of committing burglary, they do have common elements. These are that there must be:

■ entry
■ of a building or part of a building
■ as a trespasser.

The difference between the subsections is the intention at the time of entry. For s 9(1)(a) the defendant must intend to do one of the four listed offences (known as ulterior offences) at the time of entering. However, there is no need for the ulterior offence to take place or even be attempted. For s 9(1)(b) what the defendant intends on entry is irrelevant, but the prosecution must prove that he actually committed or attempted to commit theft or grievous bodily harm.

12.2.1 Entry

'Entry' is not defined in the Theft Act 1968, but there have been several cases on the meaning of the word. The first main case on

Figure 12.2 Different ways of committing burglary

| Burglary | |
s 9(1)(a)	s 9(1)(b)
Enters a building or part of a building as a trespasser.	Having entered a building or part of a building as a trespasser.
With intent to: ■ steal ■ inflict grievous bodily harm ■ do unlawful damage.	■ steals or attempts to steal or ■ inflicts or attempts to inflict grievous bodily harm.

this point was *Collins* (1972) (see section 12.2.3 for the facts of *Collins*). In this case the Court of Appeal said that the jury had to be satisfied that D had made 'an effective and substantial entry'.

However, in *Brown* (1985) this concept of 'an effective and substantial entry' was modified to 'effective entry'.

BROWN (1985)

D was standing on the ground outside but leaning in through a shop window rummaging through goods. His feet and lower part of his body were outside the shop, but the top part of his body and his arms were inside the shop. The Court of Appeal said that the word 'substantial' did not materially assist the definition of 'entry' and his conviction for burglary was upheld as clearly in this situation his entry was effective.

However, in another case, *Ryan* (1996), the need for an 'effective' entry does not appear to have been followed.

RYAN (1996)

In this case the defendant was trapped when trying to get through a window into a house at 2.30 am. His head and right arm were inside the house but the rest of his body was outside. The fire brigade had to be called to release him. This could scarcely be said to be an 'effective' entry. However, the Court of Appeal upheld his conviction for burglary, saying that there was evidence on which the jury could find that the defendant had entered.

12.2.2 Building or part of a building

The Theft Act 1968 gives an extended meaning to the word 'building' so that it includes inhabited places such as houseboats or caravans, which would otherwise not be included in the offence. However, it does not give any basic definition for 'building'. Usually there is no problem. Clearly houses, blocks of flats, offices, factories and so on are buildings. The word also includes outbuildings and sheds.

The main problems for the courts have come where a structure such as a portacabin has been used for storage or office work. There are two cases on whether a large storage container is a building. In these cases the court came to different decisions after looking at the facts.

- In *B and S v Leathley* (1979) a 25-foot-long freezer container which had been in a farmyard for over two years was used as a storage facility. It rested on sleepers, had doors with locks and was connected to the electricity supply. This was held to be a building.
- In *Norfolk Constabulary v Seekings and Gould* (1986) a lorry trailer with wheels which had been used for over a year for storage had steps, provided access and was connected to the electricity supply was held not to be a building. The fact that it had wheels meant that it remained a vehicle.

Part of a building

The phrase 'part of building' is used to cover situations in which the defendant may have permission to be in one part of the building (and therefore is not a trespasser in that part) but does not have permission to be in another part.

A case example to demonstrate this is *Walkington* (1979).

WALKINGTON (1979)

D went into a counter area in a shop and opened a till. This area was clearly marked by a three-sided counter. D's conviction for burglary under s 9(1)(a) was upheld as he had entered part of a building (the counter area) as a trespasser with the intention of stealing.

The critical point in *Walkington* was that the counter area was not an area where customers were permitted to go. It was for the use of staff. So D was a trespasser.

Other examples include storerooms in shops where shoppers would not have permission to enter or a hall of residence where one student would be a trespasser if he entered another student's room without permission.

12.2.3 As a trespasser

In order for D to commit burglary he must enter as a trespasser. If a person has permission to enter they are not a trespasser. This was illustrated by the unusual case of *Collins* (1972). The facts of this case are set out below.

COLLINS (1972)
The defendant, having had quite a lot to drink, decided he wanted to have sexual intercourse. He saw an open window and climbed a ladder to look in. He saw there was a naked girl asleep in bed. He then went down the ladder, took off all his clothes except for his socks and climbed back up the ladder to the girl's bedroom. As he was on the window sill outside the room, she woke up, thought he was her boyfriend and helped him into the room where they had sex.

Collins was convicted of burglary under s 9(1)(a), ie that he had entered as a trespasser with intent to rape. (Note that before 2004 entering as a trespasser with intent to rape was also included under s 9(1)(a), but is now an offence under the Sexual Offences Act 2003. Also note that Collins could not be charged with rape as the girl agreed that she had consented to sex.) He appealed on the basis that that he was not a trespasser as he had been invited in. The Court of Appeal quashed his conviction because there was no evidence that he was a

---

trespasser; the girl had invited him into the room.

The court said that there could not be a conviction for entering premises 'as a trespasser' unless the person entering did so either knowing he was a trespasser or was reckless as to whether or not he was entering the premises of another without the other person's consent.

So, to succeed on a charge of burglary, the prosecution must prove that defendant knew he was trespassing or that the defendant was subjectively reckless as to whether he was trespassing.

Going beyond permission

Where the defendant is given permission to enter but then goes beyond that permission, he may be considered a trespasser. This was decided in *Smith and Jones* (1976).

SMITH and JONES (1976)
Smith and his friend, Jones, went to Smith's father's house in the middle of the night and took two television sets without the father's knowledge or permission. The father stated that his son would not be a trespasser in the house; he had a general permission to enter. The Court of Appeal upheld their convictions for burglary, ruling that:

'a person is a trespasser for the purpose of s 9(1)(b) of the Theft Act 1968 if he enters premises of another knowing that he is entering in excess of the permission that has been given to him to enter, or being reckless whether he is entering in excess of that permission'

This decision is in line with the Australian case of *Barker v R* (1983) where one person who was going away asked the defendant, who was a neighbour, to keep an eye on the house and told the defendant where a key was hidden should he need to enter. The defendant used the key to enter and steal property. He was found guilty of burglary.

There are many situations where a person has permission to enter for a limited purpose. For example, someone buys a ticket to attend a concert in a concert hall, or to look round a historic building or an art collection. The ticket is a licence (or permission) to be in the building for a very specific reason and/or time. If D buys a ticket intending to steal one of the paintings from the art collection these cases mean he is probably guilty of burglary.

Shoppers have permission to enter a shop. It is obvious that if a person has been banned from entering a shop they will be entering as a trespasser if they go into that shop. Such a person would be guilty of burglary if he entered intend to steal goods (s 9(1)(a)) or if, having entered, he then stole goods (s 9(1)(b)).

The case of *Smith and Jones* takes matters further than this as it means that any person who enters a shop intending to steal is going beyond the permission to enter the shop in order to buy goods. They will be guilty of burglary under s 9(1)(a). However, it is rare for anyone to be charged with this as, unless D admits he intended to steal when he entered, it is difficult for the prosecution to prove the intent.

The law is also clear where D gains entry through fraud, such as where he claims to be a gas meter reader. There is no genuine permission to enter and D is a trespasser.

12.2.4 Mental element of burglary

There are two parts to the mental element in burglary. These are in respect of:

■ entering as a trespasser and
■ the ulterior offence.

First, for both s 9(1)(a) and s 9(1)(b) the defendant must know, or be subjectively reckless, as to whether he is trespassing. In addition, for s 9(1)(a) the defendant must have the intention to commit one of the three offences at the time of entering the building. Where D is entering intending to steal anything he can find which is worth taking, then this is called a conditional intent. This is sufficient for D to be guilty under s 9(1)(a) even if there is nothing worth taking and he does not actually steal anything.

For s 9(1)(b) the defendant must also have the *mens rea* for theft or grievous bodily harm when committing (or attempting to commit) the *actus reus* of one of these offences.

Figure 12.3 Key facts chart on burglary

Elements	Commen	Case/section
Entry	This has changed from: ■ 'effective and substantial' entry to ■ 'effective' entry to ■ evidence for the jury to find D had entered.	*Collins* (1972) *Brown* (1985) *Ryan* (1996)
Building or part of a building	Must have some permanence.	*B and S v Leathley* (1979) *Norfolk Constabulary v Seekings and Gould* (1986)
	Includes inhabited vehicle or vessel.	s 9(4) Theft Act 1968

KEY FACTS

	Can be entry of part of a building.	*Walkington* (1979)
As a trespasser	If has permission is not a trespasser.	*Collins* (1972)
	If goes beyond permission then can be a trespasser.	*Smith and Jones* (1976)
Mens rea	Must know or be subjectively reckless as to whether he is a trespasser	
	PLUS EITHER	
	Intention at point of entry to commit: ■ theft or ■ grievous bodily harm or ■ criminal damage	s 9(1)(a) Theft Act 1968
	OR	
	Mens rea for theft or grievous bodily harm at point of committing or attempting to commit these offences in a building.	s 9(1)(b) Theft Act 1968

Activity

In each of the following, explain whether or not a burglary has occurred and, if so, whether it would be an offence under s 9(1)(a) or s 9(1)(b).

1 Jonny has been banned from a local pub. One evening he goes there for a drink with a friend. While he is waiting for the friend to get the drinks at the bar, Jonny sees a handbag under one of the chairs. He picks it up and takes a £10 note from it. He then puts the handbag back under the chair.

2 Ken and his partner, Lola, have split up and Ken has moved out of the flat he shared with Lola, taking most of his belongings with him. One evening he goes back there to collect the rest of his belongings. Lola is out and he asks the neighbour to let him have the spare key which the neighbour keeps for emergencies. While Ken is packing his clothes, Lola returns. They have an argument and Ken beats up Lola, causing her serious injuries.

3 Nyasha works as a shelf-filler in a DIY store. One day when he is putting packs of batteries out on to a shelf, he slips one in his pocket. He does not intend to pay for it. Later in the day he sees the manager leave her office. Nyasha goes in and takes money from the desk. The door to the office has a notice saying 'Private'.

4 Nigella, who is a pupil at the local comprehensive, goes to the school buildings late in the evening, after school. She intends to damage the science lab as she hates the teacher. She gets in through a window but is caught by the caretaker before she does any damage.

12.3 PROBLEMS IN THE LAW ON ROBBERY AND BURGLARY

12.3.1 The element of theft in robbery

Robbery requires a theft to be completed. However, there is a difference in the way that the law on theft is applied in robbery to the way the courts have applied it in theft cases. In theft cases it has been held that appropriation occurs at one point in time. This is illustrated by the case of *Atakpu and Abrahams* (1994) where the defendants hired cars in Germany and Belgium using false driving licences and passports. They were arrested at Dover and charged with theft. The Court of Appeal quashed their convictions because the moment of appropriation under the law in *Gomez* (see below) was when they obtained the cars. So the thefts had occurred outside the jurisdiction of the English courts and as the defendants had already stolen the cars in Germany and Belgium, keeping and driving them in England was not an appropriation.

However in robbery in the cases of *Hale* (1979) and *Lockley* (1995) the courts have been prepared to view appropriation as a continuing act. In *Lockley* the defendant used force to escape after he had stolen. Despite the fact that the appropriation for the theft occurred before the force the Court of Appeal still held that the defendant was guilty of robbery. This conflicts with the courts' approach in theft cases.

The theft has to be completed otherwise there is no robbery. It can be argued that a completed theft should not be necessary. This would bring the law into line with burglary. In burglary a defendant is guilty under s 9(1)(a) where he intends to steal (or do various other offences) at the moment he enters as a trespasser. Also, in s 9(1)(b) a defendant is guilty if having entered as a trespasser he attempts to steal. If it is thought to be just that a defendant can be guilty of burglary where he intends or attempts then there seems no reason why the same rules should not have been applied to robbery. To bring the law into line with burglary the law would need to be altered to include that a person would be guilty of robbery if he used force intending to steal or if he attempted to steal using force for that purpose.

12.3.2 Level of force in robbery

The level of force required for robbery is very low. There is also the problem that in *Dawson and James* (1976) the Court of Appeal held that 'force' was an ordinary word and it was for the jury to decide if there had been force. So it is left to the jury in each case to decide whether force has been used. There are not likely to be any problems where higher levels of force have been used such as pointing a gun at the victim or punching them. The problems arise where the force is minimal and different juries may come to different decisions as to whether or not there has been force.

In fact some of the decisions on the amount of force seem to contradict what was intended by the Criminal Law Revision Committee when they proposed the law. They said in their report that they would not regard 'mere snatching of property, such as a handbag, from an unresisting owner as using force for the purpose of the definition [of robbery], though it might be so if the owner resisted'. Despite this the Court of Appeal in the case *Clouden* (1987) upheld the defendant's conviction for snatching a handbag from the victim.

12.3.3 Intention in burglary

There are anomalies between the different ways of committing burglary under s 9(1)(a) and s 9(1)(b). Under s 9(1)(a) the defendant at the time of entering must have the intention to inflict grievous bodily harm, steal something from inside the building, or damage the building or anything in it. For s 9(1)(b) there is no need to prove what the defendant's intention was at the time of entry but it must be shown that once in the building he stole (or attempted to) or inflicted grievous bodily harm (or attempted to).

Protecting people or property

The first point is that the defendant need only intend some damage (even slight) to be guilty under s 9(1)(a). Yet so far as injuring a person is concerned the prosecution must prove an intention to inflict grievous bodily harm. This difference appears to be placing the protection of property above the protection of people.

However, under s 9(1)(b) only theft or inflicting grievous bodily harm will trigger the required elements for burglary. This has the effect that under s 9(1)(a) a defendant who enters a building as a trespasser with the intention of causing damage is guilty of burglary while under s 9(1)(b) a defendant who enters a building as a trespasser with no particular intention and then when in the building damages it or other property has not committed burglary.

There seems no reason why damage should not be included as one of the trigger offence for s 9(1)(b).

Conditional intention

As already pointed out, a defendant can be guilty of burglary based on his intention when he enters the building as a trespasser. The courts have interpreted this as including where the defendant only intends to steal if there is something worth taking, as in *Walkington* (1979) where the defendant would have stolen from the till in the shop if there had been anything in it to steal. This is known as conditional intention. It can be argued convicting of the completed offence of burglary on conditional intention is unjust. Conditional intention does not permit a conviction for the full offence in other situations. In particular in robbery there must be a completed theft, intention to steal is not sufficient for the offence.

Going beyond permission

Another area of the law on burglary which can be criticised is where judges have decided that a person who is not a trespasser can become one when he goes beyond the permission given to him. In *Smith and Jones* (1976) the Court of Appeal ruled that the son of the householder was a trespasser where he had entered and stolen two television sets even though the father stated that his son would not be a trespasser in the house; he had a general permission to enter. This decision could mean that a guest at a dinner party in someone's house may become a trespasser if they go into another room, such as a bedroom, uninvited. If they then steal in that room then they could be guilty of burglary.

The concept of burglary originally was to protect people's homes and other buildings from trespassers who intended to (or did) steal etc. There is no need to extend the law on burglary to include people who have permission to be in the house, even though they have gone beyond their permission. A thief, as in *Smith and Jones*, can still be charged with theft.

Examination question

Jennifer owes a lot of money. One night she notices that the house next door, which belongs to Sharma, is in darkness. Jennifer thinks that Sharma is out so she goes next door and breaks a small window pane at the back of the house, intending to steal anything of value which she may find inside. Sharma was asleep in her front room and wakes up when she hears the noise of breaking glass and goes to investigate.

Jennifer picks up a £20 note that is lying on the kitchen table and puts it in her pocket. She is just opening a bag belonging to Sharma when Sharma enters the kitchen. In a panic Jennifer drops the bag and violently pushes Sharma to the floor, breaking Sharma's arm. Jennifer then runs out of the house empty-handed hoping that Sharma has not recognised her. In fact, Sharma sees that it is Jennifer.

Discuss Jennifer's criminal liability.

(OCR, Unit 2572, January 2005)

CHAPTER 13 | Criminal damage

The law on criminal damage is contained in the Criminal Damage Act 1971. This Act creates four offences which are:

■ the basic offence of criminal damage
■ aggravated criminal damage
■ arson
■ aggravated arson.

This chapter deals only with the basic offence, as the other offences are not included in the OCR specification.

13.1 THE BASIC OFFENCE

The basic offence is set out in s 1(1) of the Criminal Damage Act 1971 which states that:

'A person who without lawful excuse destroys or damages any property belonging to another intending to destroy or damage any such property or being reckless as to whether any such property would be destroyed or damaged shall be guilty of an offence.'

The *actus reus* of the basic offence is made up of three elements. These are that the defendant must:

■ destroy or damage
■ property
■ belonging to another.

The *mens rea* is set out in the following words from the section:

'intending to destroy or damage any such property or being reckless as to whether any such property would be destroyed or damaged.'

This shows that a defendant can have the necessary *mens rea* in one of two ways:

■ specific intention to destroy or damage the property or
■ recklessness as to whether the property is destroyed or damaged.

The *actus reus* and the *mens rea* are shown in Figure 13.1.

13.1.1 'Destroy or damage'

This phrase is not defined in the Act. However, the same phrase was used in the law prior to the 1971 Act and old cases ruled that even slight damage was sufficient to prove damage. For example, in *Gayford v Chouler*

Actus reus		Mens rea	
D must damage or destroy property belonging to another	**+**	D must intend to damage or destroy the property or realise there is a risk that the property will be damaged or destroyed and take that risk (recklessness)	**= criminal damage**

Figure 13.1 *Actus reus* and *mens rea* of criminal damage

(1898) trampling down grass was held to be damage. The cases prior to the Criminal Damage Act 1971 are, of course, no longer binding but they may still be used as persuasive precedent.

'Destroy' is a much stronger word than 'damage' and it includes where the property has been made useless even though it is not completely destroyed.

Damage covers a wide range of situations. In *Roe v Kingerlee* (1986) the Divisional Court said that whether property has been damaged was a 'matter of fact and degree'.

ROE v KINGERLEE (1986)
D had smeared mud on the walls of a police cell. It cost £7 to have it cleaned off. It was held that this could be damage even though it was not permanent.

Other cases have also held that non-permanent damage can come within the definition of 'damage'. In *Morphitis v Salmon* (1990) it was said:

'"Damage" … should be interpreted widely so as to include not only permanent or temporary physical harm, but also permanent or temporary impairment of value or usefulness.'

In some cases the courts have considered whether it cost money, time and/or effort to remove the damage. If so then this comes within the definition 'of damage'. This is illustrated in the following two cases.

HARDMAN v CHIEF CONSTABLE OF AVON AND SOMERSET CONSTABULARY (1986)
CND protesters, to mark the fortieth anniversary of the dropping of the atomic bomb on Hiroshima, painted silhouettes on the pavement with water soluble paint. The local council had had the paintings removed with water jets. The defendants argued that the damage was only

---

temporary and the paintings would have quickly been erased by the weather and by people walking on them and there was no need for the local council to go to the expense of having the paintings removed by high-pressure water jets. The court held that this was damage.

BLAKE v DPP (1993)
D wrote a biblical quotation on a concrete pillar. This needed to be cleaned off and so it was held to be criminal damage. This follows the decision in *Roe v Kingerlee* (1986) (above) where costs were incurred in removing mud from a cell wall.

The 'temporary impairment of value or usefulness' was the key factor in *Fiak* (2005).

FIAK (2005)
D was arrested on suspicion of being in charge of a vehicle when he was over the limit for alcohol, and for assault on a police officer. He was taken to a police station and placed in a cell. He put a blanket in the toilet in the cell and flushed the toilet several times. This caused water to overflow and flood the cell and two adjoining cells. The blanket was not visibly soiled but it had to be cleaned and dried before it could be used again. The cells had to be cleaned. This was held to be criminal damage.

If there are no costs or effort in clearing up, and the property can continue to be used, then there is no offence. This is shown by *A (a juvenile) v R* (1978).

A (A JUVENILE) v R (1978)
The defendant spat at a policeman and spit landed on the policeman's uniform. It was held that this was not damage as it could be wiped off with a wet cloth with very little effort.

Figure 13.2 Key cases on what is damage

Case	Facts	Law
Roe v Kingerlee (1986)	D smeared mud on cell wall. It cost £7 to have it cleaned off.	Held this could be damage even though it was not permanent.
Hardman v Chief Constable of Avon and Somerset Constabulary (1986)	D used water-soluble paint to paint silhouettes on the pavement as part of a CND protest.	Held this was damage even though it would have been erased by weather and people walking on it.
Fiak (2005)	D blocked a toilet in a cell causing water to flood the cell and two adjoining cells.	Held this was damage as the blanket and the cells were made unusable until they had been cleaned and dried.
Blake v DPP (1993)	D wrote a biblical quotation on a pillar to protest about military force being used in the Gulf War.	Held that this was damage as it could only be removed by cleaning.
A (a juvenile) v R (1978)	D spat on a policeman's uniform.	Held this was not damage as it could be removed with a wet cloth.
Morphitis v Salmon (1990)	D caused scratches to a scaffolding pole.	Held this was not damage as scaffolding was likely to get scratched in ordinary use and a scratch did not affect its usefulness or integrity.

It is possible that a different decision would have been reached if the spit had landed on a light coloured T-shirt and left a stain, so that the T-shirt needed washing or dry cleaning. As cost would be incurred in those circumstances, it could be considered as damage.

The type and purpose of the property may be relevant as in *Morphitis v Salmon* (1990) where it was held that a scratch on a scaffolding pole was not damage. Scaffolding poles are likely to get quite scratched in the ordinary course of use and it does not affect their usefulness or integrity. However, a scratch on a car would almost certainly be considered damage.

Activity

Explain whether or not there is damage within the meaning of the Criminal Damage Act 1971 in each of the following situations.

1 Aisha throws a bucket of clean water over Beth. The water thoroughly wets Beth's jacket and skirt. Would it make any difference to your answer if the water was muddy?

2 Conrad writes with white chalk on the brick wall of the local town hall.

3 Dan is working on a construction site. He throws a spanner down. It hits a wall which is being constructed and causes a small piece of brick to chip off. The spanner also hits a scaffolding post and causes a small dent in it. The spanner itself is slightly bent as a result.

13.1.2 Property

'Property' is defined in s 10(1) of the Criminal Damage Act 1971. This section says that 'property' means property of 'a tangible nature, whether real or personal, including money'. It includes wild creatures which have been tamed or are ordinarily kept in captivity. It also includes other wild creatures or their carcasses if they are in someone's possession.

Personal property covers all items which can be owned by people. It is very wide and includes clothing, furniture, electronic equipment, tools, cars, boats etc. The list is almost endless. Real property means land and buildings or other structures attached to the land.

However, property for the purposes of criminal damage does not including mushrooms growing wild on any land or flowers, fruit or foliage of a plant growing wild on any land.

The wording in the 1971 Act is similar to the Theft Act but there are two main differences. First, land is property which can be damaged although it cannot normally be stolen and secondly, intangible rights cannot be damaged, though they may be stolen.

13.1.3 'Belonging to another'

The definition of 'belonging to another' is set out in s 10(2) and is similar to the definition which is used for the purposes of theft. Property is treated as belonging to any person:

a having the custody or control of it or
b having in it any proprietary right or interest or
c having a charge on it.

This gives the same wide definition of 'belonging to' as in theft. It is not restricted to the owner. In fact a co-owner can be guilty of criminal damage as the other co-owner has a proprietary right in the property.

SMITH (1974)

D removed some electrical wiring, which he had earlier fitted in the flat which he rented. In doing this he damaged some of the fixtures he had put in. In civil law these fixtures belong to the landlord and this was property 'belonging to another'. However, D was found not guilty because he lacked the necessary *mens rea* (see 13.2.1).

It is important to note that for the purposes of the basic offence the property affected must belong to another. A person cannot be guilty of the basic offence if the property he destroys or damages is his own. But for the aggravated offence a person can be guilty even though it is his own property (see section 13.2).

13.2   *MENS REA* OF CRIMINAL DAMAGE

The defendant must do the damage or destruction either intentionally or recklessly. For the meanings of 'intention' and 'recklessness' the Law Commission, who recommended the reform of the law which led to the passing of the Criminal Damage Act 1971, meant the previous principles of *mens rea* used in criminal damage cases to continue to apply.

Before the passing of the Criminal Damage Act 1971 the law on criminal damage was contained in the Malicious Damage Act 1861. This Act used the phrase 'unlawfully and maliciously'. Maliciously was taken to have the meaning of either intending the damage or knowing there was a risk of damage and taking that risk. This type of risk taking is known as subjective recklessness.

When the Law Commission recommended reform of the law they identified the essential mental element in the malicious damage offences as 'intent to do the forbidden act or recklessness in relation to its foreseen consequences'. They suggested replacing the old-fashioned word of 'maliciously' with the phrase 'intending or being reckless'. This was meant to have the same meaning as the courts had given to the word 'maliciously'.

13.2.1 Intention

The defendant must intend to destroy or damage property belonging to another. Proving the act is not enough; there must be intention to do the damage, as was seen in the old case of *Pembliton* (1874).

> ### PEMBLITON (1874)
> D threw a stone at some men with whom he had been fighting. The stone missed them but hit and broke a window. D was not guilty of causing damage to the window as he had no intention to damage the window (or any other property) even though he intended to throw the stone.

The second point is the need to intend to damage property 'belonging to another'. This was illustrated in *Smith* (1974). Smith mistakenly believed that the property he was damaging was his own. His conviction was quashed by the Court of Appeal who said:

'Honest belief, whether justifiable or not, that the property is the defendant's own negatives the element of mens rea.'

13.2.2 Recklessness

Initially the courts used the meaning of subjective recklessness; that is that the defendant must have realised the risk of damage to the property. In *Stephenson* (1979) the defendant was a tramp who sheltered in a hollow in a haystack and, because he was cold, lit a fire there. The haystack caught fire and was destroyed. The Court of Appeal quashed D's conviction on the grounds that, although an ordinary person would realise the risk of the haystack catching fire, he did not realise this as he suffered from schizophrenia and this point should have been left to the jury to decide.

However, in *Metropolitan Police Commissioner v Caldwell* (1981) the House of Lords changed the law. They ruled that a person was reckless if he did an act which in fact created an obvious risk that property will be destroyed and, when he did the act he either:

- had not given any thought to the possibility of there being any risk; (objective) or
- had recognised that there was some risk involved, and has nonetheless gone on to take it (subjective).

This was known as '*Caldwell* recklessness' and, as can be seen, it included both subjective and objective recklessness. The objective test considered whether the risk was obvious to an ordinary prudent person. If so, then the fact that the defendant did not give any thought to the possibility of there being any risk was enough to make the defendant guilty.

This objective test was harsh in its application, particularly where the defendant was young or mentally backward. This was seen in *Elliott v C* (1983) where the defendant was incapable of appreciating the risk but was still guilty under this test.

> ### ELLIOTT v C (1983)
> D was a 14-year-old girl with severe learning difficulties who had been out all night without food or sleep. She got into a garden shed and, in an effort to get warm, poured white spirit on to the carpet and set light to it. The magistrates found that she had given no thought to the possibility that the shed might be destroyed. They also found that in the circumstances the risk would not have been obvious to her and they acquitted her. The prosecution appealed by way of case stated to the Queen's Bench Divisional Court which ruled that as the risk would have been obvious to a reasonably prudent man, the magistrates had to convict the girl.

Figure 13.3 Key cases on intention in criminal damage

KEY CASES

Case	Facts	Law
Pembliton (1874)	D threw a stone at some men with whom he had been fighting. The stone broke a window.	Held that he was not guilty as he had no intention of damaging the window.
		Comment if D realised there was a risk of damage to the window, he would be guilty.
Smith (1974)	D removed some electrical wiring which he had fitted. In doing this he damaged some of the fixtures he had put in. Legally these fixtures belonged to the landlord of the property.	Held that an honest belief that the property he was damaging was his own negatived the *mens rea* of the offence.
Stephenson (1979)	D was a schizophrenic tramp who lit a fire in a haystack for warmth. The haystack caught fire.	Held that he was not guilty as he did not realise the risk of damage to the haystack. He was not subjectively reckless.
Elliott v C (1983)	D was a 14-year-old with severe learning difficulties. She lit a fire in a shed to keep warm. The shed was badly damaged.	Held, following the ruling in *Caldwell*, that D was guilty as an ordinary prudent individual would have realised the risk.
G and another (2003)	Two young boys set fire to some newspapers under wheelie bin in a shop yard. The fire spread and damaged the shop and other buildings.	Held that the objective test in *Caldwell* was wrong. A subjective test should be applied. Ds would only be guilty if they realised the risk of damage to the shop and other buildings.

This objective test was used up to 2003. Then, in *G and another* (2003), the House of Lords overruled *Caldwell* and re-instated the subjective test for recklessness.

G AND ANOTHER (2003)

The defendants were two boys aged 11 and 12 years. During a night out camping, they went into the yard of a shop and set fire to some bundles of newspapers which they threw under a large wheelie bin. They then left the yard. They expected that as there was a concrete floor under the wheelie bin the fire would extinguish itself. In fact the bin caught fire and this spread to the shop and other buildings, causing about £1 million worth of damage. The boys were convicted under both s 1 and s 3 of the Criminal Damage Act 1971.

The trial judge directed the jury that whether there was an obvious risk of the shop and other buildings being damaged should be decided by reference to the reasonable man, ie the reasonable adult. He told them that the ordinary reasonable man is an adult and that no allowance could be made by the law for the youth of the two boys.

The House of Lords quashed their convictions and ruled that a defendant could not be guilty unless he had realised the risk and decided to take it. They overruled the decision in *Caldwell* holding that in that case the Law Lords had 'adopted an interpretation of section 1 of the 1971 Act which was beyond the range of feasible meanings'.

In *G and another*, the House of Lords emphasised that the Law Commission had intended that there should be no change in the *mens rea* required for criminal damage. The Law Commission were only replacing the old expression 'maliciously' by the more familiar expression 'reckless'. Parliament must also have intended this as they accepted the Bill in the form drafted by the Law Commission.

The effect of this decision is that 'reckless' in s 1 of the Criminal Damage Act 1971 is now clearly subjective in its meaning. The defendant can only be guilty if he realised there was a risk of damage.

13.3 WITHOUT LAWFUL EXCUSE

The Act defines two lawful excuses in s 5(2). These are available only for the basic offence. They apply where the defendant honestly believes either that:

a the owner (or another person with rights in the property) would have consented to the damage or
b other property was at risk and in need of immediate protection and what he did was reasonable in all the circumstances.

In these situations the important point is that the defendant must honestly believe one of these. It does not matter whether the belief is justified or not provided it is honestly held.

13.3.1 Belief in consent

In *Denton* (1982) the defendant, who worked in a cotton mill, thought that his employer

had encouraged him to set fire to the mill so that the employer could make an insurance claim. The Court of Appeal quashed his conviction as he had a defence under s 5(2)(a).

13.3.2 Intoxicated mistakes

The combination of s 5(2)(a) and s 5(3) allows a defence of mistake to be used, even where the defendant makes the mistake because they are intoxicated.

> **JAGGARD v DICKINSON (1980)**
> D, who was drunk, went to what she thought was a friend's house. There was no-one in and so she broke a window to get in as she believed (accurately) her friend would consent to this. Unfortunately in her drunken state she had mistaken the house and had actually broken into the house of another person.
>
> The Divisional Court quashed her conviction holding that she could rely on her intoxicated belief as Parliament had 'specifically required the court to consider the defendant's actual state of belief, not the state of belief which ought to have existed'.

The reasoning behind the decision in *Jaggard v Dickinson* was that a belief may be honestly held even though that belief is caused by intoxication, stupidity, forgetfulness or inattention.

Belief that other property was in immediate need of protection

Section 5(2)(b) could give a defence in situations where trees are cut down or a building demolished to prevent the spread of fire. A case in which the defence was successful pleaded in a jury trial was in April 2000 when Lord Melchett and several other members of Greenpeace damaged genetically modified (GM) crops in order to prevent non-GM crops in neighbouring fields being contaminated with pollen from the GM crops. The judge allowed the defence to go to the jury, but they were unable to agree on a verdict. A retrial was ordered and this time the jury acquitted the defendants.

If D has another purpose in doing the damage, then the court may rule that the defence is not available to him. This is shown by the case of *Hunt* (1978).

HUNT (1978)
The defendant helped his wife in her post as deputy warden of a block of old people's flats. He

---

set fire to some bedding in order, as he claimed, to draw attention to the fact that the fire alarm was not in working order. The judge refused to allow a defence under s 5(2)(b) to go to the jury as his act was not done in order to protect property which was in immediate need of protection. The Court of Appeal upheld his conviction, despite the very subjective wording of s 5(2)(b). There was no immediate need for protection.

In the case of *Blake v DPP* (1993) the defendant put forward defences under both s 5(2)(a) and s 5(2)(b).

Figure 13.4 Key cases on lawful excuse and s 5 defences

KEY CASES

Case	Facts	Law
Denton (1982)	D set fire to a cotton mill in the belief that the owner wanted him to do this.	D had a defence under s 5(2)(a) of the Criminal Damage Act 1971 as he honestly believed that the owner would have consented to the damage.
Jaggard v Dickinson (1980)	D, who was drunk, broke a window in order to get into what she mistakenly though was a friend's house.	s 5(2)(a) and s 5(3) of the Criminal Damage Act 1971 gave D a defence as she honestly believed she had the owner's consent to breaking the window.
Hunt (1978).	D set fire to some bedding in order to draw attention to the fact that the fire alarm in a block of old people's flats was not working.	Held that there was no defence under s 5(2)(b) as no property was in immediate need of protection.
Blake v DPP (1993)	D wrote on a concrete pillar in order to try to prevent military action in the Gulf War. He claimed that this was needed to protect property in Kuwait from damage.	Held that he had no defence under s 5(2)(b) as what he did was not capable, on an objective view, of protecting property in Kuwait.
Baker and Wilkins (1997)	D1 and D2 believed that D1's daughter was being held in a house. They damaged the door in an effort to gain entry to the house	Held that s 5(2)(b) only provides a defence where other property is in immediate need of protection. It does not provide a defence where a person may be at risk.

Figure 13.5 Key facts chart on the basic offence of criminal damage

Element	Comment	Cases
Destroy or damage	'Destroy' includes making an item useless, even if it is not completely destroyed.	
	Damage includes non-permanent damage if it requires effort to remove it.	*Roe v Kingerlee* (1986) *Hardman v Chief Constable of Avon* (1986)
	It is damage if the property is temporarily unusable.	*Fiak* (2005)
	It is not damage if it can be easily wiped off.	*A (a juvenile) v R* (1978)
Property	Must be tangible, includes real and personal property.	
	Includes wild animals in captivity or possession of another.	
Belonging to another	This is wider than 'owner.'	
	Includes custody, control or proprietary right.	*Smith* (1974)
Mens rea	Intention or recklessness in doing the damage.	
	Only subjective recklessness can make D liable.	*G and another* (2003)
Lawful excuse	Believed owner would consent to damage: s 5(2)(a).	*Denton* (1982)
	Even an intoxicated belief is a defence.	*Jaggard v Dickinson* (1980).
	Believed damage needed to protect other property s 5(2)(b).	

BLAKE v DPP (1993)

D was a Vicar who believed that the Government should not use military force in Kuwait and Iraq in the Gulf War. He wrote a biblical quotation with a marker pen on a concrete post outside the Houses of Parliament. He claimed that:

■ he was carrying out the instructions of God and this gave him a defence under s 5(2)(a) as God was entitled to consent to the damage of property, and

■ the damage he did was in order to protect the property of civilians in Kuwait and Iraq and so he had a defence under s 5(2)(b).

He was convicted and appealed, but both the claims were rejected. The court held that God could not consent to damage and that what he did was not capable of protecting property in the Gulf judged objectively, again despite the apparent subjective wording of both s 5(2)(a) and (b).

Oddly enough, the Act does not provide a defence where D believes he is acting to protect a person from harm. In *Baker and Wilkins* (1997) the two defendants believed that Baker's daughter was being held in a house. They tried to enter the house, causing damage to the door. They were convicted. Their conviction was upheld on appeal as s 5(2)(b) only provides a defence where other property is in immediate need of protection.

Activity

Read the following extract from *The Kent and Sussex Courier* of 9th January 2004 and answer the questions below.

CLINGFILM-WRAPPED YOB WRECKS LIGHTS

'A killjoy wrapped in clingfilm caused £700 worth of damage as he climbed up Tonbridge town centre's Christmas tree and smashed some of the decorative lights.

Police are investigating after the vandal wreaked festive havoc at 3.30 am on December 12.

The man, who was caught on CCTV, groped at the colourful illuminations as he clambered up the branches of the tree. In doing so he managed to break some of the decorations.

Tonbridge and Malling Borough Council has since revealed that it cost hundreds of pounds to repair the lights.'

Questions

1 Explain the *actus reus* of the basic offence of criminal damage.
2 Explain whether the *actus reus* of the offence has been committed in the scenario above.
3 Explain the *mens rea* of the basic offence of criminal damage.

---

4 Discuss whether, if a prosecution was brought in the above situation, the defendant could argue that he did not have the *mens rea* for the offence.

13.4 PROBLEMS IN THE LAW

The main problem in the law on criminal damage used to be the application of the objective test for recklessness for the *mens rea* of the offence. This objective test was harsh in its application, particularly where the defendant was young or mentally backward as in *Elliott v C* (1983). However, this aspect of the law has been reformed by the House of Lords decision in *G and another* in 2003 (see section 13.2.2). The test for recklessness is now subjective based on the defendant's realisation of any risk of damage.

The use of the subjective test brings this area of the law into line with that on assault and battery, s 47 and s 20 of the Offences against the Person Act 1861. All these use a subjective test whenever recklessness is relied on. The use of the same level of blameworthiness in different areas of the law makes it fairer and easier to apply.

However there are still some areas of the law on criminal damage which can be criticised.

13.4.1 Non-permanent damage

Damage includes non-permanent damage. In principle this is just as, otherwise, serious instances of graffiti would not be a criminal act. However, the courts have extended damage to include mud on a wall (*Roe v Kingerlee* (1986)) and, in an Australian case, *Samuels v Stubbs* (1972), it was ruled that a dent to a policeman's cap was damage. There was no evidence of any cost or real trouble in returning the cap to its original shape.

Despite this, it was ruled there was damage as there was a 'temporary functional derangement' of the cap.

This raises the question of whether there should be more permanent damage to property for there to be an offence.

13.4.2 *Jaggard v Dickinson*

For offences where recklessness is sufficient for the *mens rea*, the defendant cannot usually rely on self-induced intoxication as defence. He has been reckless in getting intoxicated and this is considered sufficient for the *mens rea*. If his intoxication causes him to make a mistake then he will only have a defence if the mistake meant that he did not have the *mens rea* for the offence and he would have made the mistake had he been sober.

However, s 5 of the Criminal Damage Act 1971 allows a defence if the defendant honestly believes that the owner of the property would consent to the damage and the same section also states that it is immaterial whether a belief is justified or not if it is honestly held.

The courts have interpreted the combination of these two provisions in s 5 as providing a defence where a defendant honestly believed that the owner of a house would consent to her smashing a window to get entry, but where the defendant made a mistake about which house belonged to her and smashed the window of a house belonging to someone else. Her mistake about which house to enter was caused by her intoxication.

This decision is not satisfactory as it allows intoxicated defendants to use this defence to a criminal damage charge, whereas for other offences they would not have a defence.

13.4.3 No defence of protection of persons

Section 5(2)(b) only provides a defence where other property is in immediate need of protection. The Act does not provide a defence where D believes he is acting to protect a person from harm. This was demonstrated by *Baker and Wilkins* (1997) where the two defendants damaged to the door when they tried to enter a house where they thought that Baker's daughter was being held.

If, in that case, they had damaged the door because they were trying to gain entry to put out a fire and prevent damage to property, they would have had a defence. It seems very strange that the law should place protection of property above protection of people.

Examination question

Critically consider what difficulties the courts have encountered in interpreting the offence of criminal damage.

(OCR, Unit 2572, January 2003)

When a person is charged with an offence there are various defences that may be available to them. Some defences are can be used for any offence; other defences can only be used for some offences. Normally, if a defence is used successfully the defendant is acquitted of the crime and is free. The exception to this is the defence of insanity where a special verdict of 'not guilty by reason of insanity' is given.

Figure 14.1 shows the availability of the defences. It also shows what, if any, limitations there are on when the defences can be used.

14.1 INSANITY

The rules on insanity are based on the M'Naghten Rules (1843). M'Naghten suffered from extreme paranoia. He thought he was being persecuted by the 'Tories' (the then Government). He tried to kill a member of the Government, Sir Robert Peel, but instead killed his secretary. Because of his mental state M'Naghten was found not guilty of murder. In fact, he was committed to a mental hospital because of his mental state but this was not a result of the verdict. The fact that he could be found not guilty and need not have

Figure 14.1 Availability of defences

Defence	Availability	Limitation
Insanity	All offences where *mens rea* is required.	Not available for strict liability offences where no mental element is required.
Automatism	All offences.	Not available for offences of basic intent if the automatic state is self-induced though drink or drugs.
Intoxication	Offences of specific intent including murder, s 18 OAPA, theft if the intoxication prevents D from forming the required *mens rea.*	Not available for offences of basic intent, manslaughter, ss 20 and 47 OAPA, assault, battery.
Duress	Most offences.	Not available for murder, attempted murder or, possibly, treason.
Necessity	Possibly all offences including murder.	BUT is very rarely successful.
Mistake	All offences where *mens rea* is required.	Not available for strict liability offences.
Self-defence	All offences.	The force used must be reasonable on the facts as D believed them to be.
Consent	Assaults where there is no injury or only a minor injury.	Never available for murder or s 18 or s 20 OAPA. Sometimes not available for s 47 OAPA.

been sent to a mental hospital caused a public outcry and led to the judges in the House of Lords being asked to answer a series of questions in order to clarify the law in respect of insanity. The answers to those questions have created the rules on insanity which are used in legal cases today.

The main rule is that:

'in all cases every man is presumed to be sane and to possess a sufficient degree of reason to be responsible for his crimes'.

For the defence of insanity to be established the defendant must prove that at the time of committing the act:

'he was labouring under such a defect of reason, from disease of the mind, as not to know the nature and quality of the act he was doing, or if he did know it, that he did not know he was doing what was wrong.'

From this it can be seen that three elements need to be proved. These are:

- a defect of reason
- which must be the result of a disease of the mind
- causing the defendant not to know the nature and quality of his act *or* not to know he was doing wrong.

The burden of proving insanity is on the defence, who must prove it on the balance of probabilities. Where a defendant is found to be insane the verdict is 'not guilty by reason of insanity'.

It used be thought that insanity was a defence to all offences. However, in *DPP v H* (1997), where the defendant was charged with driving with excess alcohol, it was held that insanity is not a defence to offences of strict liability where no mental element is required.

14.1.1 Defect of reason

This means that the defendant's powers of reasoning must be impaired. If the defendant is capable of reasoning but has failed to use those powers then this is not a defect of reason. This was decided in *Clarke* (1972) where it was held that the defect of reason must be more than absent-mindedness or confusion.

CLARKE (1972)

D went into a supermarket, picked up three items including a jar of mincemeat, put them into her own bag and then left the store without paying. She was charged with theft but claimed in her defence that she lacked the *mens rea* for theft as she had no recollection of putting the items into her bag. Indeed, she did not even want the mincemeat as neither she nor her husband ate it. She was said she was suffering from absent-mindedness caused by diabetes and depression. The trial judge ruled that this amounted to a plea of insanity, so she then pleaded guilty to the theft but appealed against it.

The Court of Appeal quashed the conviction. They held that the phrase 'defect of reason' in the M'Naghten Rules applied only to 'persons who by reason of a "disease of the mind" are deprived of the power of reasoning'. The Court of Appeal also said that the rules of insanity do not apply to people who simply have moments of confusion or absent-mindedness.

14.1.2 Disease of the mind

The defect of reason must be due to a disease of the mind. This is a legal term not a medical one. The disease can be a mental disease or a physical disease which affects the mind. An example of this is seen in *Kemp* (1956).

KEMP (1956)

D was suffering from hardening of the arteries which caused a problem with supply of the blood to the brain. This caused D to have moments of temporary loss of consciousness. During one of these he attacked his wife with a hammer, causing her serious injury. He was charged with inflicting grievous bodily harm under s 20 of the Offences Against the Person Act 1861.

At his trial the question arose as to whether this condition came with the rules on insanity. D admitted that he was suffering from a 'defect of reason' but said that this was not due to a 'disease of the mind' as it was a physical illness causing the problem and not a mental illness. He was found 'not guilty by reason of insanity' and appealed against this finding. The Court of Appeal upheld this finding, stating that the law was not concerned with the brain but with the mind. Kemp's ordinary mental faculties of reason, memory and understanding had been affected and so his condition came within the rules on insanity.

In *Sullivan* (1984) the House of Lords was asked to decide whether epilepsy came within the rules of insanity.

SULLIVAN (1984)

D, aged 51, had suffered from epilepsy since childhood. He was known to have fits and had shown aggression to those trying to help him during a fit. He injured an 80-year-old man during a friendly visit to a neighbour's flat. The trial judge ruled that on the facts he would be directing the jury to return a verdict of 'not guilty by reason of insanity'. As a result of this, D pleaded guilty to assault occasioning actual bodily (s 47 OAPA). D then appealed. Both the Court of Appeal and the House of Lords confirmed the conviction.

The House of Lords ruled that the source of the disease was irrelevant. It could be 'organic, as in epilepsy, or functional', and it did not mater whether the impairment was 'permanent or transient and intermittent', provided that it existed at the time the defendant did the act.

This ruling in *Sullivan* means that for the purpose of the M'Naghten Rules the disease can be of any part of the body provided it has an effect on the mind. In *Hennessy* (1989) high blood sugar levels because of diabetes were classed as insanity because the levels affected the mind. *Hennessy* was a diabetic who had not taken his insulin for three days. He was seen to get into a car which had been reported stolen and drive off. He was charged with taking a motor vehicle without consent and driving while disqualified. He had no recollection of taking or driving the car. The disease of diabetes was affecting his mind so this came within the definition of insanity.

In *Burgess* (1991) it was decided that in some instances sleep-walking was also within the legal definition of insanity. The defendant and his girlfriend had been watching videos. They fell asleep and in his sleep Burgess attacked the girl. There was no evidence of any external cause for the sleep-walking and a doctor at the trial gave evidence was that in this instance it was due to an internal cause: a sleep disorder. The judge ruled that this was evidence of insanity and the defendant was found 'not guilty by reason of insanity'. The Court of Appeal upheld the finding.

However, if the sleep-walking is due to an external cause, such as a blow to the head, then it is not insanity but will allow the defendant the defence of automatism (see section 14.2).

External factors

Where the cause of the defendant being in a state where he does not know what he is doing is not a disease but an external cause then this is not insanity.

QUICK (1973)

D was a diabetic who had taken his insulin but then not eaten enough. This causes low blood sugar levels which can affect the brain. In this state D, who was a nurse at a mental hospital, assaulted a patient. The Court of Appeal ruled that his condition did not come within the definition of insanity. It was caused by an external matter; in this case the drug insulin. This meant that D could rely on the defence of automatism (see section 14.2) and was entitled to be acquitted of the charge.

The decisions in *Hennessy* and *Quick* highlight the problems with the law. People with diabetes can go into an automatic state in which they do not know what they are doing. This state can be caused by:

- the disease itself which causes high levels of blood sugar (hyperglycaemia) or
- the drug, insulin, which is used to control the levels of blood sugar: if, after taking insulin, D fails to eat, the blood sugar level will become too low (hypoglycaemia).

If it is the disease which causes the automatic state then, as shown in *Hennessy*, the defendant is considered to come within the rules of insanity as it is an internal cause. If it is the drug which causes the automatic state then, as shown in *Quick*, they are not within the rules on insanity but can rely on the defence of automatism.

It seems ridiculous that a physical disease such as diabetes is classed as insanity, but it is even more ridiculous that diabetics have to rely on different defences available according to whether it was the drug or the disease itself which caused the automatic state.

14.1.3 Not knowing the nature and quality of the act

Nature and quality refers to the physical character of the act. There are two ways in which the defendant may not know the nature and quality of the act. These are:

a because he is in a state of unconsciousness or impaired consciousness or
b when he is conscious but due to his mental condition he does not understand or know what he is doing.

If the defendant can show that either of these states applied to him at the time he did the act, then he satisfies this part of the M'Naghten Rules.

An example of not knowing the nature and quality of the act is where a nurse threw a baby on to a fire, believing it to be piece of wood.

Where the defendant knows the nature and quality of the act he still can use the defence of insanity if he does not know that what he did was wrong. Wrong, in this sense, means legally wrong, not morally wrong. If the defendant knows the nature and quality of the act and that it is legally wrong, he cannot use the defence of insanity. This is so even if the defendant is suffering from a mental illness.

WINDLE (1952)

D's wife constantly spoke of committing suicide. One day the defendant killed her by giving her 100 aspirins. He gave himself up to the police and said 'I suppose they will hang me for this'. He was suffering from mental illness, but these words showed that he knew what he had done was legally wrong. As result he could not use the defence of insanity and was found guilty of murder.

Note that this case was in 1952 and the special defence of diminished responsibility to a charge of murder did not exist. That defence was only created in 1957, so Windle could not use it.

14.1.4 The special verdict

When a defendant successfully proves insanity, then the jury must return a verdict of 'not guilty by reason of insanity'. Up to 1991 the judge then had to send the defendant to a mental hospital regardless of the cause of the insanity or the offence committed. This was

clearly not suitable for cases where the defendant suffered from diabetes or epilepsy or hardening of the arteries. So, in 1991 the Criminal Procedure (Insanity and Unfitness to Plead) Act was passed to extend the options for the judge.

The judge can now impose:

■ a hospital order (with or without restrictions as to when the defendant may be released)
■ a guardianship order
■ a supervision and treatment order
■ an absolute discharge.

Figure 14.2 Key facts chart on insanity

	Law	Case
Definition	D must be labouring under a defect of reason, from disease of the mind: and must either not know the nature and quality of the act he was doing, or not know he was doing wrong.	*M'Naghten* (1843)
Defect of reason	D's powers of reasoning must be impaired. Absent-mindedness is not enough.	*Clarke* (1972)
Disease of the mind	This is a legal term NOT a medical one. There must be an internal cause. It need not be permanent; it can be 'transient and intermittent'. An external cause is not sufficient.	*Kemp* (1956) *Sullivan* (1984) *Quick* (1973)
Not know nature and quality of act OR Not know he is doing wrong	This means that D must not know it is legally wrong: if he does he cannot rely on the defence of insanity.	*Windle* (1952)
Special verdict	Not guilty by reason of insanity. Judge can impose: ■ a hospital order ■ a guardianship order ■ a supervision and treatment order ■ an absolute discharge.	Criminal Procedure (Insanity and Unfitness to Plead) Act 1991.

KEY FACTS

If the defendant is charged with murder then the judge must impose an indefinite hospital order. This means that the hospital can only release the defendant from the hospital if the Home Secretary gives his consent.

14.1.5 Problems with the law of insanity

The first major problem is that the definition of insanity was set by the M'Naghten Rules in 1843. At that time medical knowledge of mental disorders was very limited. Much more is known today about mental disorders and a more modern definition should be used.

Another major problem is that the definition has become a legal one rather than a medical one. This causes two problems.

1 People suffering from certain mental disorders do not come within it; for example, those suffering from irresistible impulses and who are psychopaths such as *Byrne* (1960). They do not come within the M'Naghten Rules as they know what they are doing and that it is wrong. However, they cannot prevent themselves from acting and have a recognised mental disorder.

2 On the other hand those suffering from physical illnesses such as diabetes (*Hennessy* (1989)), brain tumours or hardening of the arteries (*Kemp* (1957)) are considered to be legally insane. Even a sleep-walker has come within the definition (*Burgess* (1991)). The justification for this is that there is an internal cause of their actions: the behaviour may recur and it may be possible to treat it.

Even the use of the word 'insanity' is unfortunate. It carries a social stigma. It is bad enough to apply it to people who are suffering from mental disorders, but it is entirely inappropriate to apply it to those suffering from such diseases as epilepsy or diabetes.

Proof of insanity

The defendant has to prove that he is insane. This places the burden of proof on him. It is possible that this is in breach of Article 6 of the European Convention on Human Rights which states that the defendant is innocent until proven guilty.

There is also the point that the jury are required to decide if the defendant is insane or not. This is not an appropriate function for a jury. It is a matter which should be decided by medical experts. Where there is dispute, the jury have to listen to medical evidence and try to understand technical and complex psychiatric issues.

Proposals for reform

There have been several proposals for reform of the law on insanity. In 1953, the Royal Commission on Capital Punishment suggested that the M'Naghten Rules should be extended so that a defendant would be considered insane if he 'was incapable of preventing himself' from committing the offence. If this had been acted upon, then those suffering from 'irresistible impulses' would have come within the definition of insanity.

However, instead of making this reform, the Government introduced the defence of diminished responsibility. This gives a special defence to those charged with murder (see section 8.1). It does not give a defence to any other offence, but judges have discretion on sentencing for all other offences.

In 1975, the Butler Committee suggested that the verdict of not guilty by reason of insanity should be replaced by a verdict of not guilty on evidence of mental disorder.

In 1989, the Law Commission's Draft Criminal Code proposed that a defendant should be not guilty on evidence of severe mental disorder or severe mental handicap.

Figure 14.3 Key cases on insanity

Case	Facts	Law
M'Naghten (1843)	Suffering from paranoia, shot Sir Robert Peel's secretary. Acquitted but House of Lords asked to clarify the law on insanity.	D must be labouring under a defect of reason, from disease of the mind: and must either not know the nature and quality of the act he was doing, or not know he was doing wrong.
Clarke (1972)	Absent-mindedly took items from a supermarket.	Mere absent-mindedness or confusion is not insanity
Kemp (1956)	Suffering from hardening of the arteries which causes blackouts.	Was within the rules of insanity as his condition affected his mental reasoning, memory and understanding.
Sullivan (1984)	Injured friend during epileptic fit.	Insanity included any organic or functional disease. It also applied even where it was temporary.
Hennessy (1989)	Diabetic who took a car after failing to take his insulin.	If the disease affects the mind then it is within the definition of insanity.
Burgess (1991)	Injured his girlfriend while he was asleep.	If the cause of sleep-walking is internal, then it is a disease within the definition of insanity.
Quick (1973)	Diabetic who failed to eat after taking his insulin.	This was an external cause (the effect of the drug) and so not insanity.
Windle (1952)	Was suffering from a mental disorder and killed his wife, who had constantly spoken of committing suicide.	Because he knew what he done was legally wrong, he was not within the *M'Naghten* rules.

None of these proposals have been made law. However, the change to the ways in which judges can deal with a defendant after they are found not guilty by reason of insanity has improved matters. As explained in section 14.1.4, a judge can now make a supervision and treatment order or even give an absolute discharge where that is suitable.

14.2 AUTOMATISM

In *Bratty v Attorney-General for Northern Ireland* (1963) automatism was defined as:

'an act done by the muscles without any control by the mind, such as a spasm, a reflex action or a convulsion; or an act done by a person who is not conscious of what he is doing such as an act done whilst suffering from concussion or whilst sleep-walking'.

In fact this definition covers two types of automatism:

a insane automatism: where the cause of the automatism is a disease of the mind within the M'Naghten rules. In such a case the defence is insanity and the verdict not guilty by reason of insanity

b non-insane automatism: where the cause is an external one. Where such a defence succeeds, it is a complete defence and the defendant is not guilty.

14.2.1 Non-insane automatism

This is a defence because the *actus reus* done by the defendant is not voluntary. In addition the defendant does not have the required *mens rea* for the offence. The cause of the automatism must be external. Examples of external causes include:

■ a blow to the head
■ an attack by a swarm of bees
■ sneezing
■ hypnotism
■ the effect of a drug.

This concept of no fault when the defendant was in an automatic state through an external cause was approved in *Hill v Baxter* (1958).

HILL v BAXTER (1958)

D drove though a halt sign without stopping and collided with another car. He was charged with dangerous driving but acquitted by the magistrates who accepted that he remembered nothing from some distance before reaching the halt sign. The Divisional Court allowed the prosecution's appeal and remitted the case back to the magistrates with a direction to convict as there was no evidence to support a defence of automatism.

The court approved the judgment in the earlier

---

case of *Kay v Butterworth* (1945) where the judge said:

'*A person should not be made liable at the criminal law who, through no fault of his own, becomes unconscious when driving, as, for example, a person who has been struck by a stone or overcome by a sudden illness, or when the car has been put temporarily out of his control owing to his being attacked by a swarm of bees.*'

In *T* (1990) it was accepted that exceptional stress can be an external factor which may cause automatism.

T (1990)

D was raped. Three days later she took part in a robbery and an assault. She claimed that at the time she was suffering from post-traumatic stress disorder as a result of the rape and that she had acted in a dream-like state. The trial judge allowed the defence of automatism to go to the jury, but D was convicted.

Reduced or partial control of one's actions is not sufficient to constitute non-insane automatism. In *Attorney-General's Reference (No. 2 of 1992)* (1993) the Court of Appeal held that there must be 'total destruction of voluntary control'.

ATTORNEY-GENERAL'S REFERENCE (NO. 2 OF 1992) (1993)

D was a lorry driver who, after driving for several hours, drove along the hard shoulder of a motorway for about half a mile. He hit a broken down car which was stationary on the hard shoulder, killing two people. He said that he was suffering from the condition 'driving without awareness' which puts a driver into a trance-like state. It may be brought on by driving for long distances on motorways. The jury acquitted him. The Attorney-General referred the point of law to the Court of Appeal who ruled that because this condition only causes partial loss of control it did not amount to automatism.

14.2.2 Self-induced automatism

This is where the defendant knows that his conduct is likely to bring on an automatic state. Examples include a diabetic, who knows the risk, failing to eat after taking insulin or a person who drinks after taking medication, when he has been told by his doctor that he must not take alcohol while on that medication. The law on this comes from the case of *Bailey* (1983).

BAILEY (1983)

D was a diabetic who had failed to eat enough after taking his insulin to control the diabetes. He became aggressive and hit someone over the head with an iron bar. The trial judge ruled that the defence of automatism was not available. The Court of Appeal held that this ruling was wrong but upheld D's conviction as there was insufficient evidence in the case to raise the defence of automatism.

Although the appeal was dismissed in *Bailey*, the Court of Appeal set out the rules on self-induced automatism. The first point was that there is a difference in the way the defence applies to specific intent offences and basic intent offences. If the offence charged is one of specific intent, then self-induced automatism can be a defence. This is because the defendant lacks the required *mens rea* for the offence.

However, if the offence charged is one of basic intent then:

a   if the defendant has been reckless in getting into a state of automatism, self-induced automatism cannot be a defence. Subjective recklessness is sufficient for the *mens rea* of crimes of basic intent;

b   where the self-induced automatic state is caused through drink or illegal drugs or other intoxicating substances the defendant cannot use the defence of automatism. This is because *DPP v Majewski* (1977) decided that becoming voluntarily intoxicated is a reckless course of conduct (see section 14.3);

c   where the defendant does not know that his actions are likely to lead to a self-induced automatic state in which he may commit an offence, he has not been reckless and can use the defence of automatism.

This third situation was seen in *Hardie* (1984).

HARDIE (1984)

D was depressed because his girlfriend had told him to move out of their flat. He took some Valium tablets which had been prescribed for his former girlfriend. She encouraged him to take the tablets, stating that it would calm him down. He then set fire to a wardrobe in the flat. He said he did not know what he was doing because of the Valium. The trial judge directed the jury to ignore the effect of the tablets and he was convicted of arson.

The Court of Appeal quashed his conviction as the defendant had taken the drug because he thought it would calm him down. This is the normal effect of Valium. So the defendant had not been reckless and the defence of automatism should have been left to the jury.

Figure 14.4 Comparison of insanity and automatism as defences

Insanity	Automatism
For defence to prove, on the balance of probabilities.	For defendant to raise, the prosecution must then disprove.
Must have a defect of reason due to disease of the mind: M'Naghten Rules.	Must be caused by an external factor.
Example: Diabetic affected by disease: *Hennessy* (1989).	Example: Diabetic affected by (drug) insulin: *Quick* (1973).
Verdict: not guilty by reason of insanity.	Verdict: not guilty.
Judge must make one of the following four orders:	Defendant is free.
■ a hospital order (with or without restrictions as to when the defendant may be released) ■ a guardianship order ■ a supervision and treatment order ■ an absolute discharge.	

Activity

Read the following extract from a newspaper article and answer the questions below.

JURY IN RAPE TRIAL ACCEPTS THE DEFENCE OF SLEEPWALKING

A man accused of raping a female friend three times in a matter of minutes was cleared yesterday after claiming that he had been sleepwalking.

After hearing his unusual defence, the jury took less than three hours to clear him of three rape charges.

York Crown Court heard that he had let the 22-year-old friend sleep in his bed when they returned to his flat after a night out with other friends.

He fell asleep on the sofa and insisted that the next thing he knew was waking up as the

'victim' was leaving the flat. She claimed she had fallen asleep and woke up to find him having sex with her.

He said nothing during the alleged rapes and afterwards climbed over her and went back to the sofa.

He said he could not deny having sex with the woman but had no recollection of doing so.

He told the police he had suffered from sleepwalking since he was 13 and had a family history of the condition. 'It's the only explanation I can come up with for this,' he said.

(*Daily Mail*, 20th December 2005)

Questions

1 What two defences may be used where the defendant did something while sleepwalking?
2 If these defences are successful what verdicts will be given by the jury?

14.3 INTOXICATION

This covers intoxication by alcohol, drugs or other substances, such as glue-sniffing. Intoxication does not provide a defence as such, but is relevant as to whether or not the defendant has the required *mens rea* for the offence. If he does not have the required *mens rea* because of his intoxicated state he may be not guilty.

Whether the defendant is guilty or not depends on:

1 whether the intoxication was voluntary or involuntary and
2 whether the offence charged is one of specific or basic intent.

Specific intent offences are generally those which require specific intention for their *mens rea*. The specific intent offences on OCR A2 specification are murder, s 18 Offences Against the Person Act 1861, theft, robbery and burglary. For WJEC A2 they are murder and s 18 Offences against the Person Act 1861.

Basic intent offences are generally those for which recklessness is sufficient for the *mens rea*. The basic intent offences on both OCR A2 and WJEC specifications are the offences of manslaughter, s 20 and s 47 OAPA and assault and battery. In addition for OCR there is the offence of criminal damage.

14.3.1 Voluntary intoxication

Voluntary intoxication is where the defendant has chosen to take an intoxicating substance. This can be by taking alcohol, illegal drugs or other intoxicants such as through sniffing glue. It can also occur where the defendant knows that the effect of a prescribed drug will be to make him intoxicated.

Voluntary intoxication and specific intent offences

Voluntary intoxication can negate the *mens rea* for a specific intent offence. If the defendant is so intoxicated that he has not formed the *mens rea* for the offence he is not guilty. This rule comes from *DPP v Beard* (1920). Beard had been charged with murder and had put forward as his defence the fact that he was too intoxicated to have formed the *mens rea* for murder. He was convicted but on appeal, Lord Birkenhead considered previous decisions and stated:

'*Where a specific intent is an essential element in the offence, evidence of a state of drunkenness rendering the accused incapable of forming such an intent should be taken into consideration in order to determine whether he had in fact formed the intent necessary to constitute the particular crime.*'

Lord Birkenhead then stated the rule which still stands today:

'*If he was so drunk that he was incapable of forming the intent required, he could not be convicted of a crime which was committed only if the intent was proved.*'

An example of where it was found that the defendants were so drunk that they did not have the *mens rea* for murder is *Sheehan and Moore* (1975). The defendants were very drunk when they threw petrol over a tramp and set fire to him. They were too drunk to have formed any intent to kill or cause grievous bodily harm. It was held that because they did not have the *mens rea* for murder their intoxication was a defence to that offence. However, they were found guilty of manslaughter as that is a basic intent offence.

Where the defendant has the necessary *mens rea* despite his intoxicated state, then he is guilty of the offence. The intoxication does not provide a defence. It has been held that a drunken intent is still; an intent. This was shown by *A-G for Northern Ireland v Gallagher* (1963).

GALLAGHER (1963)

D decided to kill his wife. He bought a knife to do the killing and also a bottle of whisky. He drank a large amount of the whisky before killing his wife. His conviction for murder was upheld.

Voluntary intoxication and basic intent offences

Where the offence charged is one of basic intent then intoxication is not a defence. This is because voluntarily getting intoxicated is considered a reckless course of conduct and recklessness is enough to constitute the necessary *mens rea*. The leading case on this is *DPP v Majweski* (1977).

DPP v MAJWESKI (1977)

D had taken both alcohol and drugs. In a very intoxicated state he then attacked people in a public house and also the police officers who tried to arrest him. He was convicted of three offences of assault occasioning actual bodily harm (s 47 OAPA) and three of assaulting a police officer in the execution of his duty. The House of Lords upheld all these convictions. His intoxicated state was not a defence as the House of Lords said:

'It is a reckless course of conduct and recklessness is enough to constitute the necessary mens rea.'

14.3.2 Involuntary intoxication

Involuntary intoxication covers situations where the defendant did not know he was taking an intoxicating substance. This may be where, for example, a soft drink has been 'laced' with alcohol or drugs. It also covers situations where prescribed drugs have the unexpected effect of making the defendant intoxicated.

The test is: did the defendant have the necessary *mens rea* when he committed the offence? If so, it was decided in *Kingston* (1994) that he will be guilty. The involuntary intoxication will not provide a defence. This is so even though the defendant would not have committed the offence without the intoxication lowering his resistance to committing the offence.

KINGSTON (1994)

The defendant's coffee was drugged by someone who wanted to blackmail him. He was then shown a 15-year-old boy who was asleep and invited to abuse him. The defendant did so and was photographed by the blackmailer. The House of Lords upheld his conviction for indecent assault. They held that if a defendant had formed the *mens rea* for an offence then the involuntary intoxication was not a defence.

Where, however, the defendant did not have the necessary intent he will be not guilty. He has no *mens rea* and so cannot be guilty of a specific intent offence. Neither can he be guilty of a basic intent offence. This is because the defendant has not been reckless in getting intoxicated. An example of this is *Hardie* (1985) (see section 14.2.2) where the defendant took Valium tablets not knowing they could make his behaviour unpredictable.

14.3.3 Drunken mistake

If the defendant is mistaken about a key fact because he is drunk, then it depends on what the mistake was about as to whether he has a defence or not.

Where the mistake is about something which means that the defendant did not have the necessary *mens rea* for the offence then for a specific intent offence he has a defence. However, where the offence is one of basic intent then the defendant has not got a defence. An example of this was the case of *Lipman* (1970).

> ### LIPMAN (1970)
> D and his girlfriend had taken the drug LSD before falling asleep at her flat. LSD causes people to have hallucinations. D thought that he was at the centre of the earth and being attacked by snakes. When he awoke he found his girlfriend was dead. He had strangled her and stuffed a sheet into her mouth believing she was a snake attacking him. His conviction for manslaughter was upheld.

Lipman did not have the specific intention for murder as he thought he was killing a snake. He did not intend to kill or cause grievous bodily harm to any human being. However, he was guilty of manslaughter because he had voluntarily taken the drug LSD. This was 'a reckless course of conduct' and so he was guilty of manslaughter.

If the mistake is about another aspect, for example the amount of force needed in self-defence, the defendant will not have a defence. This was stated in *O'Grady* (1987) and confirmed in *Hatton* (2005).

> ### O'GRADY (1987)
> After D and V, who was a friend, had been drinking heavily, they fell asleep in D's flat. D claimed that he awoke to find V hitting him.

> D picked up a glass ashtray and hit V with it, D then went back to sleep. When he woke the next morning he found that V was dead. D was charged with murder but was convicted of manslaughter. The Court of Appeal upheld this conviction.

O'Grady was convicted of manslaughter which is a basic intent offence. This is clearly in line with the decision in *DPP v Majewski* (1977) as getting drunk is a 'reckless course of conduct' and recklessness is sufficient for a basic intent offence such as manslaughter.

The interesting point in the case was that the Lord Chief Justice, Lord Lane, also stated that an intoxicated mistake as to the amount of force needed in self-defence was not a defence to a specific intent offence. This has been confirmed by *Hatton* (2005).

> ### HATTON (2005)
> D had drunk over 20 pints of beer. He and another man (V) went back to D's flat. In the morning D claimed he found V dead from injuries caused by a sledgehammer. D said he could not really remember what had happened but thought V had hit him with a five-foot-long stick and he had defended the attack. D was convicted of murder. The Court of Appeal held that the decision in *O'Grady* was not limited to basic intent crimes, but also applied to specific intent crimes. A drunken mistake about the amount of force required in self-defence was not a defence.

By refusing to allow a drunken mistake as the amount of force required, the law is trying to balance the need to be just to the defendant with the protection of victims.

An exception to the rule on intoxicated mistake is *Jaggard v Dickinson* (1981) (see section 13.4.3 for full details). This exception is because s 5 of the Criminal Damage Act 1971 allows an honest belief that the person

Figure 14.5 Key facts chart on intoxication as a defence

KEY FACTS

	Specific intent crimes	Basic intent crimes
Voluntary intoxication	If defendant has *mens rea* he is guilty: *Gallagher* (1963). If defendant has no *mens rea* he is not guilty.	Becoming intoxicated is a reckless course of conduct: *Majewski* (1977) The defendant is guilty of the offence.
Involuntary intoxication	If defendant has *mens rea* he is guilty (Kingston). If defendant has no *mens rea* he is not guilty: *Hardie* (1984).	The defendant has not been reckless in becoming intoxicated, so not guilty: *Hardie* (1984).
Drunken mistake	If the mistake negates *mens rea* the defendant is not guilty. If the mistake is about the need to defend oneself, it is not a defence. The defendant will be guilty. This so for both specific and basic intent offences: *O'Grady* (1987) *Hatton* (2005).	This is a reckless course of conduct, so the defendant is guilty.

to whom the property belonged would have consented to the damage or destruction as a lawful excuse to a charge of criminal damage, whether or not the belief is justified. This has been interpreted as giving a defendant a defence even where the mistake was made through intoxication.

14.3.4 Problems in the law

It can seem odd that a drunken mistake can afford a defence where the mistake means that the defendant does not have the necessary intent for an offence yet does not afford him a defence where he makes a drunken mistake about the amount of force needed. However, this is in line with the law on mistake even when the defendant is not drunk. See section 14.4 for the law on mistake and section 14.4.1 for the law on mistake about the amount of force required.

There are also problems resulting from the decision in *DPP v Majewski* (1977). The

decision in this case, that the defendant is guilty of a basic intent offence because getting drunk is a 'reckless course of conduct', ignores the principle that *mens rea* and *actus reus* must coincide. The decision to drink may be several hours before the defendant commits the *actus reus* of any offence. For example, in *O'Grady*, the defendant had fallen asleep and only committed the act of hitting his friend some hours afterwards.

In addition, the recklessness in becoming intoxicated is that the defendant takes a general risk of doing something 'stupid' when drunk. At the time of getting intoxicated the defendant has no idea that he will actually commit an offence. Normally, for offences where recklessness is sufficient for the *mens rea* of an offence, it has to be proved that D knew there was a risk of the specific offence being committed.

This point was considered by the Law Commission in a consultation paper in 1993. They said in that paper that the *Majewski* rule was arbitrary and unfair. However, the Law Commission's proposals for changing the law were severely criticised and by the time they published firm proposals for reform of the law in 1995 they had changed their opinion. By this time they thought that the present law operated 'fairly, on the whole, and without undue difficulty'.

The rule that a defendant is guilty of a basic intent offence has the effect, for homicide cases and non-fatal assaults, that even thought the defendant is not guilty of the more serious specific intent offence, he can be found guilty of a basic intent offence. These are manslaughter where murder is charged or an offence under s 20 of the Offences Against the Person Act 1861 where a s 18 offence has been charged.

However, for other crimes, there is often no 'fall-back' offence. If a defendant is charged with theft and successfully claims that he did not form the *mens rea* for theft because he was too intoxicated, he will be not guilty of any offence.

A final point where the law could be thought to be in need of reform is where the defendant's inhibitions are broken down by being made intoxicated involuntarily. The decision in *Kingston* (1994) makes such a defendant guilty if he formed the necessary *mens rea*. This ignores the fact that the defendant was not to blame for the intoxication. Such a defendant would be not guilty of a basic intent offence where the prosecution relied on recklessness (as in *Hardie* (1984)). This appears to be unfair to defendants in Kingston's situation.

14.4 MISTAKE

To be a defence a mistake must be a mistake about a fact. The mistake must have the effect that if the facts had been as the defendant believed them to be, it would mean:

- either there was no *mens rea* for the offence or
- that the defendant would have been able to rely on another defence.

Simple situations illustrate these concepts:

- if A picks up an umbrella from a stand as he is leaving a restaurant in the mistaken belief that it is his own umbrella, he does not have the *mens rea* required for theft as he is not dishonest
- if B, in the mistaken belief that V is pointing a gun at him, throws a stone at V and knocks him out, B can plead he should be judged on the basis that his action was in self-defence.

In these situations, provided the defendant genuinely made a mistake, there is a defence. This is so, even if the mistake is unreasonable. This rule was first stated in *DPP v Morgan and others* (1976).

DPP v MORGAN AND OTHERS (1976)
D, who was a senior officer in the RAF, invited three junior officers to come to his house to have sex with his wife. The three queried this, but said they were persuaded by D that his wife did want to have sex with them. He told them that she would pretend to refuse in order to stimulate her own excitement. So, the men had sex with the wife, despite the fact that she screamed and called for her son to call the police. The judge told the jury that their belief in the wife's consent had to be based on reasonable grounds. They were convicted.

The Court of Appeal held that the judge had misdirected the jury as the belief in consent had to be genuine but need not be reasonable. However, the Court of Appeal upheld their convictions as they thought a jury correctly directed would still have convicted.

In *Williams* (1987) it was ruled that the defendant should be judged according to his genuine mistaken view of the facts, regardless of whether this mistake was reasonable or unreasonable. This allowed Williams to use the defence of protection of others.

WILLIAMS (1987)

D was on a bus when he saw what he thought was a man assaulting a youth. In fact it was a man trying to arrest the youth for mugging an old lady. D got off the bus and asked what was happening. The man said that he was a police officer arresting the youth, but when D asked him to show his police ID card he could not do so. There was then a struggle between D and the man in which the man was injured. D was convicted of assault after the judge directed them that D only had a defence if his mistake was a reasonable one.

The Court of Appeal quashed his conviction because the jury should have been told that if they thought the mistake was genuine they should judge the defendant according to his genuine mistaken view of the facts, regardless of whether this mistake was reasonable or unreasonable.

Excessive force

If the jury accept that defendant's mistake meant that he genuinely thought he was acting in self defence or using force in the prevention of crime, then the jury have to decide whether the amount of force used was reasonable in the circumstances as the defendant believed them to be. If the amount of force was unreasonable in those circumstances then the defendant has not got a defence.

Drunken mistakes

See section 14.3.3.

14.5 SELF-DEFENCE/PREVENTION OF CRIME

This covers not only actions needed to defend oneself from an attack, but also actions taken to defend another or prevent crime. The defence can be a defence to any crime, including murder as the defendant is justifying the use of force. Section 3(1) of the Criminal Law Act 1967 states that:

'a person may use such force as is reasonable in the circumstances in the prevention of crime'.

14.5.1 Reasonable force

In deciding whether the force used was reasonable, the fact that the defendant had only done what he honestly and instinctively thought was necessary in a moment of unexpected anguish is very strong evidence that the defensive action taken was reasonable.

In looking at the circumstances, the defendant must be judged on the facts as he genuinely believed them to be. In *Williams* (1987) (see section 14.4) the defendant had to be judged on his genuine but mistaken view that a youth was being attacked by a man.

If the force is used after all danger from the assailant is over (ie as retaliation or revenge), the defence of self defence is not available.

14.5.2 Excessive force

The amount of force used to defend oneself or another must be reasonable in the circumstances. If excessive force is used the defence will fail. In *Clegg* (1995) the defendant was a soldier on duty at a checkpoint in Northern Ireland. A car came towards the checkpoint at speed and with its headlights full on. One of the soldiers shouted for it to stop but it did not. Clegg fired three shots at the windscreen of the car and one as it passed him. This final shot hit a passenger in the back and killed her. The evidence showed that the car had gone past Clegg by the time this last shot was fired. So it was held that he could not use self-defence as a defence because there was no danger when he fired that shot. The force was excessive in the circumstances and his conviction for murder was upheld.

Activity

Explain whether there would a defence available in the following situations.

1 Alice took some illegal drugs. She is told that while she was under the influence of the drugs, witnesses saw her hit Peter in the face with a saucepan, breaking his jaw. Alice cannot remember doing this. What defence(s) might be available to her if she is charged with offences under s 18 and s 20 of the Offences against the Person Act 1861?

2 Courtney is a diabetic. One morning he gets up late and in his rush to get to work he forgets to take his insulin. As a result he becomes violent later in the day and punches Jemima in the face. What defence(s) might be available to him if he is charged with an offence under s 47 of the Offences Against the Person Act 1861?

3 Zahir is hit on the head by a slate which accidentally falls off a building. He loses consciousness briefly but is then able to walk home. Later that day he attacks his partner, Lynne, causing serious injuries to her. He has no recollection of doing this. What defence(s) might be available to him if he is charged with offences under s 18 and s 20 of the Offences Against the Person Act 1861?

4 Martha has an argument with her husband, Desmond. Desmond then goes into the kitchen and a few minutes later comes out shouting abuse at her. Martha sees what she thinks is a knife in his hand, although it is actually a child's toy. Believing that he is about to stab her, Martha throws an ash-tray at Desmond's head. This hits him on the temple and kills him. What defence(s) might be available to her if she is charged murder?

14.6 DURESS

Duress is a defence based on the fact that the defendant has been effectively forced to commit the crime. The defendant has committed the offence because he has been threatened with death or serious injury. The law therefore allows a defence. The defendant has to choose between being killed or seriously injured or committing a crime. In such a situation there is no real choice. The defendant can be considered as so terrified that he ceases 'to be an independent actor'. However, despite this the defendant knowingly does the *actus reus* for the offence and has the required *mens rea*. So, if the law did not allow the defence, he would be liable for the offence.

Duress can be either through a direct threat by another (duress by threats) or through external circumstances (duress of circumstances). Duress of circumstances overlaps with the defence of necessity.

14.6.1 What crimes is duress available for?

Duress can be used as a defence to all crimes, except murder, attempted murder and, possibly, treason. It was originally held in *DPP for Northern Ireland v Lynch* (1975) that the defence of duress was available to a secondary party on a charge of murder. This meant it was available for defendants who had participated in a murder, such as a get-away driver, but had not actually performed the act of killing. However in *Howe*

(1987) the House of Lords ruled that the defence was not available to anyone charged with murder, even if they were only a secondary party and had not done the killing themselves.

HOWE (1987)

D, with others, took part in torturing and abusing a man who was then strangled by one of the others. On a second occasion another man was tortured, abused and then strangled by D. D claimed that he took part in the killings because of threats to him. The trial judge ruled that duress was available to D for the first killing where D was only a secondary party to the killing, but that it was not available for the second killing where D was a principal offender. The Court of Appeal ruled that this was correct but the House of Lords held that duress was not available as a defence for either murder.

The reason why duress was held not to be a defence was explained by Lord Hailsham when he said in the judgment:

'I do not at all accept in relation to the defence of murder it is either good morals, good policy or good law to suggest ... that the ordinary man of reasonable fortitude is not to be supposed to be capable of heroism if he is asked to take an innocent life rather than sacrifice his own.'

In the case of *Howe* the House of Lords said they thought the defence should not be available on a charge of attempted murder. This was an *obiter dicta* statement and so not binding. However, in *Gotts* (1992) the Court of Appeal decided to follow this *obiter* statement.

GOTTS (1992)

D was a 16-year-old boy whose parents were separated. D was threatened with violence by his father unless he agreed to stab his mother. D attacked his mother but did not kill her. He

was convicted of attempted murder. The Court of Appeal upheld his conviction on the basis that the defence of duress was not available to him.

14.6.2 Duress by threats

Duress by threats is where a person's will is overborne by threats of death or serious injury, so that he commits an act which he would not otherwise do. So, where another person threatens the defendant with serious violence unless the defendant commits an offence, and the defendant then commits the offence, he is acting under duress. For example, if an armed man pointed a gun at the defendant, gave him a fake credit card, and ordered him to use it in a cash point machine to get money. The defendant is stealing the money but he is only doing it because of the threat.

The threat of violence is directed at the defendant by another person who demands that the defendant commit a specific crime or else he will be shot.

Seriousness of the threat

The threat must be of death or serious injury; lesser threats do not provide a defence. For example, a threat to disclose a previous conviction is not sufficient for duress. However, provided there are serious threats, then the cumulative effect of the threats can be considered. This was decided in *Valderrama-Vega* (1985).

VALDERRAMA-VEGA (1985)

The defendant illegally imported cocaine. He claimed he had done this because of death threats made by a mafia-type organisation involved in drug-smuggling and also because of threats to disclose his homosexuality and because of financial pressures. The trial judge said that the defence was only available to him if the death threats were the sole reason for his committing the offence. The Court of Appeal quashed his conviction as the jury were entitled to look at the cumulative effects of all the threats.

If there had not been a threat of death, then the other threats in this case would not be enough on which to base a defence of duress. But as there had been a threat of death the jury were entitled to consider the whole of the threats.

Threat to whom?

It used to be thought that the threat had to be to the defendant himself. But in an Australian case in 1967 it was accepted that threats to kill or seriously injure the defendant's common law wife were sufficient.

In recent cases in England it has been accepted that threats to family or even to friends can be a basis for the defence of duress. In *Martin* (1989) in a case of duress of circumstances the wife of the defendant threatened to commit suicide unless he drove whilst disqualified (see section 14.6.9). This was held to be sufficient. In *Conway* (1988) the threats were to a passenger in the defendant's car. These were accepted as forming the basis for the defence of duress (see section 14.6.9).

There has been no decision on whether a threat to a complete stranger would be enough to give a defence of duress, but it seems likely that the courts would now allow this. Supposing an armed man seizes hold of someone you do not know and then orders you to go to and firebomb a particular building and cause severe damage to it or else he will kill the stranger. If you do damage the building, can you use the defence of duress? You would be able to if the threat was to a member of your family or, under *Conway*, to a friend. So, it would be reasonable to say that you should have a defence if you choose to commit a crime rather than let an innocent stranger die. In fact, the Draft Criminal Code proposed that that this should be the law.

14.6.3 Subjective and objective tests

In deciding if the defence should succeed the jury must consider a two-stage test. This involves both subjective and objective tests. These are:

- was the defendant compelled to act as he did because he reasonably believed he had good cause to fear serious injury or death? (a mainly subjective test) and
- if so, would a sober person of reasonable firmness, sharing the characteristics of the accused have responded in the same way? (an objective test).

These tests were laid down by the Court of Appeal in *Graham* (1982) and approved by the House of Lords in *Howe* (1987).

GRAHAM (1982)

D was a homosexual who lived with his wife and another homosexual man, K. K was violent and bullied D. After both D and K had been drinking heavily, K put a flex around the wife's neck and told D to pull the other end of the flex. D did this for about a minute. The wife died. D claimed he had only held the flex because of his fear of K. D's conviction for murder was upheld.

Subjective test

The first part of the test is based on whether the defendant did the offence because of the threats he believed had been made. This is subjective, but it was thought that this had to be a reasonable belief in the sense that an ordinary person would have believed it. This made it a partially objective test.

However, in *Martin (DP)* (2000), the Court of Appeal interpreted this part of the two-stage test as being whether the defendant may have reasonably feared for his safety. So, in considering this test, the jury could take into account any special characteristic of the defendant which may have made him more likely to believe the threats.

> **MARTIN (DP) (2000)**
> The defendant suffered from a condition known as schizoid-affective state, which would lead him to regard things said to him as threatening and to believe that such threats would be carried out. He claimed he had been forced to carry out two robberies by two men who lived on the same estate. The judge ruled that the schizoid-affective disorder was irrelevant to the first part of the test, although it was a characteristic which could be included in the second part of the test.
>
> The defendant appealed saying that the correct test should have been whether, in view of his condition, he may have reasonably feared for his own or his mother's safety.
>
> The Court of Appeal allowed the appeal and quashed his conviction. They held that duress and self-defence should be treated in the same way in regard to belief of the circumstances. In self-defence a mistaken belief by the defendant can be a defence provided it is a genuine mistake. The same applies to duress and so the defendant's mental condition is relevant in deciding whether he reasonably believed that his (or his family's) safety was at risk.

This decision is now in doubt following the House of Lords' decision in *Hasan (formerly Z)* (2005) (see section 14.6.8) which confirmed the decision in *Graham* that the defendant's belief in the threats must be reasonable and genuine.

Objective test

The second part of the test is based on whether the reasonable man would have responded in the same way. However, the jury are allowed to take certain of the defendant's

characteristics into account as the reasonable man is taken as sharing the relevant characteristics of the defendant.

What characteristics can be taken into account was decided in *Bowen* (1996). In this case the defendant had a low IQ of 68 and he obtained goods by deception for two men who had told him they would petrol-bomb him and his family. It was held that this was irrelevant in deciding whether the defendant found it more difficult to resist any threats. The relevant characteristics must go to the ability to resist pressure and threats. In *Bowen* it was accepted that the following could be relevant:

- age: as very young people and the very old could be more susceptible to threats
- pregnancy: there is the additional fear for the safety of the unborn child
- serious physical disability: which could make it more difficult for the defendant to protect himself
- recognised mental illness or psychiatric disorder; this could include post-traumatic stress disorder or any other disorder which meant that a person might be more susceptible to threats: this did not include a low IQ
- sex: although the Court of Appeal thought that many women might have as much moral courage as men.

14.6.4 No safe avenue of escape

Duress can only be used as a defence if the defendant is placed in a situation where he has no safe avenue of escape. In *Gill* (1963) the defendant claimed that he and his wife had been threatened unless he stole a lorry. However, there was a period of time during which he was left alone and so could have raised the alarm. As he had a 'safe avenue of escape' he could not rely on the defence of duress.

It has also been held that if police protection is possible then the defendant cannot rely on duress. However, in the case of *Hudson and Taylor* (1971) it was accepted that police protection might not always be effective.

HUDSON and TAYLOR (1971)

The defendants were two girls, aged 17 and 19, who were prosecution witnesses in a case against a man called Wright who was charged with wounding another man. When giving evidence in court they lied and said they could not identify Wright as the attacker. They were then charged with perjury (lying in court under oath). In their defence at their trial for perjury they said they lied because a man called Farrell, who had a reputation for violence, had told Hudson that if she gave evidence against the attacker, he would 'cut her up'. They were convicted and appealed. The Court of Appeal quashed their conviction.

At the appeal the prosecution argued that the girls could have sought police protection. On this point the Court of Appeal pointed out that there were cases in which the police could not provide effective protection. They said that in deciding whether going to the police for protection was a realistic course, the jury should consider the age of the defendant, the circumstances of the threats and any risks which might be involved in trying to rely on police protection.

However, the decision in *Hudson and Taylor* was criticised by the House of Lords in *Hasan (formerly Z)* (2005) (see section 14.6.8). It is now doubtful that a defendant could use the defence of duress where there was opportunity to go to the police.

14.6.5 Imminence of threat

The threat must be effective at the moment the crime is committed. But this does not mean that the threats need to be able to be carried out immediately. In *Hudson and Taylor* the trial judge in their perjury case ruled that the defence of duress was not available to the two girls. This was because the threat could not be immediately put into effect while the girls were giving evidence, so there was no reason why they could not have given truthful evidence.

On this point the Court of Appeal said that the threat had to be a 'present' threat but that this was in the sense that it was effective to neutralise the will of the defendant at the time of committing the offence. If the threat is hanging over the defendant at the time he or she commits the offence, then the defence of duress is available.

This was further considered in *Abdul-Hussain* (1999), a case on duress of circumstances.

ABDUL-HUSSAIN (1999)

The defendants, who were Shiite Muslims, had fled to Sudan from Iraq because of the risk of punishment and execution because of their religion. They feared that they would be sent back to Iraq and so they hijacked a plane. The plane eventually landed in the UK. The defendants were charged with hijacking and pleaded duress. The trial judge decided that the danger they were in was not sufficiently 'close and immediate' as to give rise to a 'virtually spontaneous reaction' and he ruled that the defence of duress could not be considered by the jury. The defendants were convicted and appealed.

The Court of Appeal quashed their convictions, holding that the threat need not be immediate but it had to be imminent in the sense that it was hanging over them.

The Court of Appeal in *Abdul-Hussain* (1999) ruled that:

- there must be imminent peril of death or serious injury to the defendant, or to those for whom he has responsibility
- the peril must operate on the defendant's mind at the time of committing the otherwise criminal act, so as to overbear his will; this is a matter for the jury
- execution of the threat need not be immediately in prospect.

The Court of Appeal also backed their ruling by giving a hypothetical example based on the history of Anne Frank whose family hid from the Nazis for a long period of time during the Second World War because they knew they would be sent to a concentration camp. Anne Frank and all the members of her family were eventually caught and all of them, except her father who survived, died in a concentration camp. The Court of Appeal said:

'If Anne Frank had stolen a car to escape from Amsterdam and been charged with theft, the English law would not, in our judgment, have denied her a defence of duress of circumstances, on the ground that she should have waited for the Gestapo's knock on the door.'

14.6.6 Threat to make defendant commit a specific offence

The defendant can only use the defence if the threats are in order to make him commit a specific offence.

> **COLE (1994)**
> D claimed that he and his girlfriend and child had been threatened (and he had been actually hit with a baseball bat) in order to make him repay money he owed. As he did not have the money D carried out two robberies at building societies to get sufficient money to repay the debt. D said he only did this because of the threats of violence to him and his family.
>
> His conviction was upheld because he had not been told to commit the robberies. The threats to him were directed at getting repayment and not directed at making him commit a robbery. This meant there was not a sufficient connection between the threats and the crimes he committed, so the defence of duress was not available to him.

This applies only to duress by threats. In duress of circumstances the defence may be used for any offence which is an appropriate response to the danger posed by the circumstances. As seen in *Abdul-Hussein* above, the danger was of torture and execution and the offence committed was hijacking which enabled them to get to a safe venue.

14.6.7 Intoxication and duress

If the defendant becomes voluntarily intoxicated and mistakenly believes he is being threatened he cannot use duress as a defence. A mistake in these circumstances is unreasonable. However, if there is no mistake and the intoxication is irrelevant to the duress the defendant can use the defence of duress. This could be, for example, where he is threatened by a man with a gun. In this situation there is duress and it is irrelevant whether the defendant is intoxicated or not.

14.6.8 Self-induced duress

This is where the defendant has brought the duress on himself through his own actions. For example where a defendant voluntarily joins a criminal gang and commits some offences, but then is forced to commit other crimes which he did not want to do under duress.

Figure 14.6 Key cases on general principles of duress

KEY CASES

Duress can be by threats or circumstances.

Duress is not available for murder (*Howe* (1987)) or attempted murder (*Gotts* (1992)).

Case	Facts	Law
Valderama-Vega (1985)	Smuggled cocaine because of death threats and threats to disclose homosexuality.	Must be a threat of death or serious injury but can consider cumulative effect of threats.
Graham (1982)	Help kill his wife because he was threatened by his homosexual lover.	Two-stage test: ■ was D compelled to act as he did because he reasonably believed he had good cause to fear serious injury or death? ■ if so, would a sober person of reasonable firmness, sharing the characteristics of the accused have responded in the same way
Martin (DP) (2000)	Suffered from a schizoid-affective state which would make D see things as threatening and believe the threats would be carried out.	Correct test should have been whether, in view of his condition, he may have reasonably feared for his own or his mother's safety.
Bowen (1996)	Had a low IQ (68) – obtained goods by deception for two men because of petrol-bomb threat.	Cannot take low IQ into account Can consider: ■ age ■ pregnancy ■ recognised mental illness ■ sex.
Gill (1963)	Threatened so that he stole a lorry but had time to escape and raise the alarm.	Cannot use duress if has a 'safe avenue of escape'.
Hudson and Taylor (1971)	Two girls lied on oath because of threats to 'cut them up'.	The threat need not be capable of being carried out immediately. Also recognised that police protection cannot always be effective. Take into account age and sex.
Hasan (2005)	D tried to burgle a safe after he was threatened by a drug dealer associate.	Criticised *Hudson and Taylor* saying that D should seek police protection.
Abdul-Hussain (1999)	Hijacked plane to escape from persecution in Iraq.	Threat must be 'imminent' and operating on D's mind when he commits the offence.

The normal rule is that where the defendant is aware that he may be put under duress to commit offences he cannot use the defence. This has been held to apply to the following situations:

- where the defendant joins a criminal gang which he knows are likely to use violence
- where the defendant puts himself in a position where he knows that he is likely to be subjected to threats of violence or actual violence. This could be by being involved in criminal activity although not part of a gang, or by becoming indebted to a drug dealer.

These situations can be illustrated by specific cases.

> **SHARP (1987)**
> D joined a gang who carried out robberies. D claimed that he had wanted to withdraw from the robberies before the last one where a sub-postmaster was shot dead. The Court of Appeal ruled that he could not use duress as a defence. D knew when he joined the gang that they were likely to use violence, so he could claim duress when they threatened him with violence.

A contrasting case to *Sharp* is the case of *Shepherd* (1987).

> **SHEPHERD (1987)**
> D had joined an organised gang of shoplifters. A group of them would enter a shop and while one of them distracted the shopkeeper the others would steal as much as they could, usually boxes of cigarettes. This activity, although criminal, was non-violent. D said he wanted to stop taking part but was then threatened with violence unless he continued. The Court of Appeal allowed his appeal and quashed his conviction. If he had no knowledge that the gang was likely to use violence then the defence of duress was available to him.

The rule that duress is not available where it is self-induced has been extended to situations where the defendant associates with violent criminals. For example, in *Heath* (2000) the defendant owed money to a drug dealer. He was then threatened and made to help in the supply of cannabis. He could not use the defence of duress as he knew that by becoming indebted to a drugs dealer he was putting himself at risk of being threatened or having violence used on him.

However, in other cases, the courts have allowed a defendant who associated with violent people to use the defence of duress. This conflict of whether self-induced duress could be a defence was resolved in *Hasan (formerly Z)* (2005).

> **HASAN (FORMERLY Z) (2005)**
> D associated with a violent drug dealer. This drug dealer told D to burgle a house in order to steal a large amount of money that was in a safe there. The dealer threatened that if D did not do this then D and his family would be harmed. D, carrying a knife, broke into the house but was unable to open the safe. He was convicted of aggravated burglary. The Court of Appeal quashed the conviction but certified the following question for the consideration of the House of Lords:
>
> '*Whether the defence of duress is excluded when as a result of the accused's voluntary association with others:*
>
> *(i) he foresaw (or possibly should have foreseen) the risk of being then and there subjected to any compulsion by threats of violence; or*
>
> *(ii) only when he foresaw (or should have foreseen) the risk of being subjected to compulsion to commit criminal offences; and, if the latter*
>
> *(iii) only if the offences foreseen (or which should have been foreseen) were of the*

Figure 14.7 Key facts chart on duress by threats

	Law	Case
Availability	All offences EXCEPT: ■ murder ■ attempted murder ■ treason (possibly).	*Howe* (1987) *Gotts* (1992)
Seriousness of threat	Must be of death or serious injury BUT can consider cumulative effect of other threats with threat of injury.	*Valderrama-Vega* (1985)
Subjective and objective tests	There are two tests: ■ was D compelled to act because he feared serious injury or death? (subjective) ■ would a sober person of reasonable firmness have responded in the same way? (objective).	*Graham* (1982)
	Some of D's characteristics can be taken into account, especially: ■ age ■ pregnancy ■ serious physical disability ■ recognised mental illness.	*Bowen* (1996)
Avenue of escape	Duress is NOT available as a defence if there is a safe avenue of escape.	*Gill* (1963)
Imminence of threat	The threat need not be immediate but it must be imminent.	*Hudson and Taylor* (1971) *Abdul-Hussain* (1999)
Self-induced duress	Duress is NOT available where: ■ D joins a criminal gang whom he knows are violent ■ D puts himself in a position where he foresaw (or should have foreseen) the risk of being subjected to compulsion.	*Sharp* (1987) *Hasan* (2005)

same type (or possibly the same type and gravity) as that ultimately committed.'

The House of Lords reinstated his conviction. They took the view that option (i) in the certified question correctly states the law. The defence of duress is excluded where D voluntarily associates with others who are engaged in criminal activity and he foresaw or ought reasonably to have foreseen the risk of being subjected to any compulsion by threats of violence.

So self-induced duress is no longer available where a defendant realises or ought to have realised that he may be threatened with violence and compelled to commit an offence.

14.6.9 Duress of circumstances

Although duress by threats has been recognised as a defence for a long time, it is only recently that the courts have recognised that a defendant may be forced to act because of surrounding circumstances. This is known as duress of circumstances.

The first case in which this was recognised was *Willer* (1986). In this case the defendant and a passenger were driving down a narrow alley when the car was surrounded by a gang of youths who threatened them. Willer realised that the only way to set away from the gang was by driving on the pavement. He did this quite slowly (about 10 mph) and having made his escape he drove to the police station to report the gang. The police charged him with reckless driving for having driven on the pavement and he was convicted.

He appealed and the Court of Appeal said that the jury should have been allowed to consider whether the defendant drove 'under that form of compulsion, that is, under duress'.

This case was followed by *Conway* (1988).

There was then a third case involving a driving offence. This was *Martin* (1989) where the defendant's wife became hysterical and threatened suicide unless he drove her son (who was late and at risk of losing his job) to work. The defendant was disqualified from driving but he eventually agreed to do this. He was convicted of driving whilst disqualified. On appeal it was ruled that duress of circumstances could be available as a defence and the same two-stage test put forward in *Graham* for duress by threats applied. So the tests were:

▨ was the defendant compelled to act as he did because of what he reasonably believed he had good cause to fear serious injury or death? and
▨ if so, would a sober person of reasonable firmness, sharing the characteristics of the accused have responded in the same way?

Although these cases established that there was a defence of duress of circumstances, all the cases involved driving offences. It was not until the decision in *Pommell* (1995) that it became clear that duress of circumstances could be a defence to all crimes except murder and attempted murder and some forms of treason.

CONWAY (1988)
A passenger in D's car had been shot at by two men a few weeks earlier. The car was stationary when the passenger saw two men running towards the car. He thought they were the two who were after him (in fact they were plain clothes policemen) and he yelled at D to drive off. Conway did so very fast and was charged with reckless driving. The trial judge refused to leave duress for the jury to consider and D was convicted. On appeal the Court of Appeal quashed his conviction and ruled that a defence of duress of circumstances was available if, on an objective standpoint, the defendant was acting in order to avoid a threat of death or serious injury.

POMMELL (1995)
D was found by police at 8.00 am lying in bed with a loaded sub-machine gun against his leg. He told police that at about 1 am he had taken it off another man who was going to use 'to do some people some damage'. D said he had intended getting his brother to give the gun into the police that morning. At his trial for possessing a prohibited weapon the judge ruled that his failure to go to the police straight away prevented him having any defence. D was convicted. He appealed to the Court of Appeal who held that the defence of duress of circumstances was available for all offences except murder and attempted murder and some forms of treason. They quashed D's conviction and sent the case for retrial.

In *Cairns* (1999) the court had to consider whether there had to be a real threat to the defendant or whether the defence was available where the defendant reasonably perceived a threat of serious physical injury or death, even though there was no actual threat.

> **CAIRNS (1999)**
> V threw himself across the bonnet and windscreen of D's car. Several of V's friends were nearby shouting and D felt threatened. D drove off with V on his bonnet and some of V's friends following. These friends were in fact trying to help rather than threaten D. When D braked for a speed hump, V fell under the car and was seriously injured. At the trial the judge directed the jury they had to consider whether D's actions were 'actually necessary'. D's conviction was quashed as he reasonably perceived a threat of serious physical injury or death.

It is sufficient for the defendant to show that he acted as he did because he reasonably perceived a threat of serious physical injury or death. He is not required to prove that the threat was an actual or real threat.

14.6.10 Problems in the law of duress

Unavailability for murder

The ruling in *Howe* (1987) that duress is not available on a charge of murder ignores situations such as a woman motorist being hijacked and forced to act as getaway driver. Lord Griffiths simply dismissed such examples on the basis that it was inconceivable that such person would be prosecuted. However, it is possible that such a person might be prosecuted and would have no defence.

What if a young mother is hi-jacked and told her two young children will be killed unless she helped terrorists plant a bomb? Lord Hailsham thought that the ordinary person should be capable of heroism if he is asked to take an innocent life rather than sacrifice his own. But in this situation the mother is being asked to sacrifice her two children. Yet she would have no defence.

The law also creates an anomaly in that duress is not available for murder but is available for a charge under s 18 of the Offences Against the Person Act 1861. The *mens rea* of intention to cause grievous bodily can be the same as for murder.

There is an additional problem where a defendant is charged with murder as this offence carries a mandatory life sentence. This has the effect the judge has to send the defendant to prison for life. The judge cannot even take the duress into account when passing sentencing. Where the defendant is charged with attempted murder the judge has discretion in sentencing. For example, in the case of the 16-year-old *Gotts* (1992), the judge placed him on probation.

The Law Commission, in its report, *Legislating the Criminal Code: Offences Against the Person and General Defences* (1993), proposed that the defence of duress should be available for all crimes.

No allowances for low IQ

In *Bowen* (1996) the Court of Appeal refused to allow the fact that the defendant had a very low IQ to be taken into account in deciding whether the defendant found it more difficult to resist any threats. This decision may be seen as harsh. A very low IQ can mean that the person fails to understand the true nature of matters. It should be taken into account.

Police protection

In *Hudson and Taylor* (1971) the Court of Appeal accepted that police protection could not be completely fool-proof. Even where a defendant had the opportunity to go to the police and tell them of the duress, many people might be so afraid of the consequences that they would not go to the police.

Unfortunately the decision in *Hudson and Taylor* has been called into question by the House of Lords' judgment in *Hasan* (2005). This leaves the law uncertain as to whether a person threatened with duress, who does not take an available opportunity to go to the police, can rely on the defence of duress.

Activity

Explain whether a defence of duress would be available in the following situations.

1 Clancy is threatened by Neil, a fellow employee, who tells Clancy that he will tell their boss about Clancy's previous convictions for theft. Neil says that Clancy has to help him shoplift from a small corner shop by distracting the counter-staff while Neil does the stealing. Clancy feels obliged to do this as he does not want to lose his job.

2 Joseph, who is of a timid nature and low intelligence, is told by Katya that she will beat him up unless he obtains goods for her from a shop using a stolen credit card. He does this and obtains a DVD player for her.

3 Natasha's boyfriend, Ross, is a drug dealer. She also knows that he has convictions for violence. He threatens to beat her 'senseless' unless she agrees to take some drugs to one of his 'customers'. She is caught by the police and charged with possessing drugs with intent to supply.

4 Sanjeet's wife has tried to commit suicide previously. She is very depressed because they are heavily in debt. She tells Sanjeet that she will throw herself under a train unless he can get the money to pay off their debts. Sanjeet obtains the money by robbing a local off-licence.

5 Tamara is due to give evidence against Alexia's boyfriend who is facing a trial for attempted murder. A week before the trial is due to take place, Alexia sends Tamara a text message saying that Tamara will be killed if she gives evidence. Tamara attends the court but lies in evidence saying, untruthfully, that the man she saw was much shorter than Alexia's boyfriend.

14.7 NECESSITY

This is where circumstances force a person to act in order to prevent a worse evil from occurring. The defence has similarities with the defence of duress of circumstances, yet the courts have been reluctant to recognise necessity as a defence in its own right. The leading case is *Dudley and Stephens* (1884).

DUDLEY and STEPHENS (1884)

The two defendants were shipwrecked with another man and V, a 17-year-old cabin boy, in a small boat about 1600 miles from land. After drifting for 20 days and having been nine days without food and seven days without water, the two defendants killed and ate the cabin boy. Four days later they were picked up by a passing ship and on their return to England were convicted of murder. Their claim of necessity to save themselves from dying was rejected.

It is interesting to note that although Dudley and Stephens were convicted of murder and sentenced to be hung, their sentence was commuted to a mere six months' imprisonment.

In *Dudley and Stephens,* the charge was of murder, so it can be argued that the law on necessity is in line with the law on duress, as duress is not available on a charge of murder. However, in the case of *Buckoke v Greater London Council* (1971) Lord Denning stated, *obiter,* that he thought the defence of necessity would not be available to emergency service drivers (fire-fighters or ambulance drivers) if they broke traffic laws in an attempt to get to an emergency quickly. He did go on to say that such a driver should be congratulated for their action and he hoped that anyone in that situation would not be prosecuted. Nevertheless, the law seems to be that such a person could be prosecuted and would not have a defence of necessity.

As there is no general defence of necessity, the traffic laws have now been changed to give emergency service drivers a special defence in certain circumstances.

14.7.1 Recognition of the defence

It is interesting that the defence has been recognised by the courts when making an order in some civil cases. An example of this is *Re F (Mental Patient: Sterilisation)* (1990).

> ### RE F (MENTAL PATIENT: STERILISATION) (1990)
> A health authority applied for a declaration that it was lawful to sterilise a girl who had very severe mental disability. The girl had formed a sexual relationship with another mental patient, putting her at risk of becoming pregnant. Doctors said that she would not be able to understand pregnancy and it could be disastrous for her precarious mental health. The girl's mother supported the application, but the Official Solicitor, who was acting on behalf of the girl as she was unable to give consent to an operation herself, thought that that performing such an operation would be illegal.

> The House of Lords granted the application and Lord Brandon stated:
>
> *'In many cases … it will not only be lawful for doctors, on the ground of necessity, to operate on or give other medical treatment to adult patients disabled from giving their consent, it will also be their common duty to do so.'*

Another case in which doctors sought a declaration that it would be lawful for them to operate was *Re A (Conjoined twins)* (2000). In this case the defence of necessity was considered and held to be available as a defence even to a potential charge of murder.

> ### RE A (CONJOINED TWINS) (2000).
> Conjoined twins were born with one of them having no proper heart or lungs. She was being kept alive by the other twin, whose heart circulated blood for both of them. Their parents refused to consent to an operation to separate them. Doctors applied for a declaration that it was lawful to operate to separate the twins, even though the weaker twin would certainly die. The Court of Appeal gave the declaration. The three judges gave very different reasons for why the operation would be lawful, but one of them, Brooke LJ said that the defence of necessity would be available to the doctors were they to be charged with murder of the weaker twin. He approved the following four principles of the defence of necessity as set out in Stephen's *Digest of Criminal Law* (1883):
>
> 1 the act was done only in order to avoid consequences which could not otherwise be avoided
> 2 those consequences, if they had happened, would have inflicted inevitable and irreparable evil
> 3 that no more was done than was reasonably necessary for that purpose
> 4 that the evil inflicted by it was not disproportionate to the evil avoided.

Figure 14.8 Key facts chart on necessity

	Law	Case
Definition	Circumstances force a person to act in order to prevent a worse evil from occurring.	
Existence	Only recognised as duress of circumstances in criminal cases.	*Dudley and Stephens* (1884)
	Civil case have recognised the defence of necessity.	*Re F (Mental Patient: Sterilisation)* (1990) *Re A (Conjoined twins)* (2000)
Tests	These were set out in Stephen's *Digest of Criminal Law* and approved in *Re A*: ■ act was done only to avoid consequences which could not otherwise be avoided ■ hose consequences would have inflicted inevitable and irreparable harm ■ no more was done than was necessary ■ the evil inflicted was proportionate to the evil avoided.	*Re A (Conjoined twins)* (2000)

KEY FACTS

Necessity was also considered in the case of *Shayler* (2002). In this case the defendant was a former member of the British Security Service (MI5). He was charged with disclosing confidential documents in breach of the Official Secrets Act 1989. He claimed the defence of necessity. His conviction was upheld by both the Court of Appeal and the House of Lords. The Court of Appeal discussed the defences of necessity and duress of circumstances and thought that they were in effect the same defence. Lord Woolf stated:

'The distinction between duress of circumstances and necessity has, correctly been by and large ignored or blurred by the courts. Apart from some of the medical cases like Re F *(1990), the law has tended to be treat duress of circumstances and necessity as one and the same.'*

The Court of Appeal held that the tests for duress of circumstances and/or necessity were:

■ the act must be done only to prevent an act of greater evil
■ the evil must be directed towards the defendant or a person or persons for whom he was responsible
■ the act must be reasonable and proportionate to the evil avoided.

It can be seen that these tests are very similar to those for necessity. But there are differences. The important one is that the evil must be directed towards the defendant or a person or persons for whom he was responsible. This demonstrates that it is wrong to treat necessity as being the same as duress of circumstances. In 'pure' necessity situations there is no requirement for this. In the case of *Re A (conjoined twins)*, the evil was not directed at the doctors. Nor were they responsible for the twins. The parents had responsibility for them.

The other major difference between duress of circumstances and necessity is that duress of circumstances cannot be used as a defence to murder, yet in *Re A (conjoined twins)*, it was accepted that necessity could be a defence to the murder of the weaker twin. In that case performing an operation, which the doctors knew would kill the weaker twin, was an act which would prevent the greater evil of both twins dying.

14.7.2 The role of necessity in other defences

Even though there are doubts as to whether necessity exists as a defence in its own right, necessity effectively forms the basis of other defences. These include:

Self-defence

The essence of this defence is that the defendant is claiming that he acted as he did because it was necessary for his protection.

Special statutory defences

An example is s 5(2)(b) of the Criminal Damage Act 1971 where it is a defence to a charge of criminal damage that other property was at risk and in need of immediate protection provided that what the defendant did was reasonable in all the circumstances.

Examination questions

1 Discuss how and why the courts have limited the availability of automatism as a defence in criminal law.
(OCR, Unit 2572, June 2004)

2 Martha suffers from epilepsy but knows that she can control her condition by taking medication at the correct times. One Saturday, shortly after leaving home to go and stay at her friend Heidi's house for a week, she realises that she has forgotten to take her medication with her. She decides that she can do without it.

The following Friday, Martha is in Heidi's front room having a cup of coffee when she has an epileptic fit, falls on the floor and starts to have convulsions. Martha lashes out uncontrollably, knocking over a jug which spills water on to Heidi's new carpet and breaks a cup that is on the coffee table. Heidi becomes upset and tries to restrain Martha by holding her down. Martha struggles violently, cutting Heidi's lip and causing her severe bruising on her arm.

Discuss any potential offence that Martha may have committed together with any defences available to her.
(OCR, Unit 2572, June 2005)

3 Carol and Diana decide to go 'clubbing' for the night. They meet at Carol's house and begin the evening by sharing half a bottle of vodka. They then go out and have some more drinks in a pub and they each take an ecstasy tablet. As they are leaving the pub, Carol takes a leather jacket from the back of a chair, mistaking it for her own very similar jacket which she has, in fact, left at home.

By the time they arrive at the club, both girls are suffering from hallucinations. The doorman, Barry, asks them for identity. Diana, who thinks Barry is an alien who wants to transport them to another planet, pokes him in the eye with her finger and then hits over the head with her umbrella, knocking him unconscious. Carol picks up the wallet which has fallen on to the pavement from Barry's pocket and they both run off.

Consider the offences that Carol and Diana may have committed and advise them of any defences they may have available to them.
(OCR, Unit 2572, June 2004)

4 The defence of intoxication represents a

satisfactory compromise between justice for an individual defendant and the demands of public policy.

(OCR, Unit 2572, June 2005)

5 Explain, by reference to decided cases, how and why the courts have limited the defence of consent in relation to non-fatal offences against the person.

(OCR, Unit 2572, June 2003)

6 To what extent can insanity or other mental impairment on the part of the accused provide a defence to a charge of murder?

(WJEC, LW5, June 2003)

7 To what extent, if at all, are duress and necessity recognised as defences to a criminal charge?

(WJEC, LW5, June 2004)

8 Daniel began to borrow heavily from his brother-in-law Jack, who is married to Daniel's sister, Samantha, although he knew that Jack made his money working for Harry, a local criminal with a reputation for violence. Jack told Daniel that Harry was going to have Samantha 'cut up' unless Daniel helped him rob the night club where Daniel worked. Jack knew that Daniel had access to the safe in the manager's office, and said that all Daniel would have to do was open the safe, and afterwards claim to have been overpowered at gun point. However, on the night of the robbery, the manager of the club, George, walked into the office while Jack was filling a suitcase with cash. Jack pulled out a gun, but Daniel forestalled him by knocking George unconscious with a heavy ashtray. Daniel and Jack left the club and got into Daniel's car. Jack told Daniel that he had arranged to meet Samantha at the airport and escape abroad. Daniel agreed to drive Jack to the airport, but on the way he noticed another car following close behind. Jack said, 'It's

Harry – he knows I've double-crossed him, and he's got a gun'. Daniel did the only thing he could think of, which was to brake hard, forcing Harry to swerve and crash.

Daniel has been charged with taking part in the robbery, wounding George, and attempting to murder Harry. Consider whether he may be able to rely on duress as a defence.

(WJEC, LW4, June 2005)

WJEC Specification

Criminal Law and Justice is Option 2 of the A2 specification for WJEC. As the title 'Criminal Law and Justice' implies, the specification includes elements of both criminal law and the criminal justice system.

The grid after the Preface in the front of the book shows which areas of criminal law are relevant to WJEC students.

This textbook is purely on criminal law, but in order to make WJEC students aware of the broader range of topics they need to study, this appendix sets out the criminal justice topics in the specification. Most these topics are covered by my textbook *The English Legal System.*

This appendix also explains the style of examination set by WJEC. Finally, it includes some Internet sources for keeping up to date on areas such as reported crime.

A1.1   CRIMINAL JUSTICE TOPICS IN THE WJEC SPECIFICATION

The Rule of Law in Law Enforcement

The meaning and scope of the concept of the Rule of Law, including the role of the courts; problems of control and accountability; impartiality of the judiciary and the police; the need for legalised force and for legal limits upon its use.

Crime and Society

Measurement of crime; reported and unreported crime; reliability of statistics; patterns of criminality; clear-up rates.

Police Powers, Admissibility of Evidence, Remedies for Breach of Police Powers

Discretionary nature of police powers; powers to stop and search persons, vehicles, property and premises; powers of arrest, detention and interrogation; rights of persons in custody; treatment of persons during detention, including role of the custody officer; admissibility of evidence; remedies for breach of police powers, including police complaints procedure.

Role of the Courts: Prosecution and Criminal Trial Process

Police discretion in the decision to prosecute, including the use of police cautions; functions of the Crown Prosecution Service, including outline of the roles of the Attorney-General and the Director of Public Prosecutions; bail and remand in custody; the trial process, including youth justice.

Sentencing

General principles of sentencing of adults and youths under the appropriate legislation; theories and objectives of sentencing; empirical data relating to sentencing; powers of the Magistrates' Courts and the Crown Court; Court of Appeal guidelines.

A1.2   THE STYLE OF EXAMINATION

Candidates have to sit three papers for A2. These are:

LW4: Problem Unit

Candidates have to answer two problem questions from a choice of four, in one and a half hours. Questions from past WJEC examination papers on the substantive criminal law have been included at the end of some of the chapters in this book. There are also problem questions on areas such as the use of police powers.

LW5: Essay Unit

Candidates have to answer two essay questions from a choice of six, in one and a half hours. There are questions on both the substantive criminal law and on the criminal justice system. Questions from past WJEC examination papers on the substantive criminal law have been included at the end of some of the chapters in this book.

The following are examples of questions on the criminal justice system.

1 Explain and evaluate the work of the Crown Prosecution Service within the criminal justice system.

(LW5, WJEC, 2003)

2 'The law relating to bail contains ample safeguards to protect the public from suspected offenders.' Discuss.

(W5, WJEC, 2004)

LW6: Synoptic Unit

Candidates have to answer one compulsory question in one hour. In the 2002 examination session this was an essay question. However, in 2003, 2004 and 2005 the compulsory question started with a scenario and then set five questions on different aspects of the scenario.

In past papers these questions have concentrated on different factors in the criminal justice system rather than any substantive areas of law. For example, there have been questions on:

▓ whether police powers were correctly used
▓ what factors the police and magistrates would take into account when deciding whether to grant or refuse bail
▓ what appeals would be open to a defendant after a trial in the Crown Court
▓ how the Court of Appeal would apply the rules of precedent.

Past papers and mark schemes can be obtained from WJEC.

A1.3 KEEPING UP TO DATE ON THE CRIMINAL JUSTICE SYSTEM

A1.3.1 Recorded crime

One of the areas of knowledge required by the specification is recorded crime. The easiest way to keep up to date on this topic is to look at the annual reports, *Crime in England and Wales*, issued each year by the Home Office. These can be found at www.homeoffice.gov.uk

Crime statistics for each area in the country are also published by the Home Office. These can be found at www.crimestatistics.org.uk

A1.3.2 Police powers

The Home Office publishes information on the use of police powers of arrest. These can be found on the main Home Office website (address given above). Also look in 'Research and Publications' on the menu.

The Serious Organised Crime and Police Act 2005 (SOCPA) makes major changes to powers of arrest. These came into effect in January 2006. The main change is that the category of 'arrestable offence' is abandoned. Instead, an arrest can be made for any offence (s 110 of SOCPA substitutes a new s 24 into PACE 1984).

However, an arresting officer can only arrest if he has reasonable grounds for believing that it is necessary to make the arrest for one of the following reasons:

▓ to enable the person's name or address to be ascertained
▓ to prevent the person from:
  ▓ causing physical injury to himself or any other person
  ▓ suffering physical injury
  ▓ causing loss of or damage to property
  ▓ committing an offence against public decency

- causing an unlawful obstruction of the highway
- to protect a child or other vulnerable person
- to allow the prompt and effective investigation of the offence or of the conduct of the person
- to prevent any prosecution for the offence from being hindered by the disappearance of the person in question.

Changes to searches of premises

The Serious Organised Crime and Police Act 2005 also makes changes to the powers to search premises. The main ones are:

- the introduction of an 'all premises' warrant to allow all premises occupied or controlled by the defendant to be searched
- allowing search warrants to provide for access on more than one occasion.

Police Codes of Practice

The police Codes of Practice can be found on the main Home Office website.

Sentencing

The Criminal Justice Act 2003 set up the Sentencing Guidelines Council. This consults on sentencing issues. It may also ask the Sentencing Advisory Panel to conduct research on sentencing. Following consultation and research, the Council issues guidelines on specific areas of sentencing.

The Council's website is at www.sentencing-guidelines.gov.uk

A1.3.3 Other useful websites

www.cjsonline.org.uk
This gives general information on the criminal justice system.

www.cps.gov.uk
This is the website for the Crown Prosecution Service. On it can be found the Service's annual reports. Look in the menu for 'Publications' and then 'Reports'.

www.ipcc.gov.uk
This is the website of the Independent Police Complaints Commission. This gives information on making complaints against the police. It also contains the Commission's annual reports. The first report was published in November 2005.

The Synoptic Unit for OCR for 2007–08

This appendix deals with the source material and style of examination for the Criminal Law Special Study Unit, 2573. This Unit is part of the six-module examination for the OCR Law A Level and will be examined in the following sessions:

- January 2007
- June 2007
- January 2008 (as a re-sit).

The source material is reproduced below at section A2.1. Booklets containing this source material are available from OCR for use in preparing for the examination. In addition, each candidate will be given a clean copy of the booklet for reference purposes within the examination room.

This source material forms the basis of the questions on the examination paper, so it is essential that all students study it carefully.

A2.1 SOURCE MATERIALS

Source 1

Extract adapted from Richard Ward, *Walker and Walker's English Legal System*, (Butterworths), pp 34–36, 42, 62–63, 75, 76, and 218–219.

The traditional view of the function of an English judge has been that it is not to make law but to decide cases in accordance with existing legal rules. Few would now deny that judges have a powerful law-making function, but there is no doubt that this traditional declaratory view of the judicial process was the theoretical foundation of binding precedent whereby the judge is not merely referred to earlier decisions for guidance, but

also bound to apply the rules of law decided by those cases. All courts stand in a definite relationship to one another. A court is bound by decisions of a court above it in the hierarchy and, usually, by a court of equivalent standing. Given that the doctrine of precedent has binding force within this framework, the question naturally arises of how the law may develop if cases are always to be determined according to ageless principles. In practice there are several ways in which the doctrine retains its flexibility . . . two basic principles [should be considered]; first, that superior courts have power to overrule decisions of inferior courts and, in certain cases, to overrule their own earlier decisions, and, secondly that any rule of law may be changed by statute. Consequently every rule of law is subject to change, either by the judges themselves or by Parliament. Although legislation is the ultimate source of law, in the sense that Parliament has within our constitution the ultimate power to make, or unmake any law, it should not in any way be regarded as a superior source of law. Although judges may well be reluctant to make major changes which involve policy better settled by Parliament, judicial law-making can provide flexibility, and relative speed, because of the demands on parliamentary time.

Every rule of law must have its origin. If it were not created by statute, then it must have been created by a court. Thus, where there is no precedent the doctrine breaks down and the judge is bound to reach a decision in accordance with the general principles. Even in modern times cases arise for which there is no precedent. These cases are described as cases of first impression and require the judge to make law rather than to apply it.

Judges do sometimes create new law. For example, Lord Denning . . . virtually did this in *Central London Property Trust v High Tree House Ltd* ([1947] KB 130). The self-assumed power of the House of Lords to depart from its own previous decisions has had the effect of bringing into sharp relief the scope of the judicial function, for the members of the House are now free, in effect, to create new law. It is fair to say that certain judges deem it to be within their function to create new principles of law while other believe that any far-reaching change should be left to Parliament, which has greater facilities for testing the possible repercussions of law reform.

Where the words of the statute are clear and unambiguous, persons affected by its provisions will regulate their conduct according to the terms of the statute and the need for judicial interpretation will not arise. However, if the meaning or extent of a statute is uncertain or ambiguous, litigation is inevitable and the statute will have to be interpreted. There is a technical distinction between interpretation and construction. 'Interpretation' is simply the process whereby a meaning is assigned to words in a statute. the courts' primary task on interpretation is to ascertain and give effect to the meaning of the words used: the first enquiry of a court should be to ask: 'what do the words themselves mean?' 'Construction', on the other hand, is the process whereby uncertainties or ambiguities in a statute are resolved. It follows that every statute that comes before a court is interpreted whereas only uncertain or ambiguous provisions require construction. The processes are not usually distinguished by judges since, in the nature of things, litigation only arises around the wording of a statute where it is ambiguous or, at least, uncertain.

The main difficulty in such cases is that the intention of Parliament must be established primarily from the words used by Parliament, although increasingly intrinsic aids may be used.

An interesting problem of construction arises when the court is faced with a factual situation for which the statute has not provided. It can only be remedied by attributing to Parliament an intention which Parliament never had. That amounts to a legislative act on the part of the judiciary and is a function which the more conservative judges are slow to adopt.

In *Magor & St Mellons v Newport Corporation* [1952] AC 189, Lord Simonds condemned the approach of Lord Denning as a 'naked usurpation of the legislative function' . . . 'If a gap is disclosed', Lord Simonds explained, 'the remedy lies in an amending Act.' Nonetheless it is a truism that hard cases make bad law and the courts have, from time to time, been prepared to assume the authority to supply omission left by the legislature.

Source 2

Extract from s 8 of the Theft Act 1968.

8 Robbery

(1) *A person is guilty of robbery if he steals, and immediately before or at the time of doing so, and in order to do so, he uses force on any person or puts or seeks to put any person in fear of being then and there subjected to force.'*

Source 3

Extract adapted from the judgment of Lord Justice Lawton in *Dawson* (1976) 64 Cr App R 170.

Mr Locke had submitted at the end of the prosecution's case that what had happened could not in law amount to the use of force. He called the learned judge's attention to some old authorities and . . . submitted that because of those old authorities there was not enough evidence to go to the jury.

The object of the Act was to get rid of all the old technicalities of the law of larceny and to put the law into simple language which juries would understand and which they themselves would use. That is what has happened in section 8 which defines 'robbery'.

The choice of the word 'force' is not without interest because under the Larceny Act 1916 the word 'violence' had been used, but Parliament deliberately on the advice of the Criminal Law Revision Committee changed that word to 'force'. Whether there is any difference between 'violence' or 'force' is not relevant for the purposes of this case; but the word is 'force'. It is a word in ordinary use. It is a word which juries understand. The learned judge left it to say whether jostling a man in the way which the victim described to such an extent that he had difficulty in keeping his balance could be said to be the use of force. The learned judge, because of the argument put forward by Mr Locke, went out of his way to explain to the jury that force in these sort of circumstances must be substantial to justify a verdict.

Whether it was right for him to put that adjective before the word 'force' when Parliament had not done so we will not discuss for the purposes of this case. It was a matter for the jury. They were there to use their common-sense and knowledge of the world. We cannot say that their decision as to whether force was used was wrong. They were entitled to the view that force was used.

Source 4

Extract adapted from the judgment of Lord Justice Eveleigh in *Hale* (1978) 68 Cr App R 415.

In so far as the facts of the present case are concerned, counsel submitted that the theft was completed when the jewellery box was first seized and any force thereafter could not have been 'immediately before or at the time of stealing' and certainly not 'in order to steal'. The essence of the submission was that the theft was completed as soon as the jewellery box was seized.

Section 8 of the Theft Act begins: 'A person is guilty of robbery if he steals . . . '. He steals when he acts in accordance with the basic definition of theft in section 1 of the Theft Act; that is to say when he dishonestly appropriates property belonging to another with an intention of permanently depriving the other of it. It thus becomes necessary to consider what is 'appropriation' or, according to section 3, 'any assumption by a person of the rights of an owner'. An assumption of rights . . . is conduct which usurps the rights of the owner. To say that the conduct is over and done with as soon as he lays hands on the property, or when he first manifests an intention to deal with it as his own, is contrary to common-sense and to the natural meaning of the words.

In the present case there can be little doubt that if the appellant had been interrupted after the seizure of the jewellery box the jury would have been entitled to find that the appellant and his accomplice were assuming the rights of an owner at the time when the jewellery box was seized. However, the act of appropriation does not suddenly cease. It is a continuous act and it is a matter for the jury to decide whether or not the act of appropriation has finished. Moreover, it is quite clear that the intention to deprive the owner permanently, which accompanied the assumption of the owner's rights, was a continuing one at all material times. This Court therefore rejects the contention that the theft had ceased by the time the lady was tied up. As a matter of common-sense the appellant was in the course of committing the theft; he was stealing.

There remains the question whether there was robbery. Quite clearly the jury were at liberty to find the appellant guilty of robbery relying upon the force used when he put his hand over Mrs Carrett's mouth to restrain her from calling for help. We also think that they were also entitled to rely upon the act of tying her up provided they were satisfied (and it is difficult to see how they could not be satisfied) that the force so used was to enable them to steal.

Source 5

Extract adapted from the judgment of Watkins J in *Corcoran v Anderton* (1980) 71 Cr App R 104.

So confining myself to the facts as found by the justices in the instant case, I think that an 'appropriation' takes place when an accused snatches a woman's handbag completely from her grasp, so that she no longer has physical control of it because it has fallen to the ground. What has been involved in such activity as that, bearing in mind the dishonest state of mind of the accused, is an assumption of the rights of the owner, a taking of the property of another. If one had to consider the definition of 'theft' as contained in the Larceny Act 1916, it is inevitable, so it seems to me, that there was here a sufficient taking and carrying away to satisfy the definition of 'theft' in that Act. In my judgment there cannot possibly be, save for the instance where a handbag is carried away from the scene of it, a clearer instance of robbery than that which these justices found was committed.

Turning to the actual question posed to this Court. 'Could the tugging at the handbag, accompanied by force, amount to robbery, notwithstanding that the co-accused did not have sole control of the bag at any time?' in my opinion, which may be contrary to some notions of what constitutes a sufficient appropriation to satisfy the definition of that word in section 3(1) of the Theft Act, the forcible tugging of the handbag of itself could in the circumstances be a sufficient exercise of control by the accused person so as to amount to an assumption by him of the rights of the owner, and therefore an appropriation of the property.

Source 6

Extract adapted from J C Smith, *Smith & Hogan Criminal Law* (10th edn, Butterworths), p 563.

No jury could reasonably find that the slight physical contact which might be involved where D picks P's pocket would amount to a use of force. But very little may be required to turn a case of theft into one of robbery and to push or nudge the victim so as to cause him to lose his balance is capable of being a use of force.

Under the former law robbery was thought of as stealing accomplished by force . . ., the force being used to overpower P's resistance and not merely to seize the property. The CLRC appeared to have the same distinction in mind for they said that they would 'not regard mere snatching of property, such as a handbag, from an unresisting owner as using force for the purpose of the definition'. The distinction was meant to be conveyed by the words in s 8 'if he steals . . . and in order to do so, he uses force . . .'. But in *Clouden* the distinction was rejected and D's conviction for robbery was upheld where he wrenched a shopping basket from P's hand and ran off with it. In the view of the court the former distinction could not stand with words of the section and it was open for a jury to find on these facts that force had been used on P with intent to steal. [In consequence] it will be robbery where, for example, a struggle, even a fleeting one, takes place for possession of a handbag, or where an earring is snatched tearing the lobe of the ear.

Source 7

Extract from s 9 of the Theft Act 1968.

'9 Burglary

(1) A person is guilty of burglary if –

   a he enters any building or part of a building as a trespasser and with intent to commit any such offence as is mentioned in subsection (2) below; or

   b having entered any building or part of a building as a trespasser he steals or attempts to steal anything in the building or that part of it or inflicts or attempts to inflict on any person therein any grievous bodily harm.

(2) The offences referred to in subsection (1)(a) above are offences of stealing anything in the building or part of a building in question, of inflicting on any person therein any grievous bodily harm, or of doing unlawful damage to the building or anything therein.

(4) References in subsections (1) and (2) above to a building shall apply also to an inhabited vehicle or vessel, and shall apply to any such vehicle or vessel at times when the person having a habitation in it is not there as well as at times when he is.'

Source 8

Extract adapted from the judgment of Lord Justice Edmund Davies in *R v Collins* [1973] 1 QB 100.

Now one feature of the case which remained at the conclusion of the evidence in great obscurity is where exactly Collins was at the moment when, according to him, the girl manifested that she was welcoming him. Was he kneeling on the sill outside the window or was he already in the room, having climbed through the window frame, and kneeling upon the inner sill? It was a crucial matter, for there were certainly three ingredients that it was incumbent upon the Crown to establish. Under s 9 of the Theft Act 1968 . . . the entry of the accused into the building must first be proved. Secondly, it must be proved that he entered as a trespasser. Thirdly, it must be proved that he entered as a trespasser with intent at the time of entry to commit rape therein.

The second ingredient of the offence – the entry must be as a trespasser – is one which has not, to the best of our knowledge been previously canvassed in the courts.

What does that involve? According to the editors of *Archbold Criminal Pleading* 'Any intentional, reckless or negligent entry into a building will, it would appear, constitute a trespass if the building is in the possession of another person who does not consent to the entry'.

A view contrary to that . . . was expressed by Professor Smith's book on *The Law of Theft*: 'D should be acquitted on the ground of lack of *mens rea*. Though, under the civil law, he entered as a trespasser, it is submitted that he cannot be convicted of the criminal offence unless he knew of the facts which caused him to be a trespasser or, at least, was reckless.'

The matter has also been dealt with by Professor Griew . . . 'What if D wrongly believes that he is not trespassing . . . for the purpose of criminal liability a man should be judged on the basis of the facts as he believed them to be. . .D should be liable for burglary only if he knowingly trespasses or is reckless as to whether he trespasses or not'.

We prefer the view expressed by Professor Smith and Professor Griew . . . there cannot be a conviction for entering premises 'as a trespasser' within the meaning of section 9 of the Theft Act unless the person entering does so knowing that he is a trespasser and nevertheless deliberately enters, or, at the very least, is reckless as to whether or not he is entering the premises of another without the other party's consent.

Having so held, the pivotal point of this appeal is whether the Crown established that this defendant at the moment he entered the bedroom knew perfectly well that he was not welcome there, or being reckless as to whether he was welcome or not, was nevertheless determined to enter. That in turn involves consideration as to where he was at the time the complainant indicated that she was welcoming him into the bedroom.

Unless the jury were entirely satisfied that the defendant made an effective and substantial entry into the bedroom without the complainant doing or saying anything to cause him to believe that she was consenting to his entering it, he ought not to be convicted of the offence charged.

We have to say that this appeal must be allowed on the basis that the jury were never invited to consider the vital question whether this young man did enter the premises as a trespasser.

Source 9

Extract adapted from Michael Jefferson, *Criminal Law* (Pearson Publishing), pp 429–430.

The Court of Appeal in *Brown* [1985] Crim LR 212 widened the *Collins* definition by holding that the entry had to be effective but need not be substantial. The question whether the entry was effective was for the jury. There was no need for the whole of the accused's body to be in the building: the top half was in a shop-front display, the bottom half outside. In *Ryan* [1996] Crim LR 320 the accused had his head and right arm inside a house but he was trapped by the neck by the window. The Court of Appeal applied *Brown*. There was evidence on which a jury could find that the accused had entered. The accused had entered a building even though only part of the body was within the building and even though he could not do anything 'effective' in the position in which he was caught. 'Effective' therefore does not mean 'effective to commit the ulterior offence'. This ruling seems right in principle. After all a person can be guilty of burglary with intent to rape when there is no person present in the building.

It is thought that 'effective' relates to the entry, not to the possibility of theft, rape, etc. The problem is this: if the accused's intention is to rape and he is in the same position as in *Brown* with the top half of his body in the building, is his entry therein effective for the purposes of the rape form of burglary? On the wording of the statute it would seem that an effective entry into the building is sufficient without the accused's going so far as to be in a position to effect his ulterior intent. *Ryan* confirmed this supposition. It may be that *Brown* and *Ryan* are leading to a position where entry need not be effective just as it need not be substantial.

Source 10

For reasons of copyright, Source 10 cannot be reproduced. Source 10 is available as part of the source material from the OCR website, www.ocr.org.uk/OCR/Website/Data/ Publication/Pre-Release%20Materials%20 (Live%20Materials)/AS_A_Level60293.pdf

Source 11

Extract adapted from the judgment of Lord Justice Geoffrey Lane in *R v Walkington* [1979] 1 WLR 1169.

The defendant was seen loitering near tills in Debenhams in Oxford Street while cashing up was in process. He then went into a till area, which was for staff only, and which was unattended. He looked into the partly open cash drawer and then slammed it shut when he saw that it was empty. He was convicted of burglary with intent to steal contrary to s 9(1)(a) Theft Act 1968 and appealed unsuccessfully.

It seems to this court that in the end one simply has to go back to the words of the Act itself and if the jury are satisfied so as to feel sure that the defendant had entered any building or part of a building as a trespasser, and are satisfied that at the moment of entering he intended to steal anything in the building or that part of the building, the fact that there was nothing in the building worth while to steal seems to us to be immaterial. He nevertheless had the intent to steal. As we see, to hold otherwise would be to make a nonsense of this part of the Act and cannot have been the intention of the legislature at the time when the Theft Act 1968 was passed. Nearly every prospective burglar could no doubt truthfully say that he only intended to steal if he found something in the building worth stealing.

Source 12

Extract adapted from C M V Clarkson and H M Keating, *Criminal Law Text and Materials* (4th edn, Sweet & Maxwell), p 834.

Reference must be made to the civil law in order to understand the term 'trespass'. Under civil law, trespass is entry without the consent of the lawful possessor. No conviction for burglary can be obtained without a finding of civil trespass but as *Collins* makes clear, more than this is required, the defendant must enter 'knowing that he is a trespasser . . . or, at the very least, is reckless whether or not he is entering the premises of another without the other party's consent'.

Even if there is consent, if the defendant acts in a way that goes beyond what the possessor would have consented to, he may be deemed to enter as a trespasser. Thus in *Jones and Smith* the defendant had left his parents' home but was a frequent, welcome visitor. One night he entered their home and stole two television sets. Despite the father's loyal statement that his son was welcome at *any* time, the court held that an inference could be drawn that he would not have consented to entry for the purposes of theft. The son was thus held to have entered as a trespasser.

A2.2 THE STYLE OF QUESTIONS

There are four questions on the paper, all of which must be answered. The first question is always on the English Legal System theme of statutory interpretation. The second question is case study on one of the cases in the source material. The third question is an essay on the substantive law of burglary and robbery. The fourth is an application question on the substantive law of burglary and robbery.

The time for answering the whole paper is one and a half hours (90 minutes). The total marks for the paper are 100. From this it can be worked out that there is less than a minute for each mark. This makes important to look at the mark allocation for each question and make sure that enough time is allowed to answer all four questions.

A2.2.1 The assessment objectives

To fully understand the type and level of answer required on this Unit, it is helpful to know the three assessment objectives which are used in marking all the units of A level law. These are:

1 **AO1 Knowledge and Understanding**
   Recall, select and develop knowledge and understanding of legal principles accurately and by means of examples and citation.
2 **AO2 Analysis, Evaluation and Application**
   Analyse legal material, issues, and situation, and evaluate and apply the appropriate legal rules and principles.
3 **AO3 Communication and Presentation**
   Present a logical and coherent argument and communicate relevant material in a clear and effective manner, using appropriate legal terminology.

Overall on this paper, the weighting of the assessment objectives is:

- 30% for AO1
- 60% for AO2
- 10% for AO3.

The weighting of AO1 and AO2 varies on each question in the Special Study Unit. The exact weighting for each type of question will be explained as we look at the four types of question asked in this Unit. The weighting of AO3 is always 10%.

A2.2.2 Statutory interpretation question

Students need to have good knowledge of the law on statutory interpretation. This will have been studied for AS Law, but it is important to realise that A2 requires a greater depth of knowledge and a higher standard of analysis.

The question will be an essay style question and will refer to specific lines of Source 1 and will be focused on a particular area of statutory interpretation. For example, the question in the June 2005 examination was this:

In Source 1 [page 3, lines 52–53 Special Study Materials]* the author suggests that the main problem with statutory interpretation is that '*that the intention of Parliament must be established primarily from the words used by Parliament*'.

Compare the literal and purposive approaches to statutory interpretation in the light of the above statement.

[30 marks]

*The page and line references are those in the Special Study Materials booklet supplied by OCR.

The 30 marks show that there is only about 27 minutes to answer the question. In fact, question 1 will always either be worth 25 or 30 marks. For 25 marks, you need to allocate about 22 minutes to the question.

There is slightly more weighting on AO2 than on AO1, but there is not a great difference in the two. This means that you need both to demonstrate your knowledge (not merely using what is in the source) and to analyse and evaluate the information you use. Merely writing down the rules of statutory interpretation will not gain marks for AO2.

There are several areas of statutory interpretation that could be examined. These include:

- the two approaches – literal and purposive
- any of the three 'rules' – the literal rule, the golden rule and the mischief rule
- the rules of language – especially the *ejusdem generis* rule
- the aids to interpretation – intrinsic and extrinsic.

It is important to be able to use case examples to explain these. Case examples are also useful for evaluation. For evaluation, you can use relevant points from the source material, but you must also bring in other points.

Use of source material

If you want to refer to the source material, this can be done by giving the source page and line reference. Do not copy out large amounts of the source: this will get you very little credit. The important points are showing an understanding of arguments in the source, being able to explain them in your own words and to use them in discussion. This applies to questions 1, 2 and 3.

A2.2.3 The case study question

Question 2 is always on a case in the source material. The question usually carries 15 marks (= about 12 minutes), but it is possible for the question to be worth 20 marks (= about 17 minutes).

The focus of the question has a link to development of the law in that particular area, for example how a particular case has developed the law or how the law has been interpreted by the courts.

The weighting of the assessment objectives is heavily on AO2 (analysis and evaluation). If the question carries 15 marks, the division of marks is 10 for AO2, 3½ for AO1 and 1½ for AO3. The reason for the weighting being on AO2 is that a considerable amount of the facts will already be in the source. The marks for AO1 are, therefore, for the extra knowledge which you show about the case – possibly details of the case – or the area of law, such as other cases on the same point.

The question for June 2005 was:

Discuss the extent to which the decision in *Hale* [Source 4 Special Study Materials] can be said to represent Parliament's intention in the Theft Act 1968 s 8.

[15 marks]

This required a discussion on the wording of s 8 (given in Source 2), making points such as:

- the words show a clear intention that, to be guilty of robbery, a defendant should use force in order to steal – was this the position in *Hale*?
- the words also show a clear intention that the force should be 'immediately before or at the time of stealing' – how does this fit with the use of force by tying up the victim after the theft?
- discussion of the particular facts in *Hale*, where one defendant tied the victim up while the other stole, in relation to the definition of robbery
- discussion of the court's interpretation of theft as being a continuous act – was this Parliament's intention?

Where relevant, use the source material to support your arguments. See section A2.2.2 for tips on how to use source material.

Note that mark schemes and examiners' reports are available from OCR.

A2.2.4 The main essay question

Question 3 is an essay on a particular area or areas of the substantive law on burglary or robbery. The question will refer to specific lines of one of the Sources in the Special Study Material booklet. It will carry either 25 (= 22 minutes) or 30 marks (= 27 minutes).

The weighting of the assessment objectives is slightly more for AO2 (analysis and evaluation) than for AO1 (knowledge). As with the statutory interpretation in question 1, this means that you need to demonstrate your knowledge (not only using what is in the source) and to make sure that you analyse and evaluate the information you use.

Use the source material where relevant. If you really know the source material well, you may be able to identify, quickly, other sources which have linked and relevant points. There is not time to read through all the sources: you need to know them well enough to be able to identify which source or sources you want to use.

A2.2.5 The application question

The final question requires you to apply the law to factual situations. There will probably be three different short scenarios, each being worth 10 marks and the total question worth 30 marks. Of these, 20 marks are for AO2, so you can see that in this question the majority of the marks will be for identifying the issues and applying the law.

Each scenario will raise a different point or points of law. For example, in burglary scenarios, there will be s 9(1)(a) and s 9(1)(b) situations. It is important to show a clear understanding of the two different types of burglary. Consider the following scenario:

Example question

Amrit is invited by Jason to his birthday party. After the meal, Amrit goes to the bathroom. In the hallway he sees an open handbag with a purse in it. Amrit takes a £20 note from the purse. Amrit then sees that the bedroom door is open and there is some jewellery on a table in there. He decides to steal the jewellery and enters the bedroom. At that moment, he hears someone coming up the stairs. He leaves the bedroom without taking anything.

Explain whether Amrit has committed burglary.

Answering the question

It is important to identify the issues. This scenario has two situations which must be considered separately.

In the first situation, involving the £20 note, Amrit is a lawful visitor in the hallway. He had been invited there by Jason and Jason would expect any guest to go through the hallway. So this means that Amrit is not a trespasser in respect of this area of the house and so cannot be guilty of burglary.

However, in the situation of the jewellery in the bedroom, Amrit probably is a trespasser. His invitation to the house does not include going, uninvited, into the bedroom. So, at the moment he enters the bedroom, he is a trespasser. As he has the intention to steal when he enters, he is guilty of a s 9(1)(a) burglary at that moment. It does not matter that he does not take anything.

An additional point to explain about the definition of burglary is that the entry as a trespasser can be to a building or 'part of a building'. Here, the entry is to the bedroom, which is part of a building. This point can be supported with the case of *Walkington* (1979) (see Source 11), where going into the till area in a store was held to be entry to part of a building. Also in *Walkington*, the defendant was guilty even though he did not steal anything (there was nothing in the till). Again, the analogy can be drawn with Amrit's situation.

The four-module A Level OCR (2008 onwards)

From September 2006 OCR specification for A Level Law will change to four modules. There will be two modules for AS which will be examined for the first time in 2007 and two modules for A2 which will be examined for the first time in 2008. The A2 modules for the Criminal Law option will be:

■ Unit 3A – worth 60% of the A2 and
■ Unit 3B – worth 40% of the A2.

The full specification, specimen papers and mark schemes can be found online at www.ocr.org.uk

A3.1 ASSESSMENT OBJECTIVES

Answers are marked on the basis of three assessment objectives. These are used in marking all the units of A Level law and are the same as used in the previous six-module specification. They are:

1 **AO1 Knowledge and Understanding**
   Recall, select and develop knowledge and understanding of legal principles accurately and by means of examples and citation.
2 **AO2 Analysis, Evaluation and Application**
   Analyse legal material, issues, and situation, and evaluate and apply the appropriate legal rules and principles.
3 **AO3 Communication and Presentation**
   Present a logical and coherent argument and communicate relevant material in a clear and effective manner, using appropriate legal terminology.

A3.2 CRIMINAL LAW UNIT 3A

This will examine all of the content area of the new specification. See the grid in the Preface for the topics covered. The question paper will have three sections:

■ Section A: essays: in which candidates are required to answer one essay from a choice of three
■ Section B: problems: in which candidates are required to answer one problem from a choice of three
■ Section C: dilemma boards (evaluation of statements) in which candidates are required to answer one from a choice of two.

A3.3 ESSAY QUESTIONS

These can be based on any area or areas of the substantive criminal law studied for the A2 option. There are 50 marks available for each essay. These are allocated to the assessment objectives as follows:

■ AO1 – maximum 25 marks
■ AO2 – maximum 20 marks
■ AO3 – maximum 5 marks.

These show that it is important both to know the law in question and to be able to analyse and evaluate it.

The questions in the specimen papers show that the style of essay questions will remain the same as those set for the previous six-module specification. All essay-style examination questions at the end of chapters in this book are taken from past OCR papers on the six-module specification, so they can be used as practice for the new four-module specification.

A3.4 PROBLEM QUESTIONS

These can also be based on any area or areas of the substantive criminal law studied for the A2 option. For these, knowledge and understanding of the law (AO1) together with identification of the relevant issues and application of the law (AO2) are required. Each question is worth 50 marks and the allocation of assessment objectives is the same as for essay questions:

- AO1 – maximum 25 marks
- AO2 – maximum 20 marks
- AO3 – maximum 5 marks.

The questions in the specimen papers show that the style of problem questions will remain the same as those set for the previous six-module specification. As with the essay questions, all problem-style examination questions at the end of chapters in this book are taken from past OCR papers on the six-module specification, so they can be used as practice for the new four-module specification.

However, it should be remembered that there may be a wider mix of topics than in the six-module examinations where areas of criminal law were examined separately on the first two criminal law modules. It is now possible for an examiner to create problem questions that include, for example, murder and assaults. Or one in which murder and defences such as duress or automatism feature. An example is given below of a question taken from an OCR examination paper pre-curriculum 2000.

Question

Richard is an 18-year-old student who lives with his domineering father, Steven, and his mother, Tilly, who is diabetic. Steven has subjected Richard to regular and quite violent beatings for many years.

Steven has been involved in a long-standing dispute with a neighbour, Vinnie.

Steven orders Richard to lie in wait for Vinnie and stab him to death. Terrified of further beatings, Richard picks up what he believes to be a hunting knife. In fact, it is a dummy knife of the type used in film and television and, as Richard stabs Vinnie, the blade slides harmlessly into the handle and Vinnie escapes unharmed.

On hearing what Steven ordered Richard to do, Tilly becomes so distressed that her diabetes becomes unstable, causing hyperglycaemia (a high blood sugar level). Whilst in this state she shoots Steven in the head with a shotgun as he lies, apparently, sleeping in bed. Medical evidence shows conclusively that before Tilly shot Steven, he had died from a heart attack.

Consider the criminal liability of Richard and Tilly.

(OCR, Summer 1997)

Potential answer

It is necessary to identify that Richard's attack on Vinnie was attempted murder. Explain the intention required for this. Then it is necessary to identify the possible defence of duress by threats. The important cases here are *Howe* (1987) and *Gotts* (1992), as these establish that duress is not available as a defence to murder or attempted murder.

Next, consider Tilly's liability. The shooting of Steven was attempted murder. It is necessary to discuss the fact that the killing was impossible but that this does not prevent it from being attempted murder under the Criminal Attempts Act 1981. Having established the offence, go on to any possible defences. Here, the diabetic state of high blood sugar is a clear hint at automatism, but because Tilly's condition is caused by an internal disease, this is insane-automatism and she will come within the M'Naghten Rules on insanity. Important cases here are *Sullivan* (1984) and *Hennessy* (1989).

A3.5 DILEMMA BOARDS/ EVALUATING STATEMENTS

The final style of questions on Unit 3A of the four-module A level examinations is known as a dilemma board or evaluating statements. This is a new style of question in which students are faced with a scenario plus four statements about it which they have to evaluate. Each dilemma board carries 20 marks. This means that you should spend considerably less time on it than on the other two questions. The marks are all for AO2.

An example of such a question is given on p. 216. It is taken from the specimen papers published by OCR.

Question

Wayne is the captain of the Northport United football team. During an important match against their local rivals, Wayne is involved in a nasty clash of heads in an incident with an opposing player, Andrew. Wayne receives a nasty bruise above his left eye and is badly concussed. Wayne insists on continuing after treatment with a cold sponge but is obviously still in a very dazed condition. A few minutes later, Wayne jumps wildly into a foul tackle on Andrew. Andrew is carried off in agony and X-rays later reveal that he has a broken ankle.

Evaluate the accuracy of **each** of the four statements A, B, C and D individually, as they apply to the facts in the above scenario.

Statement A: Andrew is liable for ABH s 47 OAPA for the bruise suffered by Wayne.
Statement B: Wayne is liable for GBH s 18 OAPA for the broken ankle sustained by Andrew.
Statement C: Andrew has a defence of consent for any charge brought by Wayne.
Statement D: Wayne has a defence of automatism for any charge brought by Andrew.

(Specimen question, OCR)

Potential answer

It is necessary to deal with each statement separately. For each one, explain whether it is a correct statement or not. Let's look at Statement A. The important points are what the scenario states that Andrew did and what the law on s 47 OAPA is.

Andrew is involved in a clash of heads with Wayne, causing a bruise. A bruise can be ABH. But is it sufficient to satisfy the test of 'interfering with the health and comfort of the victim? (*Miller* (1954))

Has Andrew realised the risk of applying unlawful force to Wayne (*Cunningham* (1957)) or has he applied unlawful force intentionally? If either of these applies, he can be liable for a s 47 offence.

The answer can be written as series of short statements. It is not meant to be an essay. It is useful to practise these types of questions, using a dilemma board and writing your answers on the board. An example of a dilemma board for this scenario is given on the next page.

A3.6 CRIMINAL LAW UNIT 3B

This is based on the Special Study Materials pre-released by OCR. The materials used in the specimen papers are given in the next appendix. This material will be used in the examination sessions for January 2008, June 2008 and January 2009.

Wayne is liable for GBH s 18 OAPA for the broken ankle sustained by Wayne

Andrew is liable for ABH s 47 OAPA for the bruise suffered by Wayne

Wayne is the captain of the Northport United football team. During an important match against their local rivals, Wayne is involved in a nasty clash of heads in an incident with an opposing player, Andrew. Wayne receives a nasty bruise above his left eye and is badly concussed. Wayne insists on continuing after treatment with a cold sponge but is obviously still in a very dazed condition. A few minutes later Wayne jumps wildly into a foul tackle on Andrew. Andrew is carried off in agony and x-rays later reveal that he has a broken ankle.

Wayne has a defence of automatism for any charge brought by Andrew

Andrew has a defence of consent for any charge brought by Wayne

In the above dilemma board use the four spaces surrounding the four statements to consider whether each is or is not appropriate to the situation outlined in the central box.

The Synoptic Unit for OCR for 2008 to 2010

This appendix deals with the source material and style of examination for the Criminal Law Special Study Unit, 2573. This Unit is part of the new four-module examination for the OCR Law A Level. It will be examined for the first time in January 2008. It will then be available for at least the following sessions:

- June 2008
- January 2009.

The source material is reproduced below at section A4.1. Booklets containing this source material are available from OCR for use in preparing for the examination. In addition, each candidate will be given a clean copy of the booklet for reference purposes within the examination room.

This source material forms the basis of the questions on the examination paper, so it is essential that all students study it carefully.

The assessment objectives are the same as those set out in Appendix 3 at section A3.1 for Unit Criminal Law 3A

A4.1 SOURCE MATERIALS

Source 1

Adapted from the judgment of Lord Lane, Lord Chief Justice, in *R v Graham* (1982) 74 Cr App R 235 (Court of Appeal, Criminal Division).

The law requires a defendant to have the self-control reasonably to be expected to the ordinary citizen in his situation. It should likewise expect him to have the steadfastness reasonably to be expected of the ordinary citizen in his situation . . .

. . . the correct approach on the facts of this case would have been as follows: (1) Was the defendant, or may he have been, impelled to act as he did because, as a result of what he reasonably believed King had said or done, he had good cause to fear that if he did not so act King would kill him or cause . . . him serious physical injury? (2) If so, have the prosecution made the jury sure that a sober person of reasonable firmness, sharing the characteristics of the defendant, would not have responded . . . by taking part in the killing?

Source 2

Adapted from the judgment of Lord Hailsham, LC, in *R v Howe* [1987] 1 AC 417.

. . . some degree of proportionality between the threat and the offence must, at least to some extent, be a prerequisite of the defence under the existing law. Few would resist threats to the life of a loved one if the alternative were driving across the red lights or in excess of 70 m.p.h. on the motorway. But it would take rather more than the threat of a slap on the wrist or even moderate pain or injury to discharge the evidential burden even in the case of a fairly serious assault. In such a case the 'concession to human frailty' is no more than to say that in such circumstances a reasonable man of average courage is entitled to embrace as a matter of choice the alternative which a reasonable man could regard as the lesser of two evils. Other considerations necessarily arise where the choice is between the threat of death or . . . serious injury and deliberately taking an innocent life. In such a case a reasonable man might reflect that one innocent human life is at least as valuable as his own or that of his loved one. In such a case a man cannot claim that he is choosing the lesser of two evils. Instead he is embracing the cognate but morally disreputable principle that the end justifies the means.

Source 3

Adapted from the judgment of Lord Griffiths in *R v Howe* [1987] 1 AC 417, HL.

As I can find no fair and certain basis on which to differentiate between participants to a murder and as I am firmly convinced that the law should not be extended to the killer, I would depart from the decision of this House in *DPP for Northern Ireland v Lynch* and declare the law to be that duress is not available as a defence to a charge of murder, or to attempted murder.

Source 4

Adapted from the judgment of Lord Jauncey in *R v Gotts* [1992] 2 AC 412, HL.

. . . I share the view of Lord Griffiths that 'it would have been better had [the development of the defence of duress] not taken place and that duress had been regarded as a factor to be taken into account in mitigation' . . . *R v Howe* . . . While it is not now possible for this House to restrict the availability of the defence of duress in those cases where it has been recognised to exist, I feel constrained to express the personal view that given the climate of violence and terrorism which ordinary law-abiding citizens now have to face Parliament might do well to consider whether the defence should continue to be available in the case of all very serious crimes . . . The reason why duress has for so long been stated not to be available as a defence to a murder charge is that the law regards the sanctity of human life and the protection thereof as of paramount importance. Does that reason apply to attempted murder as well

as to murder? As Lord Griffiths points out [in *Howe*] . . . intent to kill must be proved in the case of attempted murder but not necessarily in the case of murder. Is there logic in affording the defence to one who intends to kill but fails and denying it to one who mistakenly kills intending only to injure . . .?

. . . withholding the defence in any circumstances will create some anomalies but I would agree with Lord Griffiths (*R v Howe*) that nothing should be done to undermine in any way the highest duty of the law to protect the freedom and lives of those who live under it. I can therefore see no justification in logic, morality or law in affording to an attempted murderer the defence which is withheld from a murderer.

Source 5

Adapted from Clarkson and Keating, *Criminal Law Text and Materials* (Sweet & Maxwell, 1998), pp. 328–329 and 335–336.

In *Valderrama-Vega* the defendant was threatened with the disclosure of his homosexuality, was under financial pressure and received threats of death or serious harm. The first two are incapable of amounting to duress but the court held that the jury was entitled to look at the cumulative effects of all of the threats. It was wrong to direct the jury that the threat of death or serious injury had to be the sole reason for him committing the crime.

In *Cole* the defendant robbed two building societies and claimed that he had done so to pay off a debt to moneylenders who had hit him with a baseball bat and had threatened him and his family. The Court of Appeal held that the defence of duress is only available if the threats are directed at the offence committed. In this case the moneylenders had not stipulated that he commit robbery . . . to meet their demands [so] there was . . . insufficient nexus between the threat and the offence.

In *Hudson and Taylor* the threats could have been reported to the police, but the two young girls, aged 17 and 19, were convinced that the police protection would be ineffective. Are we to blame them for their failure to seek official protection? It would appear that their response was typical of the response of most ordinary girls of that age faced with such a predicament. It would surely be ludicrous to assert that the defence of duress would only be available to them if there had been a sniper sitting in the court ready to execute his threats immediately. These views were echoed by Lord Griffiths in *Howe*:

'*if duress is introduced as a merciful concession to human frailty it seems hard to deny it to a man who knows full well that any official protection he may seek will not be effective*'.

The Draft Criminal Law Bill 1993 has, however, not responded to these calls . . .

Source 6

Adapted from Duncan Bloy and Philip Parry, *Principles of Criminal Law* (Cavendish, 2000), pp 259–260.

The defence is likely to be denied if the accused has voluntarily joined a criminal organisation, because he has put himself into a position where he may expect others to use force to exert their will over him, particularly if he should try to resile from their operations. The leading case is *Sharp* (1987) where Lord Lane CJ stated the principle thus:

'*Where a person has voluntarily, and with knowledge of its nature, joined a criminal organisation or gang which he knew might bring pressure on him to commit an offence and was an active member when he was put under such pressure, he cannot avail himself of the defence of duress.*'

[In] *Shepherd* (1987) a number of men would enter the shop, some would distract the shopkeeper while the others took the goods. S claimed that after the first expedition he wanted to withdraw but was threatened by other gang members with violence to him and his family and so he felt compelled to carry on. The trial judge ruled that duress was not available. The appeal was allowed. This case can be distinguished from [*Sharp*] on the basis that the defendant was not at the outset joining a gang with a known propensity for violence and who could anticipate what might happen if his nerve failed. In this case there would be no immediate assumption that should he wish to withdraw then he might be faced with serious violence. As the court said:

'. . . *there are certain kinds of criminal enterprises the joining of which, in the absence of any knowledge or propensity to violence on the part of one member, would not lead another to suspect that a decision to think better of the whole affair might lead him into serious trouble. In such cases, if trouble materialises unexpectedly and puts the defendant into a dilemma in which a reasonable man might have chosen to act as he did, the concession to human frailty is available to the defendant.*'

Source 7

Adapted from Michael Jefferson, *Criminal Law* (Pitman, 1997), pp 236–239.

Looking at the law one might expect that necessity should be made consistent with duress by affording a defence in similar circumstances.

Surely there must be some kind of a defence in circumstances such as those which occurred in *Kitson* (1955), which is one of the more ludicrous cases in post-war English law. The passenger in a car, having taken drink, fell asleep. He awoke to find the driver gone and the car coasting downhill. He grabbed hold of the steering-wheel and in doing so prevented a crash. Surely he should be congratulated not prosecuted. [and] If prosecuted . . . he should have a defence.

Recently – and the law is not yet settled – the courts have shown themselves more amenable than previously in creating a defence. The Court of Appeal in *Conway* established a defence called 'duress of circumstances ' The defendant . . . said that he had driven recklessly because he feared that two men who approached his car were going to kill his passenger. The court allowed his appeal. The judges held that the facts amounted to duress of circumstances; that duress was an example of necessity; and that whether duress of circumstances was called duress or necessity did not matter.

The court in *Conway* believed themselves bound by their decision in *Willer* (1986) [where] the term 'duress of circumstances' was not used.

These two cases were followed in *Martin* where the Court of Appeal drew the boundaries of the defence. There had to be a fear of death or serious bodily harm, and a question to be asked was whether a person of reasonable firmness sharing the defendant's characteristics would have responded as the accused did.

Source 8

Adapted from the judgment of Lord Justice Kennedy in *Pommell* [1995] 2 Cr App R 607.

The strength of the argument that a person ought to be permitted to breach the letter of the criminal law in order to prevent a greater evil [to] himself or others has long been recognised . . . but has, in English law, not given rise to a general defence of necessity, and . . . to . . . murder, the defence has been specifically held not to exist (see *Dudley and Stephens*) . . .Even in relation to other offences there are powerful arguments against recognising the general defence . . .

However, that does not really deal with the

situation where someone commendably infringes a regulation in order to prevent another person from committing what everyone would accept as being a greater evil with a gun. In that situation it cannot be satisfactory to leave it to the prosecuting authority not to prosecute . . .

. . . in the present case the defence was open to the appellant . . . [but] a person who has taken possession of a gun in circumstances where he has the defence of duress of circumstances must 'desist from committing the crime as soon as he reasonably can' . . .

Source 9

Adapted from Clarkson and Keating, *Criminal Law Text and Materials* (Sweet & Maxwell, 1998), pp 357–358.

In 1974 the Law Commission proposed that a general defence of necessity be introduced into English law. However, three years later it rejected the idea, going so far as to say that if a defence of necessity already existed at common law it should be abolished. It felt that allowing such a defence to a charge of murder could effectively legalise euthanasia in England. The Law Commission felt that specific statutory provisions already covered those areas where the defence might be most needed. For minor offences it argued that prosecutions were unlikely and, in any event, the sentencing policy of the English courts was such that people convicted in these situations would probably receive a minimal sentence, say, an absolute or conditional discharge.

. . . at the same time as making these 'totally negative' proposals, the Law Commission was recommending that duress be extended to *all* crimes. The absurdity of this position was exposed by the . . . Criminal Code Bill [which] emphasised that it was unacceptable to rely on prosecutorial discretion [and] instead proposed a defence of necessity called 'duress of circumstances'.

. . . it is unfortunate that the Draft Bill perpetuates the terminology of 'duress of circumstances'. Perhaps it was introduced in *Willer* and *Conway* because the threats there came from other persons rather than from objective circumstances. However, *Martin* was a classic case of necessity and should be recognised as such.

The courts have come a long way in a short time in recognising that blame is inappropriate in circumstances of necessity.

Source 10

Adapted from the judgment of Lord Justice Ward in *Re A (Conjoined Twins)* [2000] NLJ Law Reports, 6th October 2000, pp 1453–1454.

J and M were conjoined twins . . . J was capable of independent existence, but an operation to separate the twins would inevitably have resulted in the death of M who was alive only because a common artery enabled her sister to circulate oxygenated blood for both of them. If there was no such operation they would both die . . . The parents would not consent . . ., but the doctors were convinced that they could carry out the operation so as to give J a life that would be worthwhile. The Trust therefore sought a declaration confirming the lawfulness of the proposed operation.

Ward LJ:
The judge was plainly right to conclude that the operation would be in J's best interest. The question was whether it would be in M's best interest. It could not be. It would bring her life to an end before its natural span. It denied her inherent right to life.

A balance had to be struck . . . The best interests of the twins was to give the chance of life to the twin whose actual bodily condition was capable of accepting the chance to her advantage even if that had to be at the cost of the sacrifice of the life which was so unnaturally supported. This was, however, subject to whether what was proposed to be done could be lawfully done.

The crucial question was whether the law should confer in any circumstances, however extreme, the right to choose that one innocent person should be killed rather than another.

. . . the doctors could not be denied a right of choice if they were under a duty to choose. They were under a duty to M not to operate because it would kill M, but they were under a duty to J to operate because not to do so would kill her. It was important to stress that it made no difference whether the killing was by act or omission.

In those circumstances the law had to allow an escape through choosing the lesser of the two evils. Faced as they were with an apparently irreconcilable conflict the doctors should be in no different position from that in which the court itself was placed . . . giving the sanctity of life principle its place in the balancing exercise that had to be undertaken. For the same reasons that led to the conclusion that consent should be give to operate, the conclusion had to be that the carrying out of the operation would be justified as the lesser evil and no unlawful act would be committed.

Source 11

Adapted from Christopher F Sharp QC, *The Manchester Conjoined Twins Case, New Law Journal*, 6th October 2000, pp. 1460–1462.

The issue for the court was whether an act by the doctors which, while saving Jodie's life, and although not primarily intended to kill Mary, would have that inevitable effect, would be unlawful or could be justified . . . This led finally to a detailed consideration of the doctrine of necessity.

The Court's approach was to accept that the doctrine of necessity, which in its related form of duress has been rejected by the House of Lords in *Howe* . . . as a defence to murder,

. . . could nevertheless in the unique circumstances of this case be extended to cover the doctors' intended action . . . Robert Walker LJ concluded that in the absence of Parliamentary intervention the law as to the defence is going to have to develop on a case by case basis . . . and this was an appropriate case to extend it, if necessary.

Ward LJ having identified the rationale of the rejection of the defence of necessity as one based on the sanctity of life, and having identified as the crucial question in this case the question posed by Lord Mackay in *Howe* whether the circumstances could ever be extreme enough for the law to confer a right to choose that one innocent person should be killed rather than another, held that . . . the law should allow an escape by permitting the doctors to choose the lesser of two evils.

Brooke LJ carried out an exhaustive review of the jurisprudence . . . From . . . Stephen, he derived three necessary requirements for the application of the doctrine:

1 the act is needed to avoid inevitable and irreparable evil
2 no more should be done than is reasonably necessary for the purpose to be achieved
3 the evil inflicted must not be disproportionate to the evil avoided.

Given that the . . . law pointed irresistibly to the conclusion that the interests of Jodie must be preferred to the conflicting interests of Mary, he considered that all three of these requirements were satisfied in this case.

A4.2 THE EXAMINATION

In addition to knowing the source material and the law on the topics, the specification also states that candidates are expected to demonstrate understanding of the development of the law and to use legal methods and reasoning to analyse material, to select appropriate legal rules and apply these in order to draw conclusions.

There will be three questions on the exam paper and candidates have to answer all three. The exam is one and a half hours long. The questions will always be in the same format. They are:

■ **Question 1** A case study based on one of the cases in the special study materials.
■ **Question 2** An essay on an specific area of law in the special study materials.
■ **Question 3** An application question in which candidates have to apply the law to different scenarios.

There is more time on this four-module Special Study Paper to develop answers, than on the previous six-module specification. So the examiners are looking for depth of answer.

There are 80 marks in total for the paper.

A4.3 USING THE SOURCE MATERIALS

If you want to refer to the source material, this can be done by giving the source page and line reference. Do not copy out large amounts of the source: this will get you very little credit. The important points are showing an understanding of arguments in the source, being able to explain them in your own words and to use them in discussion.

A4.4 THE CASE STUDY QUESTION

Question 1 is always on a case in the source material. The question in the specimen material carries 12 marks and you should spend about 18 minutes on this question. The 12 marks are all given for Assessment Objective 2 (analysis and evaluation).

A4.5 THE ESSAY

Question 2 can be on any area of criminal law in the Special Study Material. The question on the specimen paper is worth 29 marks and you should spend about 36 minutes on this question.

Both AO1 and AO2 are tested in this question, with approximately equal marks available for each. For AO1, you will need to bring in extra knowledge, not merely rely on the source material. For AO2, the level of analyse and evaluation is the important aspect.

A4.6   THE APPLICATION QUESTION

There will usually be three mini-scenarios, each of which will raise different points of law. On the specimen paper each mini-scenario is worth 10 marks. Overall on this question you should spend about 36 minutes. Overall in the question 10 marks are available for AO1 and 20 marks for AO2. The question from the specimen paper is given below.

Question

Mara, Ian and Clare are all students of Christine's in the law school where Christine works as a lecturer. Consider whether or not Christine would have a defence of duress available in each of the following situations.

a Mara, who has failed EU law, comes to Christine's room with a gun and threatens to kill Christine unless Christine goes directly to the EU lecturer's room and kills her with the knife that Mara gives her. Christine goes to the room, enters and attempts to kill the lecturer but she quickly holds a large book up in front of her, preventing the knife from touching her.

[10 marks]

b Ian comes to Christine's room and threatens that unless Christine immediately steals volumes of law reports for Ian from the research library he will reveal to the Dean of School that Christine is having an affair with one of the third-year students. Christine steals the law reports for Ian.

[10 marks]

c Claire, who has failed all her first-year modules, phones Christine from Spain during the vacation after hearing her results and threatens Christine that unless Christine burns down the law school she will kill her when she returns form Spain. Christine does set fire to the law school.

[10 marks]

Each of these scenarios raises different points in the law on duress. It is necessary to identify the particular aspect of duress required and to apply the law correctly. Use case law to support answers.

A4.7   QUALITY OF WRITTEN COMMUNICATION

On this paper the marks for Assessment Objective 3 (AO3) are given as an overall mark (out of a maximum of 9) for the whole paper. To get to the top level of marks for communication and presentation, the specimen mark scheme states:

'A Level 4 response is likely to present material in a well-planned and logical sequence, with a clearly defined structure and communicate clearly and accurately with confident use of appropriate terminology and demonstrate few, if any errors of grammar, punctuation and spelling.'

Examination tips

A5.1 ANSWERING SCENARIO QUESTIONS

Both OCR and WJEC examination papers require candidates to answer problem questions. In these a scenario is set out and candidates have to explain whether someone is liable for a criminal offence.

There are four key points to remember when answering such questions. These are:

- *identify* the offence (and possible defences)
- *define* the law on the offence (or defence)
- *expand* that definition with relevant sections and/or cases
- *apply* the law to the facts given in the scenario.

As you will see, the first letters of these four points spell out the word IDEA. So, go into the exam remembering your great IDEA!

As well as these general points, there are also ways of approaching scenarios on specific areas of law to make sure that you do Identify the relevant points to be discussed. The next sections look at these.

A5.1.1 Scenarios on homicide

When considering a murder problem in an examination question, always considered whether the *actus reus* and or the *mens rea* need discussion for the specific scenario that you have been given. For example, if the facts in the question state that V was shot dead, then there is no need to discuss the *actus reus* or any aspect of causation. However, if you are told that D was shot and taken to hospital where he was given the wrong blood and died, then causation is very relevant.

Also, remember that the scenario may involve other points. It may be a situation where it is uncertain whether D had the *mens rea* for murder or not. It will therefore be necessary to consider involuntary manslaughter (see Chapter 9) as an alternative.

Alternatively, there may be a defence available to the defendant. Different types of defence have different effects on the verdict. For example, in Chapter 8 the special defences of diminished responsibility and provocation are explained. If either of these is successful then the verdict is not guilty of manslaughter but guilty of voluntary manslaughter.

In Chapter 14, the general defences are considered. If the defendant proves he was insane at the time of the killing he will be not guilty by reason of insanity. If the defendant successfully pleads automatism, mistake or self defence he is entitled to be acquitted of murder. If he is intoxicated he may not have the necessary intention for murder.

The following flowchart takes you through the different points you may have to consider.

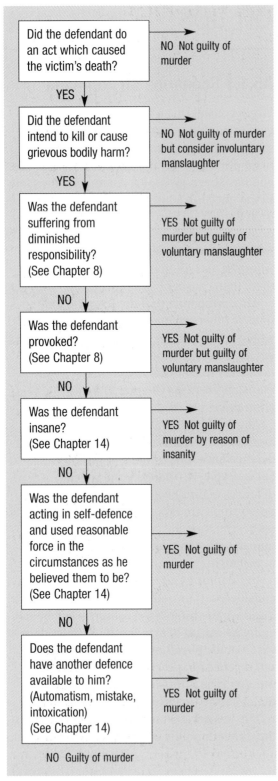

Figure A5.1 Flowchart on murder and possible defences

A5.1.2 Assault scenarios

Examination scenario questions on assaults will set the scene with a possible assault and will almost always include possible defences. For example, look at the examination questions at the end of Chapter 10. In Question 1, about Mark and Kate, there is a question of whether consent can be a defence to the branding. Then, when Kate lashes out 'uncontrollably', the defence of automatism has to be considered.

However, the first point to remember when answering the question is that you must identify the possible offences first. *Never* start with a defence.

When looking at any possible offence, start with the level of injury. This limits which offence can be charged. If there is no injury then it can only be an assault or battery. If there is only actual bodily harm (such as Kate's nose bleed in Question 1 in Chapter 10) then the only possible offence is s 47 OAPA 1861. If there is a wound or grievous bodily harm the offence may be either s 18 or s 20 OAPA 1861: the *mens rea* becomes important in deciding which it is.

Remember that examiners may well give a situation which is on the borderline, so that you may need to discuss whether the injury is, for example, actual bodily harm or grievous bodily harm. However, if the injury is clearly serious (such as Eric's serious internal injuries in Question 2 in Chapter 10) then don't waste time considering actual bodily harm.

There will usually be more than one incident and/or more than one person involved. The clearest way to deal with these multiple issue scenarios is to take one person and one incident at a time.

Don't forget to support your answers with case law.

The following flowchart may help you identify the issues in a question.

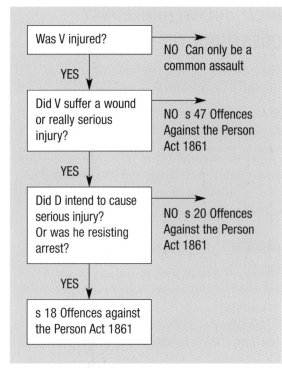

Figure A5.2 Flowchart on offences against the person

Once you have worked out the offence, now consider any possible defences.

A5.1.3 Offences against property scenarios

There are only four offences against property which have to be considered. These are:

- theft
- robbery
- burglary
- criminal damage.

A scenario on offences against property will almost certainly have several incidents to consider. Also in the new four-module OCR specification, it is possible to have offences against the person and offences against property in the same scenario. Isolate each incident and deal with them separately.

Identifying the offence

To decide if the situation is just about theft or also included robbery and burglary, the best starting point is to check whether:

- the incident involved theft and force (need to discuss robbery) or
- the incident took place in a building (need to discuss burglary) or
- something was damaged (criminal damage).

If none of these applies, then the question is just about issues on theft.

Identifying theft issues

The law on theft is set out in Chapter 11. One way of working out what area on law on theft is involved is by considering the elements in the definition of theft in turn. These we saw are all defined in different section of the Theft Act 1968:

- s 2 – dishonestly
- s 3 – appropriates
- s 4 – property
- s 5 – belonging to another
- s 6 – with the intention of permanently depriving the other of it.

You need to identify which one or more of these are relevant. It is very unlikely that all five issues will be involved. You only need to deal with the part of the definition of theft that is in issue.

Let's look at an example.

Example

Millie wants to go shopping. She knows that her neighbour is out and that he keeps his bike in an unlocked shed. She takes her neighbour's bike and rides it to the shops. She goes into a supermarket and puts a bottle of vodka into the wire shopping basket that is provided for shoppers. She also puts in several items of food. As she approaches the checkout, she realises that she has not got enough money to pay for all the items so she hides the bottle of vodka in her coat pocket.

When she leaves the shop, she sees a purse on the ground just outside the exit door. She picks it up. Millie places the purse on a shelf outside the shop so that if the owner comes looking for it, they will see it. Millie then goes to look at the programmes on at the local cinema. She returns to the supermarket 10 minutes later. The purse is still on the shelf. Millie takes it. She then rides the bike home. As she gets near her house, she sees that her neighbour has returned home. She does not want him to know she has used his bike so she leaves the bike propped against a wall at the end of the road.

Consider the criminal liability of Millie.

There are three incidents in this scenario. These involve:

- the bike
- the bottle of vodka
- the purse.

By riding the bike to the shops, Millie has appropriated it, it is property and it clearly belongs to another, so none of those points needs to be discussed. The two issues are whether Millie was dishonest (don't forget to discuss s 2(1)(b) of the Theft Act 1968 also) and whether she intended permanently to deprive her neighbour of the bike.

Regarding the bottle of vodka, Millie appropriated it the moment she placed it the wire basket. (*Morris* (1983)) But at that point she is not dishonest, that element of theft comes into play when she decides not to pay for it. The bottle is clearly property belonging to another and Millie intends permanently to deprive the store of it, so there is no need to discuss these points.

Finally, the purse, the main issue here is dishonesty. You need to explain s 2(1)(c) of the Theft Act 1968 and apply to the situation.

A5.2 ANSWERING ESSAY QUESTIONS

The two main points to remember when writing an essay are that you must:

- focus on the issues raised in the question and
- remember to analyse and evaluate.

You should also try to structure your essay and it helps to make a brief plan before you start writing the essay. Let's look at the essay question set out at the end of Chapter 11.

Question

The *actus reus* of theft as defined in the Theft Act 1968 is 'appropriating property belonging to another'.

Discuss the difficulties that the courts have encountered in interpreting and applying these words.

Note that the question is focused on the *actus reus* of theft. Do not write anything about the *mens rea*: you will not get any marks for doing so.

The other focus is the 'difficulties that the courts have encountered'. This directs you to the type of evaluation that the examiner wants. Don't just list all you know about the

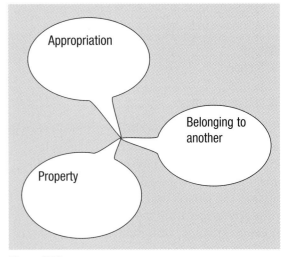

Figure A5.3

actus reus of theft: you must also discuss the
difficulties and analyse them.

A suggested way of planning the essay is by
creating a spider diagram with three arms,
one for each of appropriate, property, and
belonging to another as shown in Figure A5.3.

Then jot down the names of key cases in
each of the arms with a couple of words on
the problem that was shown by the case. Try
doing that now. You don't have to use a spider
diagram. You could use three columns
instead. The main point is to get used to
planning an essay in a way that you find
helpful.

Index

Page numbers followed by f signify a figure, e.g. 82f.